RESEARCH IN ECONOMIC HISTORY

RESEARCH IN ECONOMIC HISTORY

Series Editors: Christopher Hanes and Susan Wolcott

HB
1
.R37
2014

RESEARCH IN ECONOMIC HISTORY

EDITED BY

CHRISTOPHER HANES
SUNY Binghamton, NY, USA

SUSAN WOLCOTT
SUNY Binghamton, NY, USA

United Kingdom – North America – Japan
India – Malaysia – China

453045

4-2-14

Emerald Group Publishing Limited
Howard House, Wagon Lane, Bingley BD16 1WA, UK

First edition 2014

Copyright © 2014 Emerald Group Publishing Limited

Reprints and permission service
Contact: permissions@emeraldinsight.com

British Library Cataloguing in Publication Data
A catalogue record for this book is available from the British Library

ISBN: 978-1-78350-487-9
ISSN: 0363-3268 (Series)

ISOQAR certified
Management System,
awarded to Emerald
for adherence to
Environmental
standard
ISO 14001:2004.

Certificate Number 1985
ISO 14001

INVESTOR IN PEOPLE

CONTENTS

LIST OF CONTRIBUTORS

Svetlozar Andreev	Department of Political Science, Sofia University, Sofia, Bulgaria; Department of Political and Social Sciences, European University Institute, Florence, Italy
Stéphane Becuwe	Bordeaux University, GREThA UMR CNRS 5113, Bordeaux, France
Bertrand Blancheton	Faculty of Economics, Bordeaux University, GREThA UMR CNRS 5113, Bordeaux, France
Leonard Carlson	Department of Economics, Emory University, Atlanta, GA, USA
Jari Eloranta	Department of History, Appalachian State University, Boone, NC, USA
Kerstin Enflo	Department of Economic History, Lund University, Lund, Sweden
Martin Henning	Department of Human Geography, Lund University, Lund, Sweden
John A. James	Departments of Economics and History, University of Virginia, Charlottesville, VA, USA
John Komlos	University of Munich, Munich, Germany; Department of Economics, Duke University, Durham, NC, USA
Pavel Osinsky	Department of Sociology, Appalachian State University, Boone, NC, USA

Lennart Schön   Department of Economic History, Lund
                         University, Lund, Sweden

David F. Weiman   Department of Economics, Barnard
                         College, New York, NY, USA

EDITORS' INTRODUCTION

Research in Economic History is a refereed journal, specializing in economic history, in the form of a book. As a book we can accommodate work that does not fit the standard journal mold, such as articles that primarily present newly constructed data sets, and historical narratives that are informed by economic theory but do not test a specific hypothesis in the usual, statistical way.

In this volume, Kerstin Enflo, Martin Henning, and Lennart Schön present new data: estimates of regional value-added in the provinces of Sweden over a very long span of time, from 1855 to 2007, based on regional data on wages and employment in economic sectors and national-level estimates of value-added by economic sector. They observe long-run convergence in output per person across provinces. At the same time, employment and economic activity became more concentrated in just a few provinces.

The article by John A. James and David F. Weiman is an informed narrative: a history of check clearing networks in the United States prior to the founding of the Fed, and the early Fed's failed efforts to enforce universal par clearing. Responding to recent literature on this topic, James and Weiman draw conclusions about the efficiency of the pre-Fed system and the wisdom of the Fed's attempted regulatory intervention.

Following a more standard journal format, Jari Eloranta, Svetlozar Andreev, and Pavel Osinsky look at 24 countries across years from 1870 through 1938 to see the relationship between the development of democracy and central government spending, distinguishing between social and military spending. They find some measures of democracy were positively associated with social spending, negatively associated with military spending.

John Komlos and Leonard Carlson present new evidence on the heights of American Indians in the nineteenth century drawn from records of Indian scouts recruited into the American army, taking care to account for the nature of selection into the scouts. Their evidence indicates that Amerindians were tall relative to contemporary Europeans, consistent with previous studies, but short relative to rural Americans of settler origin.

Changes over time in the heights of Amerindians indicate their living conditions remained stable or improved through the Civil War and declined thereafter.

Stéphane Becuwe and Bertrand Blancheton examine the French tariff system over 1850–1913, particularly differentials in rates depending on an import's country of origin, which they call "tariff dispersion." They find that France often charged differentially high rates on certain products from certain countries, even countries that ostensibly had "most favored nation" status. They conclude that studies using measures of tariff rates to understand phenomena such as trade flows and domestic industrial development must take care to account for tariff dispersion.

In geographic coverage, two articles are on American history; two are on European history; one makes comparisons across a number of countries. We want to publish more articles on African and Asian economic history. If you have a paper on an African or Asian topic, please submit it to us! In these fields new data sets and informed narratives have especially great value, because so many basic facts are still to be established. A disappointing feature of current economic research is the relative lack of such work, despite the large numbers of students from China, India, and Korea being trained in American and European graduate economics programs. Many facts about American and British economic history were established in a massive wave of research that took place from the 1890s through the 1960s. Statistics created by the scholars of that era, published in journals such as the *Review of Economic Statistics* (now the *Review of Economics and Statistics*), book series such as *Studies in Income and Wealth* and numerous publications of the (American) National Bureau of Economic Research, are fundamental to economic research today. We hope that *Research in Economic History* will be an outlet for a coming wave of historical statistics on African and Asian countries.

Christopher Hanes
Susan Wolcott
Series Editors

DEMOCRATIZATION AND CENTRAL GOVERNMENT SPENDING, 1870–1938: EMERGENCE OF THE LEVIATHAN?

Jari Eloranta, Svetlozar Andreev and Pavel Osinsky

Hitherto I have set forth the nature of man, whose pride and other passions have compelled him to submit himself to government ... But because he is mortal, and subject to decay, as all other earthly creatures are; and because there is that in heaven, though not on earth, that he should stand in fear of, and whose laws he ought to obey ...

Hobbes, 1651, Chapter XXVIII

ABSTRACT

Did the expansion of democratic institutions play a role in determining central government spending behavior in the 19th and 20th centuries? The link between democracy and increased central government spending is well established for the post-Second World War period, but has never been explored during the first "wave of democracy" and its subsequent

---

Research in Economic History, Volume 30, 1–46
Copyright © 2014 by Emerald Group Publishing Limited
All rights of reproduction in any form reserved
ISSN: 0363-3268/doi:10.1108/S0363-326820140000030001

1

reversal, that is 1870–1938. The main contribution of this paper is the compilation of a dataset covering 24 countries over this period to begin to address this question. Utilizing various descriptive techniques, including panel data regressions, we explore correlations between central government spending and the institutional characteristics of regimes. We find that the data are consistent with the hypothesis that democracies have a broader need for legitimization than autocracies as various measures of democracy are associated with higher central government spending. Our results indicate that the extension of franchise had a slight positive impact on central government spending levels, as did a few of the other democracy variables. We also find that early liberal democracies spent less and monarchies more than other regimes; debt increases spending; and participation in the Gold Standard reduced government spending substantially.

Keywords: Democratization; central government spending; social and military spending; liberal democracies; autocracies; institutions

JEL classifications: E62; H10; H50; H60; N40

INTRODUCTION

This article aims to build a framework for answering the following question: What aspects of democracy and related institutions are correlated with central government spending in the crucial formation period, namely the late 19th century and early 20th century? The sample period (1870–1938) features major global crises (*global war*: the First World War; *economic crisis*: the Great Depression) as well as extensive variability in the underlying regime characteristics.

The primary goal of this article is to analyze different facets of democracy and other institutions as possible explanatory factors in central government spending and expansion in 1870–1938. We maintain that the level of central government expenditures (CGE) in this period was affected by the underlying socio-political processes, political enfranchisement, and the democratization of the political institutions – and their decline in the 1930s. As far as individual categories of central government spending are concerned, the basic model we advance suggests that the level of democracy increased social spending and central government debt, yet decreased military spending. Our model is therefore based on the premise that there is a link between central government spending and the ways that regimes try to legitimize themselves internally and externally.

The core sample of countries for which we have complete data are: Argentina, Austria(-Hungary), Belgium, Brazil, Canada, Denmark, France, Italy, Japan, the Netherlands, Norway, Portugal, Spain, Sweden, the United Kingdom, and the United States. These countries have the most uniform data for the time period in question. They also form a comprehensive panel data sample, since they include some of the most important international players and geographic regions of the period. We expand the sample when possible to extend the variation in regime type. For the interwar period we supplement the sample with Australia, Finland, Greece, and New Zealand. In a few of the cases if so noted, we add Chile, Germany, Russia, and Switzerland. Therefore, the picture emerging from the analyses is based on a rich comparative sample.

We will utilize central government spending figures (Central or Federal Government Expenditures = CGE) arising from various historical statistics collection efforts, growth accounts, and other databases. Our measure of CGE will include payment on debt, and thus will capture a country's ability to borrow. We have also gathered figures on subcategories of CGE – on military spending (Military Expenditures = ME, for sources see Eloranta, 2002, 2004) and on social spending (Social Expenditures = SE) – as well as other indicators of the characteristics of government.[1] These datasets are essentially consistent with the OECD and growth accounting criteria for decomposed parts of central government spending. The country-by-country coverage of the figures, sources, and definitions is presented in Table A.1.

The majority of political regimes in the late 19th and early 20th century had little in common with modern liberal democracies. Fig. 1 illustrates the shares of democracies and autocracies represented by all countries covered in the Polity IV data set over the period 1816–1996.[2] The period 1870–1938 experienced the first real "wave of democracy," as well as its reversal in the 1930s. It is important to study the dynamics of the process of democratization in a historical perspective, especially the roots of these processes before the Second World War. The political regimes from this period constitute an ample basis for the analysis of the early evolution of democracies, and thus will provide new evidence about the evolution of contemporary liberal democracies and the legitimacy functions of emerging democracies in general. However, one should be conscious of the fact that

Fig. 1. Percentage of Democracies and Autocracies in the World, 1816–2004. *Source*: Calculated from the Polity IV data generated with EUGene Version 3.204, software available from http://eugenesoftware.org. Democracy = 6 or more on the Polity democracy scale; autocracy = 5 or more on the Polity autocracy scale. The rest of the states were in neither category, comprising nations with varying degrees of political turmoil and transitional regimes.

the standards for characterizing the process of democratization now and then are hugely different. This is one of the reasons why there has been little reliable data on the economic and societal aspects of regime shifts with respect to the early rise of democracy in Europe, the United States, and other parts of the world.

This paper will serve as a preliminary overview of the data on regimes and CGE. We will begin with a discussion of models of fiscal spending, and then discuss models of how governments establish legitimacy. These models will inform our examination of the data we have gathered. We then proceed to look at the time trends of important variables, dividing the presentation by regime type. Next, we examine bivariate correlations over time, and finally examine the data using regression techniques. At this stage in the analysis of these data, we will be describing correlations and comparing those correlations to the predictions of the models. We will not be able to establish causality. As this is the first examination of a consistently compiled data series for many regimes over a long, and historically important, period, even this relatively straightforward data exercise will bring new information to the discussion.

FISCAL EXPANSION OF THE STATE AND DEMOCRATIZATION

There have been several studies in the last 30 years or so that have tackled some aspect of explaining central government spending or its components. Relatively few of them have focused explicitly on the long-term analysis of central government spending. Here we are conflating the focus to three approaches in particular: (1) the Webber–Wildavsky model of budgeting; (2) the Richard Bonney model of fiscal systems; (3) the Niall Ferguson model of interaction between public debts and forms of government. Caroly Webber and Aaron Wildavsky (1986) maintain essentially that each political culture generates its characteristic budgetary objectives; namely, productivity in market regimes, redistribution in sects (= specific groups dissenting from an established authority), and more complex procedures in hierarchical regimes. Thus, according to them the respective budgetary consequences arising from the chosen regime can be divided into four categories: despotism, state capitalism, American individualism, and social democracy. All of these categories in turn have implications for the respective regimes' revenue and spending behavior.

This model, however, is essentially a static one. It does not provide insights as to why nations' behavior may change *over time*. Richard Bonney has addressed this problem in his studies of the early modern states (1999). He has emphasized that the states' revenue and tax collection systems, the backbone of any militarily successful nation state, have evolved over time. During the Middle Ages, the European fiscal systems were relatively backward and autarchic, with mostly predatory rulers (or roving bandits, as Mancur Olson (1993) has coined them). In the Bonney model this would correspond with the so-called tribute state. Next in the evolution came, respectively, the domain state (with stationary bandits, providing some public goods), the tax state (more reliance on credit and revenue collection), and finally the fiscal state (embodying more complex fiscal and political structures). A superpower like Great Britain in the 19th century in fact had to be a fiscal state to be able to dominate the world, due to all the burdens that went with an empire (Ferguson, 2003, 2004; see also Przeworski, 2009 on extension of franchises). This evolution was propelled forward by various types of crises, especially wars (see also Higgs, 1989 on a crisis-driven model of government growth).

While both of the models mentioned above have provided important clues as to how and why nations have experienced fiscal expansion over time, the most war-centered account of this process has been provided by Niall Ferguson (2001). He has maintained that wars have shaped all the most relevant institutions of modern economic life: tax-collecting bureaucracies, central banks, bond markets, and stock exchanges. Moreover, he argues that the invention of public debt instruments has gone hand-in-hand with more democratic forms of government and military supremacy — hence, the so-called Dutch or British model. These types of regimes have also been the most efficient economically, which has in turn reinforced the success of this fiscal regime model. In fact, military expenditures may have been the principal cause of fiscal innovation for most of history. Ferguson's model highlights the importance, for a state's survival among its challengers, of the adoption of the right types of institutions (especially public debt), technology, and a sufficient helping of external ambitions (Macdonald, 2003).

Following Peter Lindert, competing theories on the growth of government can be divided into five categories: (1) theories implying a monotonic rise of the government spending share; (2) theories implying an end to the rise; (3) theories implying an eventual reversal; (4) more conditional predictions; (5) history-dependent hypotheses testing. The first of these includes such well-known explanatory frameworks as the *Wagner's Law* and *Baumol's Disease* (Eloranta, 2004; Webber & Wildavsky, 1986), which essentially argue that government spending has an income elasticity of more than one. In this paper we will not test any of these theories directly. Rather, we will describe the evolution of the fiscal behavior of states both across time, and according to various characteristics. The data presented will show a wide range of spending patterns for all types of regimes. As recent research into the military spending behavior and the impact of democracy has shown, the impact of democracy has not been uniform in this period. For example, it appears that only full democracies were less aggressive in terms of military spending after the First World War (Rota, 2011).

Modern data tell a different story. It is well established that modern democratic governments spend more than nondemocratic ones (see, e.g., Acemoglu & Robinson, 2006; Boix, 2001, 2003; Brown & Hunter, 1999; Deacon, 2009; Huber, Mustillo, & Stephens, 2008; Lake & Baum, 2001; Norris, 2012; Stasavage, 2005). In contrast to authoritarian rulers, who are insulated from their subjects, democratic leaders, who are to be elected and reelected, have much stronger incentives to incorporate voters' preferences into state policies. In democratic polities public preferences tend to exert a significant influence over spending decisions (Brooks & Manza, 2006; Lindert, 2004). Carles Boix (2001) has argued that the growth of the public sector is a joint result of the process of economic development and the political institutions in place. Therefore, economic modernization leads to the growth of the public sector, especially when: (1) the state intervenes to provide certain collective goods; and (2) industrialization and aging population increase the demand for social transfers. Boix argued that democracy (with full electoral participation) increases public spending levels.

Despite the fact that the overwhelming amount of modern evidence supports the social responsiveness argument, it is only part of the explanation for the expansion of modern states in the post-Second World War period. Like most theories of especially the welfare state (see especially Esping-Andersen, 1990, 1999, 2004), it highlights endogenous factors of public service provision but neglects other, exogenous mechanisms that might had made democracies more generous than they otherwise could have been. Many studies of social spending examine a relationship between political institutions and policy outcomes after 1945 (e.g., Hicks & Misra, 1993; Huber, Ragin, & Stephens, 1993; Huber & Stephens, 2001; Schmidt, 1997). Furthermore, a great number of such studies focus on developing countries (Avelino, Brown, & Hunter, 2005; Brown & Hunter, 1999; Huber et al., 2008; Kaufman & Segura-Ubiergo, 2001; Stasavage, 2005). One needs to take into account two circumstances when assessing these findings. First, the period *after* the Second World War was associated with a greater normative value of democratic governance, which was globally promoted by the United States and its allies (Mann, 2012, 2013). At that time global normative models exerted much greater influence on national policies than before. Second, the postwar period was associated with the emergence of international political organizations (such as United Nations) and international financial institutions (the IMF, the World Bank) that also promoted particular economic and policy models across the globe. That does not necessarily mean that they promoted greater spending. The problem is that political institutions and policy choices of the developing countries could have been subject to pressures from abroad, which makes it difficult to gauge the "net effect" of their endogenous democratization.

The majority of political regimes in the late 19th and early 20th century, on the contrary, had little in common with modern liberal democracies. Democracies in this earlier period emerged in a world dominated by non-democracies. Some of the authoritarian regimes of this period developed a broad range of public services supported by substantial social spending (e.g., France under Napoleon III, Germany under Bismarck). Furthermore, the first half of the 20th century was marked by the emergence of mass mobilization dictatorships (e.g., communist, fascist, corporatist, etc.) that were guided by radical redistributive ideologies. These regimes' political control allowed them to implement redistribution in practice. The redistributive policies appealed to some segments of the electorate in the democratic societies (Berman, 2006; Capoccia, 2005; Luebbert, 1991; Muller, 2011). In this way, democracies became involved in a contest for legitimacy with nondemocratic parties, in which provision of social goods became one of the key instruments of legitimization. That is why it is important to study the dynamics of the process of democratization in a historical perspective, especially before the Second World War. In addition, democracies had to compete for economic and political resources on a global stage, which forced them to compete militarily. Having a relatively strong military force was a necessity in order to protect trade routes and global empires, as well as ensure that internal order was maintained through various crises.

DEMOCRACIES AND LEGITIMACY

Scholars studying legitimacy problems in various political contexts have largely disagreed on what legitimacy is and how to define this concept precisely. They, nevertheless, have concurred that it has something to do with support, especially popular support for political decisions, personalities, and institutions (Blondel, 1995; Lord, 2000). It has been both practically and theoretically determined that no regime, even the most autocratic ones, can survive without the *support of its citizens*. That is why the majority of regimes around the world try to capitalize upon popular support by creating the appropriate fiscal incentives as well as political and social institutions, and by cultivating special relations with the representatives of civil society. It should be emphasized that the rule of law plays an important part in this process, especially constitutional rule, as a means of establishing and formalizing different channels and acts of support.

The support granted by both individuals and organizations of democratic rule may vary substantially depending on the circumstances. Hence, legitimacy should not be perceived as a clear-cut and fixed point, but more as a continuum. Authors working on legitimacy issues have indicated it can also be both general (for the overall political system) and specific (for individual policies) (Blondel, 1995; Easton, 1965). At the same time, acts of government can be perceived as legitimate for what they achieve (substantive legitimacy) and for how they do it (procedural legitimacy) (Weber, 1946). Therefore, legitimacy implies the existence of a trade-off between efficiency and stability, on the one hand, and normative justice and political style, on the other (Diamond & Lipset, 1995; Lipset, 1983).

Seymour Martin Lipset posits that "legitimacy involves the capacity of the system to engender and maintain the belief that the existing political institutions are the most appropriate ones for the society" (1984). Philippe Schmitter defines legitimacy as "a shared expectation among actors in an arrangement of asymmetric power, such that the actions of those who rule are accepted voluntarily by those who are ruled because the latter are convinced that the actions of the former conform to the preestablished norms. Put simply, legitimacy converts power into authority – *Macht* into *Herrschaft* – and, thereby, simultaneously establishes an obligation to obey and a right to rule" (2001; see also Schmitter, 2010).

Alongside the complicated question of defining what legitimacy actually is, political scientists have also puzzled over the possible methods of assuring legitimate authority for a government. This process is called legitimization, and it is different from the concept of legitimacy, which is the *object* of this act. In his classic work "The Theory of Social and Economic Organisation," Max Weber identified three ways of legitimization (or "three pure types of legitimate authority"): rational, traditional, and charismatic (1964). More recently, Fritz Scharpf has made a useful point that legitimacy can be secured either on the input or output side of government: input legitimacy implying democratic selection of office holders, public consultation and electoral approval of political programs, while output legitimacy refers to directly meeting public needs and values, and ensuring that policy follows public opinion and attitudes (1997).

Despite their disagreements on exactly how to define legitimacy, scholars working on legitimacy problems have identified four essential means by which regimes achieve legitimacy (Höreth, 1998, 2001; Scharpf, 1994, 1999; Weiler, 1993, 1999):

1. *Output legitimacy:* Efficiency and effectiveness of the ruling regime's problem-solving ability and capability, **government** *for the people*.
2. *Input legitimacy:* Direct democratic legitimization of national/international politics through citizen participation and representation, **government** *by the people*.
3. *Indirect (formal) legitimacy (Constitutional legitimacy):* Indirect democratic legitimization of the polity via the democratically elected institutions, procedures, and the rule of law, **government** *of the people*.
4. *International legitimacy:* Legitimization through participation in *alliances*, or "borrowed" through the international institutions and their standards, **government** *by group of peoples*.

How can we operationalize these theoretical concepts? Based on the earlier premises, our initial, *basic* model is summarized in Fig. 2. Therefore we argue that: (1) a rise in the level of democracy increases income and vice versa (=*Hypothesis 1*); (2) income increases (similar to many of the frameworks listed before, e.g., Wagner's Law) central government spending (=*Hypothesis 2*); (3) a rise in the level of democracy will increase central government spending (=*Hypothesis 3*). In the descriptive section which follows, we will show that income and democracy are correlated as suggested by Hypothesis 1. But the main focus of the paper is exploring links between spending and regime characteristics.

We also investigate the different types of central government spending and their correlations with regime characteristics. Therefore, to the extent the data allow, we evaluate whether: (1) increase in democracy will increase, following Lindert (2004), social spending; (2) increase in democracy will decrease, moderately, military spending (as found in numerous studies); (3) the trade-off between military and social spending will be imperfect – namely, as Niall Ferguson (1999, 2001) has pointed out, these expenditures did not really compete with one another in the beginning of this period, and moreover, there was very little trade-off between these types of expenditures in the budgetary process later on in the period. Also, democracies would have more access to external and internal debt, which would make them less prone to impose such budgetary trade-offs. Therefore, an increase in democracy is hypothesized to increase central government spending.

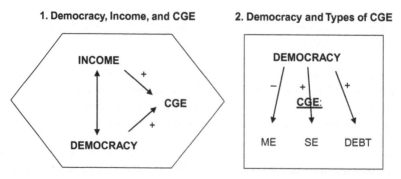

Fig. 2. Causal Inferences in the Basic Model. *Note*: CGE, central government spending; ME, military expenditures; SE, social expenditures; DEBT, central government debt.

We will provide insights into all of these purported patterns, although we cannot investigate them conclusively, given the space constraints of this article. These assertions are here first explored by examining time trends in various spending categories for different regime types. Then, we examine the correlations between the variables by decades. And finally, we use a more nuanced multivariate analytical framework to describe linkages. The right-hand variable in the multivariate regressions will be the ratio of central government expenditures to GDP (percentage). As explanatory variables, following the distinction between different types of institutional functions of regimes, we will utilize *input* variables (e.g., extension of franchise, disaggregated democracy variables); *output* variables (primary school enrollment, spending trade-offs, wars); *constitutional* variables (type of legal system, type of executive, effectiveness of the legislative branch); *international* system variables (military alliance(s), central government debt burden, membership in the Gold Standard).

Our earlier discussion suggests the signs we should expect to observe in this exercise. As we argued in the introduction, existing theoretical models suggest democracies will have a broader need for legitimizing their existence and actions than autocracies, thus the variables associated with increased democratization should be statistically significant and drive up central government spending. Military alliances (if credible) should decrease military spending, due to free riding, and possibly decrease central government spending. Common law systems, essentially a way to gauge the importance and impact of early liberal democracies (as well as lingering colonial legacies) in the sample can also be expected to have a negative impact on spending. If monarchies do not need to establish legitimacy, they should be associated with decreased government spending.

Information on the institutional foundations of the regimes and the levels of democracy (or autocracy, respectively – abbreviated as DEM), as well as the various subcategories of these indices, come mainly from the Polity IIID database assembled by Kristian Gleditsch (2000) and its more recent incarnation, Polity IV.[3] Some of the other indicators on the quality of the regimes in question come from Arthur Banks' (1976) database (which is used sparingly due to its inconsistencies), Peter Lindert's database on political voice and growth (2003), and the Correlates of War (Singer & Small, 1993) data on the relative size of the military (vis-à-vis the population). The reason for using the Polity database is that it is not only comprehensive, but it is also comparative and covers a relatively long historical period, unlike certain other social and political databases. However, its methodology of describing the countries' democratization over time, and its way of coding various factor-variables, have been often criticized by democracy scholars (Bollen & Paxton, 2000; Munck & Verkuilen, 2002).

SOME DATA PUZZLES AND IMPLICATIONS

When one inspects the long-term central government spending patterns of Western states, it seems that there have been at least four separate "phases" in the 19th and 20th centuries (Eloranta, 2004). Fig. 3 depicts the long-run spending patterns of some of the great powers over the entire period for which we have data. Central government spending levels for most of the great powers were fairly devoid of any growth trend until the First World War, although there were obvious differences between the spending patterns of the various polities. Government spending started to increase in

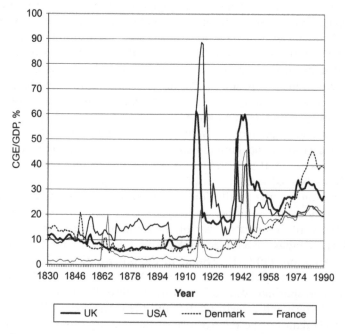

Fig. 3. Long-Run Spending Patterns: Central Government Spending for the United Kingdom, the United States, France, and Denmark, 1830–1990. *Source*: See Table A.1. Note that this only includes countries with long-run data on central/federal government spending.

the interwar period, especially in the 1930s. The increase was partly due to the costs of the war and rebuilding efforts afterwards. After the Second World War, the effect of the emerging welfare state, along with the Cold War arms race, can be observed until the 1980s. The last phase seems to be the leveling off stage or a very modest decline for the modern welfare states.

We now narrow the focus to just the years 1870–1938, but widen our view to include many more polities. The central government spending levels of many of the smaller or more peripheral countries increased modestly until the First World War, and then they entered into more turbulent, expansionary fiscal situations following the war. Here we have divided the 24 countries that we have full or partial data for into four groups to compare their government spending behavior during this period: (1) rich consistent democracies; (2) rich consistent or transitional autocracies; (3) poor transitional democracies; and (4) poor consistent or transitional autocracies. The parameters for the groupings are explained in Figs. 4a–d. Let us

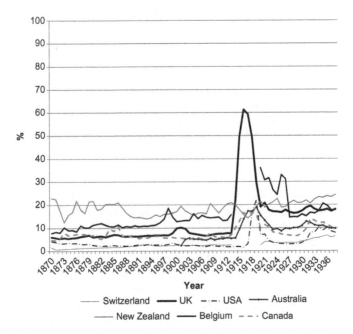

Fig. 4a. Rich Consistent Democracies: Central Government Spending, 1870–1938. *Source*: See Table A.1. Countries included had a GDP per capita level of 2,500 Geary-Khamis USD or more in 1900, and a democracy score of 5 or more *consistently* during all the cross-section years.

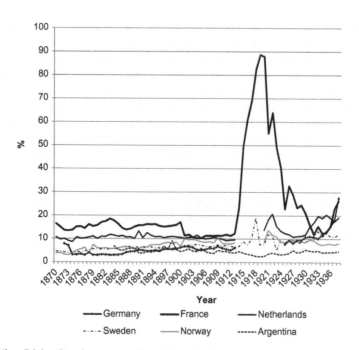

Fig. 4b. Rich Consistent or Transitional Autocracies: Central Government Spending, 1870–1938. *Source*: See Table A.1. Countries included had a GDP per capita level of 2,500 Geary-Khamis USD or more in 1900, and democracy score of less than 5 for *most or all* of the cross-section years.

first look at the central/federal government spending as a percentage of GDP of rich countries. As seen in Fig. 4a, the spending levels of the countries in this group were fairly consistent until the First World War, and then the war forced many of them, for example the United Kingdom, to increase their spending dramatically. Most of the rich democracies spent consistently less than 10 percent of their GDP on government. The exceptions to this were New Zealand, which spent around 20 percent, with a lot of annual fluctuation; Belgium, which spent less than 10 percent in the beginning of the period but about 20 percent at the end of it; and the United Kingdom, which almost tripled its government spending during the period in question. Rich autocracies (Fig. 4b), a group which includes several transitional regimes (i.e., those switching between autocratic and democratic forms of government) and regimes that became solid democracies in the interwar period, behaved, for the most part, in a similar fashion.

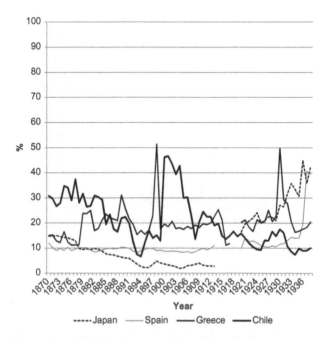

Fig. 4c. Poor Transitional Democracies: Central Government Spending, 1870–1938. *Source*: See Table A.1. Countries included had a GDP per capita level of less than 2,500 Geary-Khamis USD in 1900, and a democracy score of 5 or more for *most* of the cross-section years.

Most countries started with a spending level of less than 10 percent, and they spent more in the 1920s and 1930s. France has a massive peak in the figure due to the First World War and its aftermath – it should be noted that we do not have data for most countries' spending during the war. Moreover, Argentina's spending levels were remarkably low compared to the others, even declining during the time period.

Poor transitional democracies were a rather eclectic group as well (see Fig. 4c), exhibiting a lot of variability in their spending behavior. For example Chile had a high level of spending in the beginning of the period (over 30 percent), which fluctuated sharply after the mid-1890s (with a peak of 46.5 percent in 1901), with diminishing spending levels toward the end of the period. This was a turbulent period overall in Chilean history, during which dictatorship gave way to splintered parliamentary rule, so an increase in the level of democracy certainly did not lead to higher spending

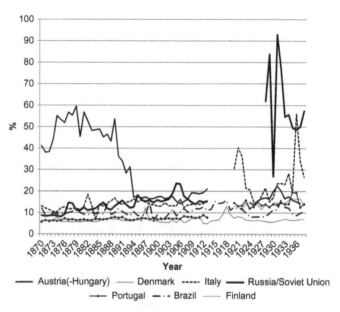

Fig. 4d. Poor Consistent or Transitional Autocracies: Central Government Spending, 1870–1938. *Source*: See Table A.1. Countries included had a GDP per capita level of less than 2,500 Geary-Khamis USD in 1900, and a democracy score of less than 5 for *all or most* of the cross-section years.

in this case, most likely due to the unsettled institutional situation. Spain's spending increased rapidly in the 1930s, when the political situation in the country deteriorated. Japan's spending declined to under 5 percent before the First World War, but it increased again in the 1920s and 1930s. Finally, Greece's fiscal behavior was almost as volatile as Chile's, and the spending level remained at over 20 percent of GDP for most of the period.

Poor autocracies, by and large, behaved in a fairly consistent manner, with a few exceptions. Most countries started the period with spending levels around 10 percent of GDP, and increased spending slightly during the period, especially after the First World War. The interwar period was also a phase that exhibited more volatility in the countries' spending patterns. For example, Austria-Hungary had very high spending level until the 1890s, and then the subsequent governments kept the spending below 20 percent for most of the remaining period. Russian spending increased steadily until the war, and the levels were quite high in the 1930s; although, we must note that the data is fairly unreliable for this period. Italy had a high level of spending in the 1920s and 1930s, which corresponds to the Fascist period.

What happened after the First World War that led to the growth phase in central/federal government spending? First of all, the gradual change began much earlier than this global conflict. The 19th century Western reforms in the fiscal sphere, for example, more efficient budgeting and taxation, were supported by the industrial revolutions and rising productivity levels, as well as accompanied by an industrialization of war and armaments production from the mid-century on. The economic challenges posed by these changes for military spending differed. Figs. 5a–5d depict the time trends in the military burden (=*ME as a percentage of GDP*) for our four types of regimes. Note that in the French case, the mean defense share of government spending (=ME as a percentage of CGE) fell to 8.9 percent in 1870–1913 compared to the early 19th century level, circa 35 percent, whereas its military burden rose modestly to 3.7 percent. So, the French CGE increased, as a total, faster than its military spending, due to its debt commitments arising from the Franco–German war of 1870–1871.

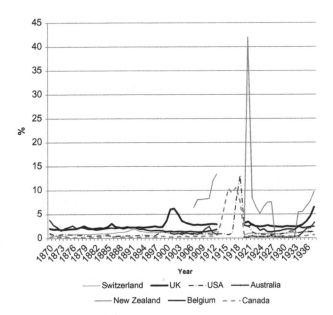

Fig. 5a. Rich Consistent Democracies: Military Burden, 1870–1938. *Source*: See Table A.1. For the parameters of country choices, see Fig. 4a.

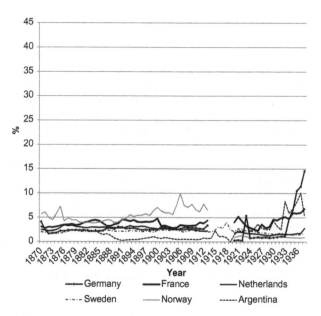

Fig. 5b. Rich Consistent or Transitional Autocracies: Military Burden, 1870–1938. *Source*: See Table A.1. For the parameters of country choices, see Fig. 4b.

In the British case, the mean defense share in total CGE in 1870–1913 declined slightly to 37.5 percent, whereas the growth of the British GDP enabled a slight military burden decline (ME) to 2.6 percent. For most countries the period leading to the First World War meant comparatively higher military burdens than in the early 19th century, as Figs. 5a–5d indicate. Furthermore, the military burdens of the Great Powers were higher and more varied than those of the small and medium powers, on average. (See Eloranta, 2007 for further details, including averages for large groups of states.) As seen in Fig. 5a, the military spending levels of rich democracies were fairly stable for the entire period, with the exception of the First World War, usually between about 1 and 3 percent of the GDP. The military spending of rich autocracies was, on average, slightly higher than the corresponding spending by rich democracies (see Fig. 5b). As we pointed out earlier, though, this group includes countries that were more transitional by nature, countries that eventually became solid democracies, like Sweden and Norway. Thus, the behavior of such countries was similar to rich democracies, except Norway's abnormally high military spending until

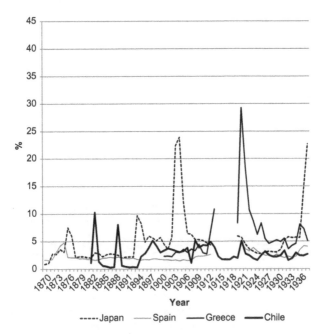

Fig. 5c. Poor Transitional Democracies: Military Burden, 1870−1938. *Source*: See Table A.1. For the parameters of country choices, see Fig. 4c.

the war. In comparison, Germany's spending was surprisingly low until the war, even respective of countries like the United Kingdom or France (Eloranta, 2007). Germany's military burden, of course, grew very fast in the 1930s under the Nazis. The other autocracies followed suit in the 1930s, jumping into the arms race more quickly than the democracies did (Eloranta, 2002).

The military spending behavior of poor transitional democracies was, like their fiscal behavior on the whole, rather erratic, as seen in Fig. 5c. Japan's military spending was strongly influenced by the Russo−Japanese war of 1904−1905 and the military expansion during the 1930s. Chile experienced lots of fluctuations in its military budgets, which meant huge peaks and troughs especially prior to the First World War. Spain's spending, in comparison, was more stable and constituted a lower percentage of GDP.

There were significant differences between the poor autocracies as well (Fig. 5d). Russia's spending was driven by the wars of the period and the

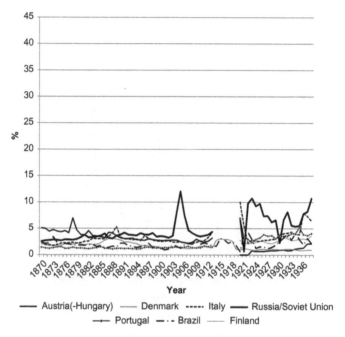

Fig. 5d.   Poor Consistent or Transitional Autocracies: Military Burden, 1870–1938.
Source: See Table A.1. For the parameters of country choices, see Fig. 4d.

priorities of Lenin and Stalin in the interwar period. Portugal spent clearly
more under Salazar in the interwar period compared to the fiscal situation
prior to the war. In general, most countries in this group spent less than
5 percent of their GDP on their military before the Great War and the
spending behavior was then more consistent than in the interwar period,
during which the levels at first dropped and then grew in the 1930s.

Social spending, as Peter Lindert (1994) has pointed out, varied greatly
across nations. For example, the social spending of the Great Powers and
smaller states alike at the national level was almost nonexistent until the
industrialization wave of the 19th century. Nonetheless, the pace of change
between these countries differed greatly. In fact, neither Germany nor the
United Kingdom played a key leadership role in this respect before the
First World War compared to for example Denmark. Weimar Germany
did emerge as a strong contender in the interwar period. Social transfers,
nonetheless, were quite rare in 1880, when traditional forms of poor relief

still persisted, although they became much more common by the turn of the century. One big watershed in this respect was the First World War, which extended the voting franchise dramatically and increased the demand for social spending in most Western countries (Lindert, 1994).

Table 1 gives Lindert's data on social spending for a few select countries. In general, the social spending levels prior to the Second World War were still fairly modest, at least compared to the 20–30 percent levels reached by the end of the century. Yet still, the future welfare state leaders like the Nordic countries and the United Kingdom had already begun to follow a different pattern than for example the United States.

What about the correlations between income, democracy, and central government spending in this period, as hypothesized in the introduction? As Fig. 6 shows, there seems to be a clear and consistent positive correlation between the level of democracy and level of economic development (measured by GDP per capita). This relationship persists throughout the period, although it changes insofar as there is a clearer division between democracies and autocracies in the 1930s during the reversal of the first wave of democracy. Countries like Great Britain were developing even faster economically than they were democratizing, thus showing up above the trend line before the First World War. Others, like Brazil in 1900, were both undeveloped economically and undemocratic, an outlier in Fig. 6 for that cross-section year. But the correlations were fairly robust, and the R^2 values were between 0.31 and 0.48 for all cross-sections except 1870.

In terms of central government spending compared with levels of democracy (Fig. 7), we cannot find such an obvious correlation, and the R^2 values were very low. In fact, if anything, central government spending, in relative terms, does not seem to increase with an increase in the level of democracy. This preliminary finding does not support the model introduced earlier.

Table 1. Social Transfers (=Social Spending Minus Education Subsidies) as a Percentage of GDP, 1880–1930.

Year	USA	UK	Finland	Sweden	Belgium
1880	0.29	0.86	0.66	0.72	0.17
1890	0.45	0.83	0.76	0.85	0.22
1900	0.55	1.00	0.78	0.85	0.26
1910	0.56	1.38	0.90	1.03	0.43
1920	0.70	1.39	0.85	1.14	0.52
1930	0.56	2.24	2.97	2.59	0.56

Source: Lindert (2004).

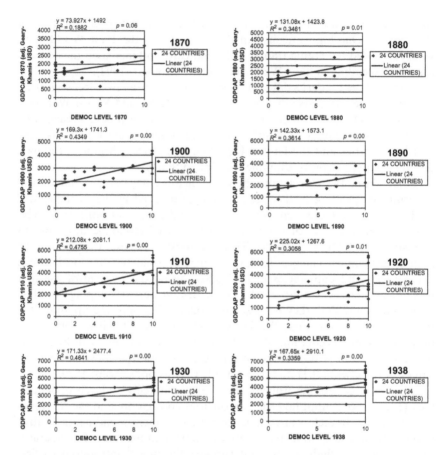

Fig. 6. Levels of Income Plotted Against Levels of Democracy, 1870–1938. *Source*: For further details, see Eloranta (2002, 2004). Levels of income represented by the real GDP per capita in 1990 Geary-Khamis dollars, obtained from Maddison (1995) and Obstfeld and Taylor (2003). Democracy scale used is the Polity IV scale, 0 indicating an autocracy, 10 indicating a "perfect" democracy. The coverage of the data for each of the countries can be found in Table A.1. Russia/USSR is also included in these figures, but excluded in the statistical analyses due to data discrepancies. *p*-values for the explanatory variable are also expressed for each figure.

There are some obvious outliers that may shed more light on this, for example, the case of Austria-Hungary. The central government spending share, as a percentage of nominal GDP, was extremely high (over 50 percent for nine of the years between 1870 and 1890), while it was not democratic. The

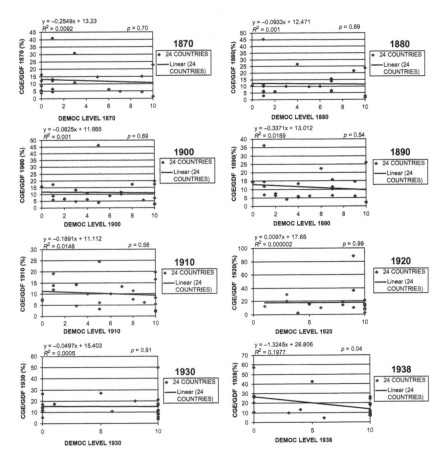

Fig. 7. Ratio of Central Government Spending to GDP (Percentage) Plotted Against Levels of Democracy, 1870–1938. *Source*: For further details, see Eloranta (2002, 2004). Additional data obtained from Mitchell (1998a, 1998b, 2003). The coverage of the data for each of the countries can be found in Table A.1. *p*-values for the explanatory variable are also expressed for each figure.

first reason for this was a weakened monarch, who had to placate many different constituencies in the late 19th century. The second was its high military burden, and the third the fact that Austria-Hungary's debt-to-GDP ratio, as a percentage, was over 150 percent in the 1890s. Japan was another outlier that had higher spending levels than suggested by its level of democracy. This was the result of massive military spending (9.7 percent of GDP in 1894, which was of course the beginning of the Sino-Japanese war of 1894–1895). We need to evaluate further whether some particular characteristic of democracy would produce such an impact, even though it does not show up in the context of the aggregate figures, perhaps because the

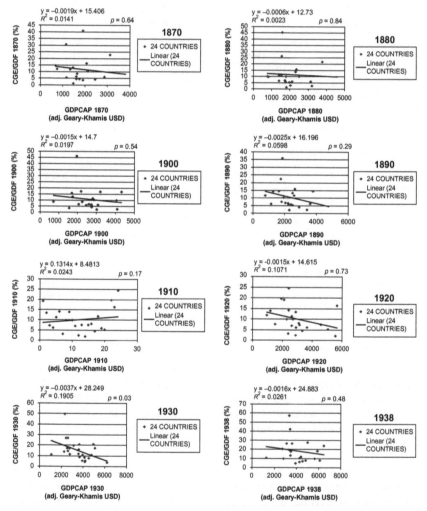

Fig. 8. Ratio of Central Government Spending to GDP (Percentage) Plotted Against Levels of Income, 1870–1938. *Source*: For further details, see previous figures. The coverage of the data for each of the countries can be found in Table A.1. *p*-values for the explanatory variable are also expressed for each figure.

impact of other variables, such as income, might be absorbing this effect. That is why a multivariate analysis is called for.

As seen in Fig. 8, there seems to be a slight negative correlation between central government spending shares and levels of income, although there are several outliers in the graphs, especially for low- to mid-range income levels. Again, Austria-Hungary was an exception, for reasons explained already. Or Japan in 1910, with spending share of 3.2 percent and an income level of 1,550 in 1990 Geary-Khamis USD. The R^2 values were quite low too for the various cross-sections. This possibly negative correlation goes against some of the assumptions presented in the introduction. Should not richer countries also spend relatively more on their governments? We would argue, first, that we need to look at the interaction of these three variables jointly to estimate their true impacts. Second, it is possible that the budgets of most states were fairly immobile and that the rapid income growth of the late 19th century provided some savings possibilities for the richer nations. Competition for lower taxes and business opportunities is another possibility. Third, we should also look at various categories of central government spending, especially military and social spending, and public debt commitments to understand this process more comprehensively.

DEMOCRACY, INSTITUTIONS, AND CENTRAL GOVERNMENT SPENDING: A MULTIVARIATE ANALYSIS

A multivariate approach is the only way to describe the interrelationships between the key variables in a more comprehensive manner. Our multivariate framework is based on the idea that states have different kinds of demand structures for central government spending based on their regime type, therefore highlighting the differences in their legitimacy functions. The reduced form equation we estimate is as follows:

$$CGE = \alpha_i + \beta_{i1}INPUT_{it} + \beta_{i2}OUTPUT_{it} + \beta_{i3}CONSTITUTIONAL_{it}$$
$$+ \cdots \beta_{i4}INTERNATIONAL_{it} + \varepsilon_{it} \qquad (1)$$

We evaluated this equation in a panel data format, yet only from 1881 onwards at eight-year increments. We do this in order to get a more representative sample and avoid some of the sporadic gaps in the individual countries' data. Measuring only at eight-year increments also allows us to avoid serial correlation, but still measure the impact of the exogenous shocks. The right-hand variable was the ratio of central government expenditures to GDP (percentage) since earlier results suggest few differences vis-à-vis the growth of this ratio. As independent variables, in order to estimate correlates with different types of legitimacy (featured in Eq. (1)), we utilized: (1) *input* variables, including the extent of the franchise (=FRAN, franchised share of adults in the population, percentage), disaggregated democracy variables (from POLITY IV: executive recruitment regulation (=XRREG), executive recruitment competition (=XRCOMP), and executive recruitment openness (=XROPEN)); (2) *output* variables, including school enrollment (primary school, in thousands = SCHOOL), ME-SE trade-off (measured as: $(ME_t + SE_t)/(ME_{t-8} + SE_{t-8})$, equal to 1 if a perfect trade-off occurs, abbreviated by MESE), war year dummies (dummy = 1 if country in a war during a given year = WAR), size of the armed forces (as a share of population, percentage = MP); (3) *constitutional* variables, including type of legal system (dummy, common law = 1, otherwise 0, abbreviated by LEGAL), type of executive branch (dummy, monarchy = 1, otherwise 0, abbreviated by EXEC), effectiveness of the legislative branch (=LEGIS, ranging from 0 to 3), following Banks' (1976) definitions; (4) *international* variables, including military alliances (dummy = 1 if country has an alliance, abbreviated by ALLIANCE), central government debt burden (central government debt as a share of GDP, percentage = DEBT), membership in the Gold Standard (dummy = 1 if a member, abbreviated by GOLD). We will also test whether a more aggregate measure of the strength of democratic institutions (Polity IV democracy values minus the autocracy values) or income (real GDP per capita) have a consistent statistically significant relationship with CGE when these other variables are included. This last step will complement the cross-plots (Figs. 7 and 8), in which we found limited evidence of correlations.

Before we go further, we need to justify the solution proposed above as how to analyze the trade-off between military and social spending, estimating this trade-off is not straightforward. In fact, there are several kinds of "guns versus butter" trade-offs. First, "guns" usually refers to military spending and the burden it causes for states. "Butter," in turn, refers to either income or redistribution implications. Some have even extended the use of this term to cover trade-offs between trade and security (see, e.g., Skaperdas & Syropoulos, 2001) or economic competition versus military competition (Grossman & Mendoza, 2001).

The other conventional way of perceiving guns versus butter trade-offs is to analyze the budgetary struggles between the proponents of military expenditures and social spending. Although some studies have been conducted on such budgetary trade-offs (Domke, Eichenberg, & Kelleher, 1983; Garand & Hendrick, 1991; Narizny, 2003; Palmer, 1990; on Second World War, see especially Harrison, 1998), there have been no systematic efforts to investigate such possible budgetary trade-offs in the long run, with either rich case studies or with large panel data samples. Moreover, there is no general agreement on how to measure this trade-off in the literature. Plotting the two against one another, as we have done in Fig. 9, does not

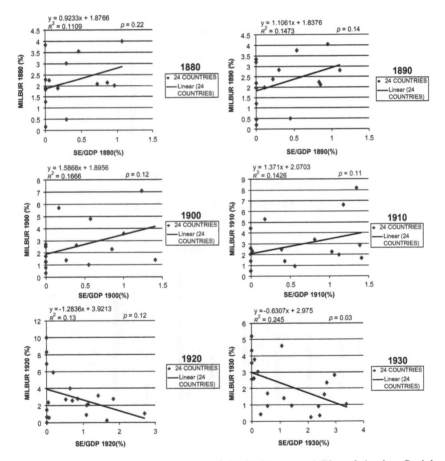

Fig. 9. Military Spending as a Share of GDP (Percentage) Plotted Against Social Spending as a Share of GDP (Percentage), 1880–1930. *Source*: For further details, see previous figures. The coverage of the data for each of the countries can be found in Table A.1. *p*-values for the explanatory variable are also expressed for each figure.

yield many clues, since for many countries social spending was zero, at least
until the First World War. And even when social spending was not zero,
there was no clear pattern to be found between social and military spending.

We propose two ways to consistently measure the guns versus butter
trade-off. One way, here dubbed Method 1, would be to add up the change
in military spending from one year to another (here at eight-year intervals)
with the change in social spending. Fig. 10 illustrates the resulting values

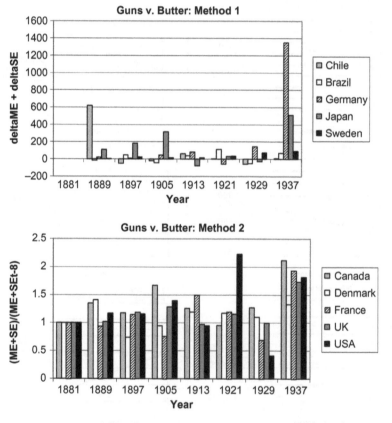

Fig. 10. Two Potential Methods of Estimating the Guns versus Butter Trade-off,
1870–1938. Guns v. Butter: Method 1 Guns v. Butter: Method 2 *Source*: For
further details, see previous figures. The coverage of the data for each of the
countries can be found in Table A.1. Delta refers to change from the previous
period to the next, at eight-year intervals.

for a few representative countries to illustrate the technique. Method 1 occasionally produces negative numbers, which is problematic for a potential conversion into logarithms. If, however we utilize Method 2, that is, divide up the net changes in the subsequent years as suggested in conjunction with the description of variables under Eq. (1), we estimate the change in relative terms in the spending levels, but with numbers greater than zero. Here we estimated the equations initially with both variables, but ultimately used the variable derived via Method 2. As for the impact of this potential guns-versus-butter trade-off, if the variable exceeded one, central government expenditures would increase, as argued by Niall Ferguson (2001). Therefore, though it is not a perfect measure, this variable will indicate if regimes allowed the sum of military and social spending to grow over time.

Further information on the sources of the income, population, debt, membership in the Gold Standard, and the size of the armed forces variables can be found in Table A.1. The data on the franchise, social spending, and school enrollment came from Peter Lindert's various studies (2003, 2004) and from Arthur Banks' (1976) database whenever needed. The Banks database also provided the data for the constitutional legitimacy measures. Data on military alliances is from the ATOP (Alliance Treaty Obligations and Provisions) database (Leeds, Ritter, Mitchell, & Long, 2000). Information on inter-state war participants is from Sarkees (2000).

Given that the panel consisted only of eight cross-section years, compared with 23 country cross-sections (for most years), the equation was first estimated with OLS (Ordinary Least Squares) with panel corrected standard errors (as advocated by Beck, 2001; Beck & Katz, 1995 when $N > T$), and additionally with period-specific SUR (*Seemingly Unrelated Regressions*) with period-SUR weighting. The variables were also tested for the existence of common unit roots, but the results were not conclusive as they were influenced by the structure of the panel.[4]

Therefore, all the regressions were performed with the original variables. Most of them were first, nonetheless, transformed into logarithms (only DEM, XRREG, XRCOMP, XRCOMP, WAR, LEGAL, EXEC, LEGIS, and GOLD were not). Those series that contained zeroes were transformed by first adding 1 to each data point. Finally, the panel data regressions were first run by using the entire sample, then with a more limited sample, namely countries that did not have any data gaps.

Tables 2 and 3 feature the descriptive statistics for some of the key variables; Table 2 has the averages for the prewar period, and Table 3 for the interwar period. In all categories the mean values were higher for the interwar period, and the standard deviations were higher as well.

Table 2. Descriptive Statistics for the Selected Variables in Total, 1870−1913.

	CGE	MILBUR	DEM	INCOME	DEBT
Mean	9.78	2.47	2.48	2,535	50.96
Median	7.32	2.14	2.00	2,360	35.29
Maximum	56.80	23.92	10.00	9,002	327.78
Minimum	1.75	0.13	−9.00	704	0.04
Std. Dev.	7.77	2.10	5.00	1,128	53.24
N	639	639	639	639	639
Number of cross sections	21	21	21	21	21

Source: See Table A.1. CGE, central/federal government expenditures as a share of GDP (percentage); MILBUR, military expenditures as a share of GDP (percentage); DEM, level of democracy, polity scale; INCOME, real GDP per capita; DEBT, level of debt as a share of GDP (percentage).

Table 3. Descriptive Statistics for the Selected Variables in Total, 1920−1938.

	CGE	MILBUR	DEM	INCOME	DEBT
Mean	14.72	2.89	5.38	3,676	56.86
Median	13.06	2.24	10.00	3,733	36.02
Maximum	87.91	42.01	10.00	6,907	237.03
Minimum	2.57	0.15	−9.00	776	0.15
Std. Dev.	9.32	3.41	6.45	1,416	56.14
N	424	424	424	424	424
Number of cross sections	23	23	23	23	23

Source: See Table A.1. Abbreviations explained in Table 2.

Overall, our regressions achieved good statistical fits, with very high adjusted R^2 figures for the SUR specifications in particular. The OLS specifications also seemed to explain about half of the variation in central government spending. Also, the coefficients of statistically relevant variables did not change much when we switched between the OLS and the period-specific SUR, which indicates that the results were fairly robust. Moreover, the limited sample (available from the authors by request) produced fairly similar results as the full sample.

As seen in Table 4, specifications 1−3 are for the cross-section weighted OLS, and specifications 4−6 for the period-specific SUR. Specifications 1 and 4 are for the base equation, specifications 2 and 5 include DEM and

Table 4. Panel Data Analysis of the Determinants of Central Government Spending, 1881–1937 (Full Sample).

Independent Variables	1 (OLS, Cross-Section Weights PCSEs): Coefficients	2 (OLS, Cross-Section Weights PCSEs): Coefficients	3 (OLS, Cross-Section Weights PCSEs): Coefficients	4 (Period-Specific SUR, Period-SUR Weights): Coefficients	5 (Period-Specific SUR, Period-SUR Weights): Coefficients	6 (Period-Specific SUR, Period-SUR Weights): Coefficients
CONSTANT	2.27***	2.04**	1.62***	2.14***	2.55***	1.91***
FRAN	0.07***	0.08***	0.07***	0.06*	0.06*	–
SCHOOL	-0.08	-0.09	–	-0.03	-0.00	–
XRREG	-1.15	-0.16	–	0.00	0.01	–
XRCOMP	0.14*	0.20*	–	0.09	0.06	–
XROPEN	0.09*	0.08*	0.11***	0.02	0.03	0.06**
MESE	0.04	0.04	–	0.01	0.01	–
WAR	0.04	0.05	–	0.14	0.11	–
MP	0.11**	0.11**	0.10**	0.12***	0.12***	0.11***
LEGAL	-0.53***	-0.53***	-0.46***	-0.38***	-0.36***	-0.40***
EXEC	0.40***	0.41***	0.28***	0.22***	0.23**	0.17***
LEGIS	-0.03	-0.02	–	-0.08	-0.08	–
ALLIANCE	0.23**	0.23**	0.18*	0.13**	0.14**	0.10**
DEBT	0.14***	0.14***	0.13***	0.13***	0.13***	0.14***
GOLD	-0.38***	-0.39***	-0.44***	-0.33***	-0.33***	-0.36***
DEM	–	-0.01	–	–	0.01	–
INCOME	–	0.03	–	–	-0.07	–
Weighted, adj. R^2	0.49	0.49	0.50	0.90	0.90	0.92
SE	0.47	0.48	0.47	0.91	0.91	0.90
N	143	143	143	143	143	143
F-statistic	10.87	9.44	18.51	NA	NA	NA

Source: See previous tables for details. *Null hypothesis of no correlation rejected at 10 percent level; **null rejected at 5 percent level; ***null rejected at 1 percent level.

INCOME, and specifications 3 and 6 represent the best statistical fits for the model.

How well do the results coincide with the theoretical framework utilized in this article? Essentially the model performed fairly well, though there are some surprises. Extension of franchise (FRAN) seemed to have a small, positive impact on central government spending levels, as expected. The military spending versus social spending trade-off effect was inconsistent and needs to be explored further. It is possible that the fact that many countries had only slowly started spending on social programs during this period explains this. Primary school enrollment (SCHOOL), which is the variable included in the regression which should be most closely linked to social expenditures, actually had a small negative coefficient, though it was not statistically significant. Military expenditures are captured in the regression by the number of military personnel expressed as a percentage of the population (MP), and the dummy for the country being in war (WAR). An increase in the number of military personnel consistently increased government spending, though the war dummy has no statistically discernible effect. Further analysis is needed to detangle the various elements that shaped the budgetary trade-offs involving social and military expenditures, a topic that the authors hope to revisit in future scholarship.

This preliminary analysis of the data indicate that alliances encouraged higher government spending, not free-riding, at least as far as central government spending was concerned. In fact, these alliances may have been less credible and binding than is often presumed (Eloranta, 2004). Higher debt levels, as a revenue tool and fiscal burden, had a positive impact, as expected. The Gold Standard, on the other hand, reduced government spending substantially. This could be explained, as Obstfeld and Taylor (2003) suggest, by the fact that the Gold Standard tended to increase a country's credibility and reduce borrowing costs, but it did so by acting as a constraint on spending.

Other than the extent of the franchise, the variables associated with democracy do not seem tightly associated with the size of central government spending. The measure of the aggregate level of democratic institutions (DEM) has only a very small coefficient which is not statistically significant. The only disaggregated democracy variables with an impact on spending is XROPEN, the openness of the recruitment of the executive. It increased spending, which is consistent with the expectations. When the executive had to rely more on the electorate for reelection purposes, historians have suggested they tended to try to placate the masses with social programs and other pork barrel spending.

Having a monarch tended to increase spending. Why? Monarchies were under threat in this period, as we have seen already for example in the case of Austria-Hungary, and had to find ways to hold on to power. Spending on social causes and finding external conflicts to fight were a way of doing that. As seen in Table 5, for example, the relative military spending of monarchies was, on average, higher than the spending by other regime types, at least until the late 1920s. Table 6 provides a bit more detail on this

Table 5.   Relative Military Spending of Monarchies versus Other Regimes, 1881–1937.

Year	Mean ME of Monarchies	Median ME of Monarchies	Mean ME of Other Regimes	Median ME of Other Regimes	Difference between Monarchies and Other Regimes' ME (Means)	Difference between Monarchies and Other Regimes' ME (Medians)
1881	2.16	1.97	1.77	1.12	0.39	0.86
1889	2.57	2.51	2.59	1.36	−0.03	1.15
1897	2.67	2.46	2.10	1.66	0.56	0.80
1905	3.78	2.44	1.68	1.36	2.10	1.08
1913	3.75	2.88	2.22	1.52	1.53	1.36
1921	7.73	2.50	2.59	2.45	5.14	0.05
1929	1.53	1.36	2.12	2.19	−0.60	−0.83
1937	4.31	2.53	4.40	3.15	−0.09	−0.63

Source: See Table A.1. ME, military spending as a percentage of GDP.

Table 6.   Relative Military Personnel of Monarchies versus Other Regimes, 1881–1937.

Year	Mean MP of Monarchies	Median MP of Monarchies	Mean MP of Other Regimes	Median MP of Other Regimes	Difference between Monarchies and Other Regimes' MP (Means)	Difference between Monarchies and Other Regimes' MP (Medians)
1881	0.88	0.71	1.23	0.60	−0.35	0.11
1889	0.68	0.81	0.98	0.31	−0.29	0.50
1897	0.66	0.72	1.09	0.47	−0.43	0.25
1905	0.65	0.63	1.04	0.50	−0.39	0.13
1913	1.08	0.71	0.94	0.60	0.13	0.12
1921	0.70	0.54	0.93	0.52	−0.23	0.02
1929	0.53	0.52	0.84	0.58	−0.31	−0.06
1937	0.53	0.49	1.03	0.62	−0.50	−0.13

Source: Singer and Small (1993). MP, military personnel as a percentage of population.

relationship, although the results are not entirely consistent. Based on the mean values, it seems that monarchies also got a lower "return" for their spending inasmuch their armies were smaller. This is just a superficial observation, since we would have to evaluate their spending in more detail (e.g., spending on troops vs. armaments) to confirm this result, especially since the median values show the opposite result.

Finally, common law countries tended to spend less on the whole, perhaps due to different institutions and historical traditions. The United States is a case in point. It has had a long tradition of resistance to higher taxation, an increased role for government, a central bank, and foreign entanglements; this tradition has carried over to the current period. Furthermore, it did not assume the role of an economic and military superpower until after the Second World War. And though Great Britain was a worldwide empire before the Second World War, the British were very keen on running their massive enterprise on the cheap (see, e.g., Ferguson, 2003).

DISCUSSION

The ideological clout of liberalism and democracy in contemporary life has become one of the essential and nearly uncontested policy principles in recent decades. Leading politicians and intellectuals have greeted enthusiastically the fall of communism and other types of autocratic rule in various parts of the globe since the Cold War. At the same time, many world leaders have called for increased global action on the basis of these somewhat undefined concepts. In fact, do we really understand what drives the so-called waves of democracy?

This paper examines data associated with the first wave of democracy. Democratization, as seen in the cross-plots, went hand-in-hand with rising incomes in the 19th and 20th centuries. Industrializing nations were able to — perhaps had to — redistribute revenue to alleviate some of the more negative consequences of aggregate growth. Carlos Boix and Susan Stokes (2003) argue that certain levels of income had to be reached before democratization could succeed. Yet, in the data presented here, we found there was little correlation between government spending and income, or government spending and democracy, contrary to our expectations.

It is also imperative to look at the data in a multivariate setting. We did this by utilizing panel data regressions, pursuing further the idea of linking spending patterns to the different legitimacy strategies of regimes. We tested input, output, constitutional, and international variables as correlates of spending. Our hypothesis was that democracies have a broader and more consistent need for legitimization than autocracies, with this broader demand driving up central government spending.

Our model performed adequately empirically, though we found that the well-established link between increased government spending and democracy seen in the post-Second World War period was more nuanced before that war. Extension of franchise seems to have had a small, positive impact on central government spending levels. The military versus social expenditure trade-off variable did not seem relevant, perhaps due to low levels of social spending for most of this period. Neither democracy in the aggregate, nor income, had much of an impact on the central government spending. Only few of the disaggregated democracy variables – essentially how open and competitive the executive branch recruitment process was – had a slight, positive impact on government spending. The common law system had a profound negative impact on government spending, reinforcing the view of limited Anglo-American welfare systems in the 20th century, although it is a bit surprising to find the roots of these differences before the Second World War. Early liberal democracies, therefore, differed in their fiscal evolution from other emerging democracies.

Also, quite surprisingly, having a monarchy had a sizable positive impact on spending, which may be explained by the growing social and military tensions of the period and the parallel rise of parliamentarism. Alliances did not encourage free-riding, but encouraged higher spending. Higher central government debt levels, as a revenue tool, had a positive impact on spending, as expected. The Gold Standard, on the other hand, reduced government spending substantially. This could be explained by the fact that the Gold Standard tended to increase a country's financial credibility and reduce borrowing costs, or that it increased credibility through acting as a real constraint on spending.

NOTES

1. Unless otherwise indicated, all spending figures are given as percentages of GDP.
2. The Polity IV Project is described on its website as a coding of the characteristics of states in the world system for purposes of comparative, quantitative analysis (http://www.systemicpeace.org/polity/polity4.htm. Accessed October 29, 2013). The

Polity IIID democracy data used here in the quantitative exercises is very similar —
the Polity IV dataset mostly includes broader country coverage.
  3. See http://www.systemicpeace.org/inscr/inscr.htm for details.
  4. Details available upon request.

ACKNOWLEDGMENTS

The assistance of several scholars is duly recognized in collecting the underlying data in this paper, especially Alan Taylor, Peter Lindert, Mark
Harrison, and Zephyr Frank. Also, the helpful criticism of several collea-
gues has improved this paper tremendously. Jari Eloranta would like to
acknowledge the support of Finnish Centre of Excellence project on long-
run structures of Finland (1400–2000), and Marie Curie fellowship awarded
by the European Union for 2002–2004.

REFERENCES

Acemoglu, D., & Robinson, J. A. (2006). *Economic origins of dictatorship and democracy.*
    Cambridge: Cambridge University Press.
Avelino, G., Brown, D. S., & Hunter, W. (2005). The effects of capital mobility, trade open-
    ness, and democracy on social spending in Latin America, 1980–1999. *American
    Journal of Political Science, 49,* 625–641.
Bakker, G. P. d., Huitker, T. A., & Bochove, C. A. v. (1990). The Dutch economy 1921–1938:
    Revised macroeconomic data for the interwar period. *Review of Income and Wealth:
    Journal of the International Association for Research in Income and Wealth, 36*(2),
    87–206.
Banks, A. S. (1976). *Cross-national time series, 1815–1973.* Ann Arbor, MI: Inter-University
    Consortium for Political and Social Research. Accessed in 2001.
Batista, D., Martins, C., Pinheiro, M., & Reis, J. (1997). New estimates for Portugal's GDP
    1910–1958. *Historia Economica, 7,* 1–128.
Beck, N. (2001). Time-series-cross-section data: What have we learned in the past few years?
    Annual Review of Political Science, 4, 271–293.
Beck, N., & Katz, J. N. (1995). What to do (and not to do) with time-series cross-section data.
    The American Political Science Review, 89, 634–647.
Berman, S. (2006). *The primacy of politics: Social democracy and making of Europe's Twentieth
    Century.* Cambridge: Cambridge University Press.
Blondel, J. (1995). *Comparative government. An introduction.* London: Prentice Hall.
Boix, C. (2001). Democracy, development, and the public sector. *American Journal of Political
    Science, 45*(1), 1–17.
Boix, C. (2003). *Democracy and redistribution.* Cambridge: Cambridge University Press.
Boix, C., & Stokes, S. C. (2003). Endogenous democratization. *World Politics, 55,* 517–549.

Bollen, K. A., & Paxton, P. (2000). Subjective measures of democracy. *Comparative Political Studies, 33*, 58−86.

Bonney, R. (1999). Introduction. In R. Bonney (Ed.), *The rise of the fiscal state in Europe C. 1200−1815.* Oxford: Oxford University Press.

Brown, D., & Hunter, W. (1999). Democracy and social spending in Latin America, 1980−1992. *American Political Science Review, 93*, 779−790.

Buyst, E. (1997). New GNP estimates for the Belgian economy during the interwar period. *Review of Income and Wealth: Journal of the International Association for Research in Income and Wealth, 43*, 357−375.

Capoccia, G. (2005). *Defending democracy: Reactions to extremism in interwar Europe.* Baltimore, MD: Johns Hopkins University Press.

Carreras, A. (1989). *Estadísticas Históricas De España: Siglos Xix-Xx/Carlos Barciela ... [Et al.]; Coordinación De Albert Carreras Colección Investigaciones.* Madrid: Fundación Banco Exterior.

Clement, P. (2000). *Government consumption and investment in Belgium: 1830−1940: The reconstruction of a database. In Studies in social and economic history* (Vol. 29). Leuven: Leuven University Press.

Deacon, R. T. (2009). Public good under dictatorship and democracy. *Public Choice, 139*, 241−262.

della Paolera, G., Taylor, A. M., & Bózzoli, C. (2003). Historical statistics. In G. della Paolera & A. M. Taylor (Eds.), *Argentina: Essays in the new economic history.* Cambridge: Cambridge University Press.

Denzel, M., Schneider, J., Schwarzer, O., & Zellfelder, F. (1997). *Währungen Der Welt/ Herausgegeben Von Jürgen Schneider, Oskar Schwarzer Und Friedrich Zellfelder Series Beiträge Zur Wirtschafts- Und Sozialgeschichte.* Stuttgart.

Diamond, L., & Lipset, S. M. (1995). Legitimacy. In S. M. Lipset (Ed.), *The encyclopedia of democracy.* Washington, DC: Lynne Rienner.

Domke, W. K., Eichenberg, R. C., & Kelleher, C. M. (1983). The illusion of choice: Defense and welfare in advanced industrial democracies, 1948−1978. *The American Political Science Review, 77*, 19−35.

Easton, D. (1965). *A system of analysis of political life.* New York, NY: Wiley.

Eloranta, J. (2002). *External security by domestic choices: Military spending as an impure public good among eleven European States, 1920−1938.* Dissertation, European University Institute.

Eloranta, J. (2004). Warfare and welfare? Understanding 19th and 20th century central government spending. In P. Vikström (Ed.), *Studying economic growth. New tools and perspectives.* Occasional Papers in Economic History No. 7, Umeå University, Umeå.

Eloranta, J. (2007). From the great illusion to the great war: Military spending behaviour of the great powers, 1870−1913. *European Review of Economic History, 11*, 255−283.

Esping-Andersen, G. (1990). *The three worlds of welfare capitalism.* Princeton, NJ: Princeton University Press.

Esping-Andersen, G. (1999). *Social foundations of postindustrial economies.* Oxford: Oxford University Press.

Esping-Andersen, G. (2004). Social welfare policy, comparisons. In N. J. Smelser & P. B. Bates (Eds.), *International encyclopedia of social and behavioral sciences.* Amsterdam: Elsevier.

Ferguson, N. (1999). *The pity of war.* New York, NY: Basic Books.

Ferguson, N. (2001). *The cash nexus: Money and power in the modern world, 1700–2000*. New York, NY: Basic Books.

Ferguson, N. (2003). *Empire: The rise and demise of the British world order and the lessons for global power*. New York, NY: Basic Books.

Ferguson, N. (2004). *Colossus: The price of America's empire*. New York, NY: Basic Books.

Garand, J. C., & Hendrick, R. M. (1991). Expenditure tradeoffs in the American States: A longitudinal test, 1948–1984. *The Western Political Quarterly, 44*, 915–940.

Gleditsch, K. (2000). *Polity IIID database*. In K. Gleditsch [Producer]. Retrieved from http:// k-gleditsch.socsci.gla.ac.uk/Polity.html. Accessed in 2000.

Global Financial Data. (2001). Retrieved from https://www.globalfinancialdata.com/index. html. Accessed in 2001.

Grossman, H. I., & Mendoza, J. (2001). Butter and guns: Complementarity between economic and military competition. *Economics of Governance, 2*, 25–33.

Harrison, M. (1998). The economics of World War II: An overview. In M. Harrison (Ed.), *The economics of World War II. Six great powers in international comparisons*. Cambridge: Cambridge University Press.

Hicks, A., & Misra, J. (1993). Political resources and the growth of welfare in affluent capitalist democracies, 1960–1982. *American Journal of Sociology, 99*, 668–710.

Higgs, R. (1989). *Crisis and leviathan: Critical episodes in the growth of American government*. Oxford: Oxford University Press.

Hjerppe, R. (1988). Suomen talous 1860–1985. Kasvu ja rakennemuutos. Kasvututkimuksia (Vol. XIII). Suomen Pankki, Helsinki.

Hobbes, T. (1651). *Leviathan*. New York, NY: Cambridge University Press. (Reprint, 1991).

Hobson, J. M. (1993). The military–extraction gap and the wary titan: The fiscal sociology of British defence policy 1870–1914. *Journal of European Economic History, 22*, 466–507.

Höreth, M. (1998). *The trilemma of legitimacy – Multilevel governance in the EU and the problem of democracy*. ZEI Discussion Papers, Bonn.

Höreth, M. (2001). *The European Commission's White Paper on governance: A 'tool-kit' for closing the legitimacy gap of EU policy-making*. ZEI Discussion Papers, Bonn.

Huber, E., Mustillo, T., & Stephens, J. D. (2008). Politics and social spending in Latin America. *The Journal of Politics, 70*, 420–436.

Huber, E., Ragin, C., & Stephens, J. D. (1993). Social democracy, Christian democracy, constitutional structure and the welfare state. *American Journal of Sociology, 99*, 711–749.

Huber, E., & Stephens, J. D. (2001). *Development and crisis of the welfare state: Parties and policies in global markets*. Chicago, IL: University of Chicago Press.

Johansen, H. C. (1985). *Dansk Historisk Statistik 1814–1980*. København: Gyldenhahl.

Kaufman, R. D., & Segura-Ubiergo, A. (2001). Globalization, domestic politics, and social spending in Latin America. *World Politics, 53*, 553–588.

Kausel, A. (1979). Österreichs Volkseinkommen 1830 Bis 1913. In *Geschichte Und Ergebnisse Der Zentralen Amtlichen Statistik in Österreich 1829–1979*. Vienna: Österreichisches Statistisches Zentralamt.

Kostelenos, G. C. (1995). *Money and output in modern Greece, 1858–1938*. Dissertation, Centre of Planning and Economic Research, University of Kent, Kent.

Krantz, O. (1987). *Offentlig verksamhet 1800–1980 Series skrifter utgivna av Ekonomisk-Historiska Föreningen i Lund 50*. Lund: Lund universitet.

Krantz, O. (1997). *Swedish historical national accounts 1800–1990 – Aggregated output series*. Mimeograph.

Lake, D. A., & Baum, M. A. (2001). The invisible hand of democracy: Political control and the provision of public services. *Comparative Political Studies, 34*, 587–621.

Leeds, B. A., Ritter, J. M., Mitchell, S. M. & Long., A. G. (2000). *ATOP (=Alliance Treaty Obligations and Provisions) database V. 1.0*. Retrieved from http://garnet.acns.fsu.edu/~aleeds/atop.html. Accessed in 2002.

Lindert, P. H. (1994). The rise of social spending, 1880–1930. *Explorations in Economic History, 31*, 1–37.

Lindert, P. H. (1996). What limits social spending? *Explorations in Economic History, 33*, 1–34.

Lindert, P. H. (2003). Voice and growth: Was Churchill right? *The Journal of Economic History, 63*, 315–350.

Lindert, P. H. (2004). *Growing public. Social spending and economic growth since the eighteenth century* (Vol. 1). Cambridge: Cambridge University Press.

Lipset, S. M. (Ed.). (1983). *Political man: The social bases of politics*. New York, NY: Doubleday.

Lipset, S. M. (1984). Social conflict, legitimacy, and democracy. In W. Connolly (Ed.), *Legitimacy and the state*. Oxford: Oxford University Press.

Lord, C. (2000). *Legitimacy, democracy and the EU: When abstract questions become practice policy problems*. Policy Paper 03/00. ESRC Programme "One Europe or Several?".

Luebbert, G. M. (1991). *Liberalism, fascism, or social democracy: Social classes and political origins of regimes in the interwar Europe*. New York, NY: Oxford University Press.

Macdonald, J. (2003). *A free nation deep in debt. The financial roots of democracy*. New York, NY: Farrar, Strauss, Giroux.

Maddison, A. (1995). *Monitoring the world economy 1820–1992*. Paris: OECD.

Mann, M. (2012). The sources of social power, *Global empires and revolutions, 1890–1945* (Vol. III). Cambridge: Cambridge University Press.

Mann, M. (2013). The sources of social power, *Globalizations, 1945–2011* (Vol. IV). Cambridge: Cambridge University Press.

Mansfield, E. D., & Snyder, J. L. (2005). *Electing to fight: Why emerging democracies go to war. BCSIA studies in international security*. Cambridge: Cambridge University Press.

Mata, E. (1993). As financas publicas portuguesas da regeneracao a primeira guerra mundial. *Historia Economica, 4*. Lisboa: Banco de Portugal.

Mitchell, B. R. (1988). *British historical statistics*. Cambridge: Cambridge University Press.

Mitchell, B. R. (1998a). *International historical statistics: Europe 1750–1993*. Basingstoke: Macmillan.

Mitchell, B. R. (1998b). *International historical statistics: The Americas 1750–1993*. London: Macmillan.

Mitchell, B. R. (2003). *International historical statistics: Africa, Asia and Oceania, 1750–2000*. New York, NY: Macmillan.

Muller, J.-W. (2011). *Contesting democracy: Political ideas in twentieth century Europe*. New Haven, CT: Yale University Press.

Munck, G. L., & Verkuilen, J. (2002). Conceptualizing and measuring democracy: Evaluating alternative indices. *Comparative Political Studies, 35*, 5–34.

Narizny, K. (2003). Both guns and butter, or neither: Class interests in the political economy of rearmament. *American Political Science Review, 97*, 203–220.

Norris, P. (2012). *Making democratic governance work: How regimes shape prosperity, welfare, and peace*. Cambridge: Cambridge University Press.

Obstfeld, M., & Taylor, A. M. (2003). Sovereign risk, credibility and the gold standard: 1870–1913 versus 1925–1931. *The Economic Journal, 113*, 241–275.

Olson, M. (1993). Dictatorship, democracy, and development. *American Political Science Review, 87,* 567–576.

Palmer, G. (1990). NATO, social and defense spending, and coalitions. *The Western Political Quarterly, 43,* 479–493.

Prados de la Escosura, L. (1993). *Spain's gross domestic product, 1850–1990: A new series.* Madrid: Banco de Espana.

Pryor, F. L. (1968). *Public expenditures in communist and capitalist nations.* London: Allen and Unwin.

Przeworski, A. (2009). Conquered or granted? A history of suffrage extensions. *British Journal of Political Science, 39,* 291–321.

Przeworski, A., Alvarez, M. E., Cheibub, J. A., & Limongi, F. (2000). *Democracy and development: Political institutions and well-being in the world, 1950–1990.* Cambridge: Cambridge University Press.

Ritzmann-Blickenstorfer, H. & David, T. (2000). *New estimates of the Swiss gross domestic product (1892–1960).* Mimeograph.

Rossi, N., Sorgato, A., & Toniolo, G. (1993). I conti economici italiani: Una ricostruzione statistica, 1890–1990. *Rivista di Storia Economica, 10,* 1–47.

Rota, M. (2011). *Military burden and the democracy puzzle.* Working Paper. Retrieved from http://ideas.repec.org/p/pra/mprapa/35254.html/. Accessed in 2013.

Sarkees, M. R. (2000). The correlates of war data on war: An update to 1997. *Conflict Management and Peace Science, 18,* 123–144.

Scharpf, F. (1994). Community and autonomy: Multilevel policy-making in the European union. *Journal of European Public Policy, 1,* 219–242.

Scharpf, F. (1997). Economic integration, democracy and the welfare state. *Journal of European Public Policy, 4,* 18–36.

Scharpf, F. (1999). *Governing in Europe. Democratic and efficient?* Oxford: Oxford University Press.

Schmidt, M. G. (1997). Determinants of social expenditure in liberal democracies: The post World War II experience. *Acta Politica, 32,* 153–173.

Schmitter, P. C. (2001). *What is there to legitimize in the European Union ... and how might this be accomplished?* Jean Monnet Working Paper. Harvard Law School European Union Program.

Schmitter, P. C. (2010). Twenty-five years, fifteen findings. *Journal of Democracy, 21,* 17–28.

Schneider, J., Schwarzer, O., Zellfelder, F., & Denzel, M. A. (1991). *Währungen Der Welt, Beiträge Zur Wirtschafts- Und Sozialgeschichte* (Bd. 44). Stuttgart: Franz Steiner Verlag.

Siegenthaler, H., & Ritzmann-Blickenstorfer, H. (1996). *Historische Statistik Der Schweiz. Statistique Historique De La Suisse. Historical Statistics of Switzerland.* Zurich: Chronos.

Singer, J. D., & Small, M. (1993). *National material capabilities data, 1816–1985.* Computer file. J. D. Singer, University of Michigan and M. Small, Wayne State University (Producers). Accessed in 2001.

Skaperdas, S., & Syropoulos, C. (2001). Guns, butter, and openness: On the relationship between security and trade. *The American Economic Review, 91,* 353–357.

Smits, J.-P., Horlings, E., & Zanden, J. L. v. (2000). *Dutch GNP and its components, 1800–1913.* Groningen. Retrieved from http://nationalaccounts.niwi.knaw.nl/pdf/newgnp1.pdf. Accessed in 2002.

Stasavage, D. (2005). Democracy and education spending in Africa. *American Journal of Political Science, 49*, 343–358.

United Nations, Dept. of Economic Affairs. (1948). *Public debt, 1914–1946*. Lake Success, NY: United Nations.

United States, Bureau of the Census. (1976). *The statistical history of the United States, from colonial times to the present = historical statistics of the United States, colonial times to 1970*. New York, NY: Basic Books.

Urquhart, M. C., & Buckley, K. A. H. (1965). *Historical statistics of Canada*. Cambridge: Cambridge University Press.

Valério, N. (1994). *As Finanças Públicas Portuguesas Entre as Duas Guerras Mundiais Portugal e o Mundo Português*. Lisboa: Edições Cosmos.

Webber, C., & Wildavsky, A. (1986). *A history of taxation and expenditure in the western world*. New York, NY: Simon and Shuster.

Weber, M. (1946). *From Max Weber: Essays in sociology* (H. H. Gerth & C. W. Mills, Trans.). New York, NY: Oxford University Press.

Weber, M. (1964). *The theory of social and economic organization* (A. M. Henderson & T. Parsons, Eds.). New York, NY: Macmillan.

Weiler, J. (1993). After Maastricht: Community legitimacy in post-1992 Europe. In W. J. Adams (Ed.), *Singular Europe. Economy and polity of the European community after 1992*. Ann Arbor, MI: University of Michigan Press.

Weiler, J. (1999). *The constitution for Europe*. Cambridge: Cambridge University Press.

APPENDIX

Table A.1. Data Coverage (Years), Sources, and Notes on Data Solutions.

Country	DEM	REAL INCOME	CGE	ME	SE	DEBT
Argentina (ARG)	Full (Gleditsch, 2000)	1884–(Obstfeld & Taylor, 2003)	Full (Mitchell, 1998)	1870–1913 (provided by Alan Taylor), 1920–1938 (Singer & Small, 1993)	Assumed 0	1884–(Obstfeld & Taylor, 2003)
Australia (AUS)	1901–(Gleditsch, 2000)	Full (Obstfeld & Taylor, 2003)	1901–(Mitchell, 2003)	1901–1913 (Banks, 1976), 1920–1938 (Singer & Small, 1993)	1881–1937 (Lindert, 1994; Lindert, 2004) (see also Appendix Table C.6)	Full (Obstfeld & Taylor, 2003)
Austria-Hungary/ Austria (AUT)	Full (Gleditsch, 2000)	Full (Obstfeld & Taylor, 2003)	Full (Mitchell, 1998)	1870–1913 (Hobson, 1993), 1920–1938 (Eloranta, 2002)	1881–1937 (Lindert, 1994, 2004) (see also Appendix Table C.6)	1881–1913, 1924–1937 (Obstfeld & Taylor, 2003)
Belgium (BEL)	Full (Gleditsch, 2000)	Full (Maddison, 1995)	Full (Mitchell, 1998) (1913 value from Banks, 1976)	Full (Clement, 2000)	1881–1937 (Lindert, 1994, 2004) (see also Appendix Table C.6)	Full (Obstfeld & Taylor, 2003)
Brazil (BRA)	Full (Gleditsch, 2000)	Full (Obstfeld & Taylor, 2003)	Full (Mitchell, 1998)	Full (Singer & Small, 1993) (1891, 1895, 1904 interpolated)	Assumed 0	1881–1913 (Obstfeld & Taylor, 2003), 1920–1938 (United Nations, Dept. of Economic Affairs, 1948)

Country						
Canada (CAN)	Full (Gleditsch, 2000)	Full (Obstfeld & Taylor, 2003)	Full (Mitchell, 1998)	Full (Urquhart & Buckley, 1965)	1881–1937 (Lindert, 1994, 2004) (see also Appendix Table C.6)	Full (Obstfeld & Taylor, 2003)
Chile (CHI)	Full (Gleditsch, 2000)	Full (Obstfeld & Taylor, 2003)	Full (Mitchell, 1998)	1882–(Singer & Small, 1993)	Assumed 0	Full (Obstfeld & Taylor, 2003)
Denmark (DEN)	Full (Gleditsch, 2000)	Full (Maddison, 1995)	Full (Johansen, 1985)	Full (Johansen, 1985)	1881–1937 (Lindert, 1994, 2004) (see also Appendix Table C.6)	1881–1913 (Obstfeld & Taylor, 2003), 1920–1938 (United Nations, Dept. of Economic Affairs, 1948)
Finland (FIN)	1917–(Gleditsch, 2000)	Full (Maddison, 1995)	Full (Eloranta, 2002, 2004)	Full (Eloranta, 2002, 2004)	1881–1937 (Lindert, 1994, 2004) (see also Appendix Table C.6)	Full (Eloranta, 2002, 2004)
France (FRA)	Full (Gleditsch, 2000)	Full (Maddison, 1995)	Full (Mitchell, 1998)	1870–1913 (Hobson, 1993), 1920–1938 (Eloranta, 2002)	1881–1937 (Lindert, 1994, 2004) (see also Appendix Table C.6)	Full (Obstfeld & Taylor, 2003)
Germany (GER)	Full (Gleditsch, 2000)	Full (Maddison, 1995)	1870–1913, 1924–1938 (Mitchell, 1998) (see also Eloranta, 2002)	1870–1913 (Hobson, 1993), 1920–1938 (Eloranta, 2002)	1881–1937 (Lindert, 1994, 2004) (see also Appendix Table C.6) (1910 & 1920 missing, interpolated)	Full (Obstfeld & Taylor, 2003)

Table A.1. (*Continued*)

Country	DEM	REAL INCOME	CGE	ME	SE	DEBT
Greece (GRE)	Full (Gleditsch, 2000)	Full (Kostelenos, 1995)	Full (Mitchell, 1998)	1901–1913 (Singer & Small, 1993), 1920–1938 (Eloranta, 2002)	Assumed 0	1920–(United Nations, Dept. of Economic Affairs, 1948)
Italy (ITA)	Full (Gleditsch, 2000)	Full (Maddison, 1995)	Full (Mitchell, 1998)	1870–1913 (Hobson, 1993), 1920–1938 (Eloranta, 2002)	1881–1937 (Lindert, 1994, 2004) (see also Appendix Table C.6)	Full (Obstfeld & Taylor, 2003)
Japan (JAP)	Full (Gleditsch, 2000)	Full (Obstfeld & Taylor, 2003)	1870–1913 (Banks, 1976), 1920–1938 (Eloranta, 2002)	1870–1913 (Hobson, 1993), 1920–1938 (Eloranta, 2002)	1881–1937 (Lindert, 1994, 2004) (see also Appendix Table C.6)	1885–(Obstfeld & Taylor, 2003)
The Netherlands (NED)	Full (Gleditsch, 2000)	Full (Maddison, 1995)	Full (Mitchell, 1998)	1870–1913 (Singer & Small, 1993), 1920–1938 (Eloranta, 2002)	1881–1937 (Lindert, 1994, 2004) (see also Appendix Table C.6)	1900–(Obstfeld & Taylor, 2003)
New Zealand (NZ)	Full (Gleditsch, 2000)	Full (Obstfeld & Taylor, 2003)	Full (Mitchell, 2003)	1907–1913 (Banks, 1976), 1920–1938 (Singer & Small, 1993)	1881–1937 (Lindert, 1994, 2004) (see also Appendix Table C.6)	1890–(Obstfeld & Taylor, 2003)
Norway (NOR)	Full (Gleditsch, 2000)	Full (Maddison, 1995)	Full (Mitchell, 1998)	1870–1904 (Banks, 1976), 1905–1913 (Singer & Small, 1993), 1920–1938 (Eloranta, 2002)	1881–1937 (Lindert, 1994, 2004) (see also Appendix Table C.6)	Full (Obstfeld & Taylor, 2003)

Portugal (POR)	Full (Gleditsch, 2000)	Full (Obstfeld & Taylor, 2003)	1870–1913 (Mata, 1993), 1920–1938 (Valério, 1994)	1870–1913 (Mata, 1993), 1920–1938 (Eloranta, 2002)	Assumed 0	Full (Obstfeld & Taylor, 2003)
Russia (RUS)	Full (Gleditsch, 2000)	Until 1913 (Maddison, 1995), then see Eloranta (2002) for further details	Sporadic (see Eloranta, 2002, 2007)	Sporadic (Eloranta, 2002, 2007)	No data	No data
Spain (SPA)	Full (Gleditsch, 2000)	Full (Obstfeld & Taylor, 2003)	Full (Carreras, 1989)	1870–1913 (Carrerasm, 1989), 1920–1938 (Eloranta, 2002)	1881–1937 (Lindert, 1994, 2004) (see also Appendix Table C.6)	Full (Obstfeld & Taylor, 2003)
Sweden (SWE)	Full (Gleditsch, 2000)	Full (Maddison, 1995)	1870–1879 (Banks, 1976), 1880– (Mitchell, 1998)	Full (Krantz, 1987)	1881–1937 (Lindert, 1994, 2004) (see also Appendix Table C.6)	Full (Obstfeld & Taylor, 2003)
Switzerland (SWI)	Full (Gleditsch, 2000)	Full (Obstfeld & Taylor, 2003)	Full (Mitchell, 1998)	1870–1913 (Siegenthaler & Ritzmann-Blickenstorfer, 1996), 1920–1938 (Eloranta, 2002)	1881–1937 (Lindert, 1994, 2004) (see also Appendix Table C.6)	1913–(United Nations, Dept. of Economic Affairs, 1948)
The United Kingdom (UK)	Full (Gleditsch, 2000)	Full (Maddison, 1995)	Full (Mitchell, 1988)	1870–1913 (Hobson, 1993), 1920–1938 (Eloranta, 2002)	1881–1937 (Lindert, 1994, 2004) (see also Appendix Table C.6)	Full (Obstfeld & Taylor, 2003)

Table A.1. (*Continued*)

Country	DEM	REAL INCOME	CGE	ME	SE	DEBT
The United States (USA)	Full (Gleditsch, 2000)	Full (Maddison, 1995)	Full (United States, Bureau of the Census, 1976)	1870–1913 (Hobson, 1993), 1920–1938 (Eloranta, 2002)	1881–1937 (Lindert, 1994, 2004) (see also Appendix Table C.6)	Full (Obstfeld & Taylor, 2003)

Additional Source Notes: All nominal GDP figures from: Mitchell (1988, 1998a, 1998b, 2003); Obstfeld and Taylor (2003), unless otherwise noted here. ARG: della Paolera, Taylor, and Bózzoli (2003); AUT: Kausel (1979); BEL: 1870–1913 (Clement, 2000), 1920–1938 (Buyst, 1997); BRA: 1870–1913 (provided by Zephyr Frank); DEN: (Johansen, 1985); FIN: Hjerppe (1988); GRE: Kostelenos (1995); ITA: 1891–(Rossi, Sorgato, & Toniolo, 1993); NED: 1870–1913 (Smits, Horlings, & Zanden, 2000), 1920–1938 (Bakker, Huitker, & Bochove, 1990); POR: 1870–1913 NNP (Mata, 1993), 1920–1938 GDP (Batista, Martins, Pinheiro, & Reis, 1997); SPA: Prados de la Escosura (1993); SWE: Krantz (1997); SWI: 1870–1913 (Siegenthaler & Ritzmann-Blickenstorfer, 1996), 1920–1938 (Ritzmann-Blickenstorfer & David, 2000). Exchange rates, when needed, obtained from: Global Financial Data (2001); Denzel, Schneider, Schwarzer, and Zellfelder (1997); Schneider, Schwarzer, Zellfelder, and Denzel (1991). For alliances, countries under foreign rule coded as being in a de facto alliance (e.g., British colonies, or Finland before 1917). *On definitions:* Following Peter Lindert (1996, 2004), social transfers equal expenditures on welfare and unemployment compensation, pensions, and health subsidies; whereas social expenditures comprise social transfers plus government subsidies to education. The definition of military expenditures utilized in this article follows Frederick L. Pryor's (1968) definition, with certain minor differences. In certain isolated cases it is possible to employ an economically more precise definition, arising out of national accounting procedures. The government debt figures refer to total central government debt (=as a share of GDP, abbreviated as *DEBT*), arising from the database collected by Maurice Obstfeld and Alan Taylor (2003), supplemented for the interwar period by the United Nations (1948) figures and other data.

SWEDISH REGIONAL GDP 1855–2000: ESTIMATIONS AND GENERAL TRENDS IN THE SWEDISH REGIONAL SYSTEM

Kerstin Enflo, Martin Henning and Lennart Schön

ABSTRACT

This paper uses a method devised by Geary and Stark to estimate regional GDPs for 24 Swedish provinces 1855–2000. In empirical tests, we find that the Swedish estimations yield results of good precision, comparable to those reported in the international literature. From the literature, we generate six expectations concerning the development of regional GDPs in Sweden. Using the GDP estimations, we test these expectations empirically. We find that the historical regional GDPs show a high correlation over time, but that the early industrialization process coevolved with a dramatic redistribution of productive capacity. We show that the regional inequalities in GDP per capita were at their lowest point in modern history in the early 1980s. However, while efficiency in the regional system has never been as equal, absolute regional differences in scale of production has increased dramatically over our investigated period.

Research in Economic History, Volume 30, 47–89
Copyright © 2014 by Emerald Group Publishing Limited
All rights of reproduction in any form reserved
ISSN: 0363-3268/doi:10.1108/S0363-326820140000030000

This process has especially benefited the metropolitan provinces. We present detailed sources of our estimations and also sketch a research agenda from our results.

Keywords: Industrialization; regional inequality; regional income; economic growth; Sweden; regional accounts

JEL classifications: N93; N94; R11

INTRODUCTION

Long-term economic growth and change is characterized by regional heterogeneity. Traditionally, historical regional development has been studied by means of, for example, distribution of population (Söderberg & Lundgren, 1982), sector employment (Lundmark & Malmberg, 1988; Söderberg & Lundgren, 1982), or regional distribution of wages and income differentials (Andersson, 1978; Persson, 1997). In some contexts, regional sector employment data may indeed be used as a way to proxy the *scale* and value of regional production. However, regional employment data frequently obscures spatial differences in economic activity, since it does not take into account differences in *efficiency* (productivity). Lack of historical regional production data has therefore partly hindered any attempt to measure a vital aspect of the spatial distribution of economic activities in the long term. To the extent that they can be estimated, historical regional factor-cost GDP data therefore provide important complementary information about the long-term economic development of regions.[1]

In 2002, Geary and Stark designed a method to *estimate* regional GDP using a minimum of historical data (we will henceforth refer to this as the G-S method). In its most basic form, the implementation of the method requires data on national value added for a set of broad industries (usually three or four), regional employment in these industries, and information about regional wage differentials. Currently, the G-S method constitutes the technical base for an ESF (European Science Foundation) effort to compile regional historical GRP data for a large number of European countries.[2] Within this wider context, the aim of this paper is (1) estimate regional GDP series for Sweden on province (län) level from 1855, (2) to describe and discuss the different data sources for the estimations in detail, and (3) to consider the quality and outcomes of the estimates compared to some literature-derived expectations concerning[3]:

- the precision of the G-S method in estimating regional GDP;
- the long-run path dependency and geographical inertia in regional production structures;
- the industrialization period as a process inducing spatial redistribution of production, followed by increased stability in spatial production patterns;
- the often stated argument that the Swedish industrialization process was not connected to and cooccurring with the urbanization process to the same extent as in many other countries.

Despite its limited economic size, Sweden is an interesting case for analyses of long-term regional economic growth and change. The country features a range of different types of regions (some differentiated in economic structure, and some extremely specialized) that are markedly separated in space. The small Swedish economy has also throughout the history of capitalism been an open one, forced to react fast to international economic trends. The spatial dynamics of the Swedish industrialization process is also said to be of a very different character compared to other countries. In terms of data, definitions of the borders of the 24 Swedish provinces (län) have been stable over the time period investigated, and national border changes and wars have had little effect on the consistency of the information used to estimate regional GDPs.

The structure of the paper is as follows. In the second section, we formulate some literature-derived expectations for the analysis of the historical Swedish GDP data. These expectations will serve both as a base for analyzing the quality of the estimations, and as a base for analyzing some aspects of the spatial dynamics of Swedish economic development over 150 years. In the third section, we explain and discuss the G-S method used to estimate the historical regional GDP. The fourth section then discusses the data sources and the implementation of the G-S method on the Swedish data. We also investigate some potential errors accruing from three specific technical features of the method. The fifth section features our final regional GDP estimations for the Swedish provinces 1855–2007. In this section, the literature-derived expectations about the Swedish economic development during the period studied are also evaluated. The sixth section concludes and suggests some further avenues of research. Appendices A and B contain some specifics about our implementation of the G-S method, while Appendix C contains the outcomes of the estimations in tabular form.

THE EXPECTATIONS

To structure the empirical description of our regional GDP estimation results in the fourth section, the discussion will evolve around six expectations about the spatial distribution of Swedish regional GDP in a historical perspective. These expectations are derived using a selection of the existing literature in the field.

The first expectation concerns the errors of the regional estimations. For many countries, historical *national* accounts already exist and are used as inputs in the G-S method. When these already known historical national GDPs are proportioned out to the regions according to the G-S method, an error will likely appear on the regional level. The estimated regional value will probably, to a greater or smaller extent, diverge from the "true" GDP of the region. Naturally, we wish to minimize this "spatial misallocation." For historical data, no information is normally available to test the precision of the regional estimations (if so, there would of course be no use to estimate regional GDP according to the G-S method). Usually, we can however compare the estimated regional GDP to official estimates for some modern year, where statistical offices have provided regional GDP calculations. In their estimations for the United Kingdom and Ireland, Geary and Stark (2002) report that their "best" specification estimates deviate with a maximum of 7.5% for one region from the official estimates (country within the United Kingdom). Using the G-S method, we should therefore expect a small error also for the Swedish data:

E1. The spatial misallocation error is small.

More to the fundamental side of how spatial economies evolve, inertia and path dependency processes can be expected to characterize historical economic development (Martin & Sunley, 2006). This means that the scale of regional production normally changes at a slow and incremental pace (provided that they are not subject to drastic chocks, see Davis & Weinstein, 2002). Moreover, recent empirical results suggest that the specific economic structures of regions *condition* their future economic evolution. For example, regions are unlikely to embark on development paths that are technologically very different from the paths that they have already established in the past (Neffke, Henning, & Boschma, 2011). Even though many clarifying issues remain about the concept of regional path dependency and how it could be quantified, it still leads us to expect that the regional distribution of GDP will show very high correlations across time in the short run. Over longer time spans, we should however expect the incremental evolution of regional production structures to result in greater changes in the regional system. One reason to expect this is because different phases of economic growth place varying emphasis on different production factors and inputs (Schön, 2000). As the access to production factors and inputs may have a distinct spatial dimension, the economic fortune of regions will also shift in the longer run. The lowered relative transport prices have, for example, over time changed the degree to which some industries need to be based in spatial proximity to their inputs. Due to these considerations, we expect to find slightly different short- and long-term correlation structures in the regional Swedish GDP data:

E2. Comparing regional distribution of GDP over time, there is very strong correlation between regional production shares in the short run.

E3. Comparing regional distribution of GDP over time, there is less strong correlation between regional production shares in the long run.

More context-informed contributions concerning periods of turbulence and stability in the Swedish regional system may however be used to form complementary expectations. When analyzing the distribution of population and income shares in the Swedish regional system between 1920 and 1975, Andersson (1978) found a very high degree of stability in regional distributions during this period. This led Andersson to argue that a long-term equilibrium of regional production and income distribution in Sweden was reached already in 1920. According to this view, the Swedish regional system essentially consisted of a number of rather self-sufficient regional economies in the beginning of the industrialization period (until around 1850). During the early industrialization period however, investments were seeking out their highest returns. Combined with a historically high mobility of capital, a comparatively large degree of production redistribution took place in the regional system during the early industrialization period. With the establishment of a new transportation and communication structure from the late 19th century (e.g., the railroads), a number of new infrastructural node-cities also became favored as economic growth centers.

The largest turbulence in terms of spatial reallocation of productive capacity therefore took place 1870–1920, according to Andersson. Workers and population migrated to equalize the spatial production/population structures, so that there would also be long-run convergence in production per capita. The regional production system remained thereafter rather stabile in a spatial sense, at least until 1975.[4] A large predicament concerning the arguments of Andersson was that he could not test his expectations in a rigorous way, partly because of imperfect substitutes to regional production data, partly because of limited time series. The arguments of Andersson (1978) may however lead us to formulate the following expectation for our dataset:

E4. There was turbulence (spatial redistribution of production) in the Swedish regional system until 1910/1920, thereafter a period of stability dominated.

From a more general perspective, international literature partly complements the expectations concerning convergence and divergence in the regional system that can be formulated using the contextual Swedish perspectives discussed above. The historical analysis of Williamson (1965) concerning regional income convergence/divergence connected to the development stage of nations, suggests that regional inequality of incomes will take an inverted u-shape over the economic evolution of a nation. Williamson uses a classification of growth stages of nations that has its origins in the works of Kuznets. Early stages of national development should, according to this perspective, be associated with regional income divergence. Lack of integration between regional markets during the early growth stage inhibits the diffusion of technological change and multipliers associated with rising income, and furthers the selective migration from less favored regions. This causes regional income to diverge spatially. Further down the growth path, integration of markets and increased factor mobility will facilitate for the traditional equilibrating forces to exert influence. Even though Williamson finds empirical evidence to support such time-bound tendencies, the data situation at the time inhibited a real long-term test of the hypothesis. The empirical exposition relies heavily on the comparison between countries in different growth stages, and on rather limited time periods. Williamson is also not very specific concerning the timing of the "peak" of inequality of income during the economic growth process. Translated to the perspective of our data that covers the period from the very start of the industrialization process in Sweden, Williamson's arguments lead us to form expectations not about income levels, but rather distribution of GDP per capita in the Swedish provinces. Taking the period around 1850 to be beginning of the "late" stages of development, we can form the following expectation (which is complementary to the discussion above):

E5. There was convergence in GDP/capita from the 1850s that equalized the regional differences in GDP/capita that were established during earlier growth regimes.

Finally, scholars have stressed the argument that the connection and cooccurrence between the industrialization and urbanization processes was weaker in Sweden than in many other countries. Söderberg and Lundgren (1982) claim by reference to historical data that the shares of manufacturing workers working in countryside locations in 1900 were vastly higher (around 60%) in Sweden than in a range of comparable nations, such as United States, Germany, and Denmark. Consequently, the regional distribution of GDP in Sweden should not unambiguously be expected to favor the bigger cities, especially not in the early industrialization period. One reason for this might be that the early industrialization process in Sweden favored many capital-intensive industries. Combined with an increasingly mobile capital, this would have led to larger shares of production taking place in areas with ample natural resource endowments rather than agglomerations of inexpensive labor. With the progression of industrialization however, one might expect migration to equalize the regional differences between shares of population and production (GDP):

E6. In beginning of industrialization a large gap quickly arises between regional shares of population and GDP. This should diminish with long-term market integration and migration, but also with a larger concentration of production to the large city areas compared to the phase of early industrialization.

REGIONAL PRODUCTION DATA AND THE GEARY–STARK METHOD

We use a method to estimate historical regional GDPs suggested by Geary and Stark (2002). The version of the method that we use requires the following input data: (1) historical national GDP estimates and industry value added, preferably also including estimates of number of workers on the national industry level, (2) regional number of employees per industry, and (3) regional wages per industry. For a specific year, it is assumed that the total national GDP at factor cost is defined as the sum of regional GDPs[5]:

$$Y_{\text{nat}} = \sum^{i} Y_i \qquad (1)$$

where Y_{nat} is the total national GDP at factor cost, and Y_i is the GRP of region i. The latter is defined as

$$Y_i = \sum^{j} y_{ij} \times L_{ij} \qquad (2)$$

where y_{ij} is the average value added per worker in region i and industry j, and L_{ij} the number of employees (workers) in region i and industry j. From this follows also the definition:

$$Y_{\text{nat}} = \sum^{j} Y_j \qquad (3)$$

where Y_j is the GDP (value added) of industry j.

The term "industry" can be used very flexibly in the context of the G-S method.[6] Normally, it here refers to the three sectors of agriculture, manufacturing, and services. One of the prime advantages with the G-S method is that it offers a solution to the predicaments that arise when there is no available data for y_{ij} (value added per employee on industry/region level). This situation is likely to arise often in historical research. y_{ij} is then proxied by taking information about the output per worker in each industry on national level, then assuming that regional differentials in labor productivity in each industry is reflected by the regional industry wage level relative to the national industry wage level (w_{ij}/w_j). Therefore, it is assumed that the final regional GDP will be given by

$$Y_i = \sum^{j} y_j \ \beta_j \left(\frac{w_{ij}}{w_j} \right) \times L_{ij} \qquad (4)$$

where β_j is a scalar that will preserve regional relative differences, but ensures that regional totals add up to the known national total for each industry. This scalar takes the form

$$\beta_j = \frac{Y_j}{\sum_i [y_j(w_{ij}/w_j)]L_{ij}} \qquad (5)$$

Essentially, the G-S method distributes already known GDP estimates on nation/industry levels regionally by making use of regional labor inputs and wage differentials. For the Swedish case, the method therefore allows for estimates of regional GRPs that are consistent with existing national estimates from the Swedish Historical National Accounts (SHNA) to 2000 (2007).

Geary and Stark (2002) show, using UK data, that their method yields results of promising precision. However, when investigating a subset of Swedish yearly estimations (for 1910, 1993, and 2006), Enflo, Svensson Henning, and Schön (2009) identify three potential problems with the method: (1) the unreliable assumption problem, (2) the sector aggregation problem, and (3) the correlation of sector/regional structure problem. The unreliable assumption problem concerns two potentially problematic aspects of the G-S method. The first is to what extent the regional wage differentials reflect the marginal productivity in the regions.[7] Of course, one could think of many reasons why this assumption would not hold. Institutional wage barriers (such as influential labor unions), inertia in wage changes, and imperfect information on the labor market are only some. For example, if there are serious obstacles in the flow of information between regions, the assumption would be dubious.

The second issue concerns the problem of how industries should be treated where no historical industry-specific regional wage data is available. We have already mentioned that lack of historical data for service wages, especially on regional level, is a common problem. In such cases, Geary and Stark (2002) suggest that an average between the regional agriculture and manufacturing wages can be used to estimate the regional service wage level. The viability of this assumption builds on the condition that between-sector labor mobility is not stalled by any major obstacles (i.e., that people are free and willing to move into sectors with higher relative wages). Indeed, investigations have shown that higher wage levels affect flows to industries positively, but also that there are quite some obstacles to migrate between sectors. Industries are for example characterized by the use of different industry-specific skills, which make a friction-free labor force transfer between industries problematic (Neffke & Svensson Henning, 2013). However, the literature on de-skilling of the labor force during the industrial revolution suggests that this might be more of a contemporary phenomenon.

The sector aggregation problem refers to the sensitiveness of the G-S method to industry aggregations. It is an important question how many different industries should be used, and what the consequences of using a broad aggregate instead of many fine-grained industries are. A conventional approach is, as mentioned above, to use an agriculture/manufacturing/ service distinction. However, regional and national specificities may cause these aggregates to bias regional estimations. An example is when a small subset of regionally concentrated activities in the agricultural sector elevates the productivity in agriculture, also on national level. But it is not self-evident that more detailed industry data is always better. Distinguishing between a large number of industries may bias estimations over time, as the risk of errors associated with problematic and unstable specifications of industries increases. Usually this is however not a major practical problem, since researches commonly do not have the possibility to choose among a wide variety of historical industry aggregations.

The correlation of sector/regional structure problem is related to the problems discussed above, and concerns the consequences of the G-S estimation principles for small regions with very specialized production portfolios. In such small regions, a broad national productivity measure can be expected to bias the GRP estimations. For example, if a small region is very specialized in a fraction of the manufacturing industries which is highly productive, using an average productivity given on a national level and for a broad set of manufacturing industries will bias the GRP estimations in that specific region. Reasonable outcomes for such regions will be very sensitive to industry productivity deviances from the national industry mean.

DATA AND IMPLEMENTATION FOR SWEDISH REGIONS AND SOME PRELIMINARY TESTS

In the implementation of the G-S method on the Swedish data we use four different data sets: (1) total population data per province, (2) historical GDP and employment data on national level from the Swedish National Historical Accounts (SNHA), (3) regional employment data from a variety of sources, and (4) regional wage data from a variety of sources.

Total Population Data Per Province (län)

The total population data per province (län) we use is provided by Statistics Sweden (www.scb.se). Table 1 lists the provinces and the average number of inhabitants 1855–2007. Stockholms län (consisting both of

Table 1. Population and Population Growth for Our 25 Analyzed
Provinces (län).

Province	Average Population 1855–2007	Population Growth 1855–2007 (%)
Stockholms län	916,357	803
Uppsala län	167,711	256
Södermanlands län	195,669	114
Östergötlands län	322,490	82
Jönköpings län	243,854	100
Kronobergs län	162,370	26
Kalmar län	232,726	10
Gotlands län	54,753	22
Blekinge län	142,258	37
Kristianstads län	246,980	52
Malmöhus län	539,657	236
Hallands län	173,363	163
Göteborg och Bohus län	486,172	324
Älvsborgs län	340,354	80
Skaraborgs län	248,059	23
Värmlands län	267,990	18
Örero län	222,108	93
Västmanlands län	182,753	152
Kopparbergs län	238,410	74
Gävleborgs län	242,302	118
Västernorrlands län	229,486	126
Jämtlands län	114,378	126
Västerbottens län	182,547	239
Norrbottens län	182,085	294
Total	6,334,833	152

Note: Own calculations from statistics Sweden data.

Stockholm city and the Stockholm province) is by far the most populated province, followed by Malmöhus län and Göteborgs och Bohus län. Gothenburg, the second largest city in Sweden, is located in the latter province. Together with the Uppsala province (close to Stockholm), the Stockholm, Göteborg, and Malmö provinces have also experienced the most dramatic population growth during the investigated period. Interestingly, quite a few provinces experienced rather meager population growth, below the national average. Many of these provinces have historically been dominated by agriculture, and some of them were also subject to large migration to the United States before and around the turn of the century 1800/1900 (e.g., Kronobergs, Kalmar, and Blekinge län).

In 2000 and 2007, an administrative change took place in the definition of the provinces. Malmöhus and Kristianstad län were merged into Skåne län. Göteborg och Bohus län, Älvsborgs län, and Skaraborgs län were merged into Västra Götalands län. As the "older" provinces give a more detailed picture of the regional development in Sweden, we use municipality data for 2000 and 2007 to adjust modern data to the older provinces, and therefore comparable over time.

Historical GDP and Employment Data on National Level

The Swedish Historical National Accounts (SHNA, Krantz, & Schön, 2007) provide national data on industry value added, number of employees, and total GDP measured at factor costs 1855−2000. In the Swedish implementation of the G-S method we generally use four different industries: agriculture, manufacturing, private services, and public services.

- "Agriculture" consists of the SHNA categories
  - Agriculture
  - Forestry
- "Manufacturing" consists of the SHNA categories
  - Manufacturing industry
  - Building and construction
- "Private services" consists of the SHNA categories
  - Transport and communication
  - Private services
- "Public services" consists of the SHNA category
  - Public services

The SHNA also identifies *services of dwellings*, which in for example 1910 contributed to about 10% of total national GDP. This industry does however not employ many people, and the incomes mainly originate from returns of house ownership. There might of course exist regional differences in productivity in this sector, but probably to a lesser extent than for other sectors. We therefore simply regionalize these incomes according to the size of regional population.

SHNA provides no estimates for 2007. For this year we have used data from the National Accounts of Statistics Sweden in our G-S estimations. To ensure consistency with the time series of the SNHA, the official 2007 figure has been depreciated with 11.3%, which is the average difference between the SNHA and official estimates 1993–2000.[8] For 2007 we also use only three industries: production of commodities (including agriculture), production of services, and public sector.

Regional Employment Data

The collection and organization of the historical regional employment data is complex and involves compiling information from a range of different original sources. Different kinds of population censuses that provide data on employees per industry per province are most frequently used.[9] For the cases where the original regional employment data is more detailed than needed for the four-industry implementation of the G-S method, we generally use the following scheme to collapse the data into four industries:[10,11]

- As "Agriculture" we define
  - Farming
  - Fishing
  - Forestry
- As "Manufacturing" we define
  - Manufacturing
  - Construction
  - Power and gas
- As "Private services" we define
  - Retail
  - Wholesale
  - Financial services
  - Transportation
  - Hotels and restaurants
  - Household services
- As "Public services" we define
  - Public administration
  - Education
  - Healthcare
  - Other services

Table 2 lists the exact sources of the regional employment information.[12,13]

Table 2.   Sources of the Regional Employment Information.

Year	Publication	Table
1855	BISOS Befolkningsstatistik 1851–1855, avd 3.	Rikets folkmängd den 31 december 1855, efter levnadsyrken och näringar. Tabell 5.
1860	BISOS Befolkningsstatistik 1856–1860, avd 3.	Rikets yrkesidkande befolkning den 31 december 1860. Tabell 5.
1870	BISOS Befolkningsstatistik 1870, avd 3.	Rikets folkmängd fördelad efter yrken och kön 31 dec 1870. Tabell 5.
1880	BISOS Befolkningsstatistik 1880, avd 3.	Folkmängden efter yrken och kön länsvis den 31 december 1880. Tabell 6.
1890	BISOS Befolkningsstatistik 1890, avd 3.	Folkmängden efter yrken och kön länsvis den 31 december 1890. Tabell 11.
1900	BISOS Befolkningsstatistik 1891–1900, avd 3.	Folkmängden efter större grupper af yrken inom härader och städer den 31 december 1900. Tabell 17.
1910	Folkräkningen 1910.	Folkmängd efter särskilda yrken. Tabell 1.
1920	Folkräkningen 1940, del V.	Folkmängd efter huvudgrupper av yrken, länsvis 1920. Tabell 4.
1930	Folkräkningen 1930, del III.	Folkmängd och förmögenhet vid slutet av år 1930. Tabell 4.
1940	Folkräkningen 1940, del III.	Yrkesverksam befolkning och deras familjemedlemmar efter näringsgren. Tabell 5.
1950	Folkräkningen 1950, totala räkningen, del IV.	År 1950 Folkmängden efter näringsgren i kommuner och församlingar. Tabell 1.
1960	SOS Folkräkningen 1960, vol VIII.	Förvärvsarbetande dagbefolkning efter näringsgren. Tabell 2.
1970	FoB 1970, del 5.	Förvärvsarbetande (20-w tim). Tabell 2.
1980	FoB 1980, del 6:2.	Förvärvsarbetande (20-w tim), dagbefolkning. Tabell 9.
1990	FoB 1990, del 5.	Förvärvsarbetande, dagbefolkning. Tabell 21.
2000	Uttag från Statistikdatabasen SCB. www.scb.se	Förvärvsarbetande 16+ år med arbetsplats i regionen (RAMS) efter region och näringsgren.
2007	Uttag från Statistikdatabasen SCB. www.scb.se	Förvärvsarbetande 16+ år med arbetsplats i regionen (RAMS) efter region, näringsgren.

Regional Wage Data

The most complicated data in our datasets, with least complete coverage, are the regional wage data series. In many cases, our ambitions have to be limited to establishing a decent proxy for the relative wage differentials. Since these data are used only to establish *relative* regional wage differentials, the inconsistency of the data over time should not pose an overwhelming problem.

For some years and for some industries, the wage information is provided for spatial aggregations that are geographically different from the provinces. The *Dyrortsgruppper* is a regional hierarchy of cities, based on estimations of living cost levels and constructed for salary adjustment purposes. Where we have data for such Dyrortsgruppper, we have used the dyrortsgrupp of the largest city in the province as a proxy for the cost level in the province as a whole. Where there is only wage data for larger regions than the provinces (*Riksområden*), we take the wage level in the area to which the province belongs to be representative of the wage level of the province itself. Admittedly, these proxies of the wage level of the region are much less than perfect. However, our tests suggests that leaving out wage differentials would cause estimations to be more biased.

Table 3 lists the sources of the regional wage data for *agriculture* together with some important remarks. Table 4 lists the sources of the regional wage data for manufacturing together with some important remarks. Table 5 lists the sources of the wage data for private services together with some important remarks.

Table 3. Sources of the Wage Data and Remarks for Agriculture.

Year	Publication	Table/Source	Remarks
1855	See 1860.		Wages 1860 were used.
1860	Jörberg (1972).	Day laborer's wages, p. 588	Wages from Blekinge län missing, proxied with wages from Kronobergs län.
1870	Jörberg (1972).	Day laborer's wages, p. 588	Wages from Blekinge län missing, proxied with wages from Kronobergs län.
1890	Jörberg (1972).	Day laborer's wages, p. 588	Wages from Blekinge län missing, proxied with wages from Kronobergs län.
1900	Jörberg (1972).	Day laborer's wages, p. 588.	Wages from Blekinge län missing, proxied with wages from Kronobergs län.
1910	Jörberg (1972).	Day laborer's wages, p. 588.	Wages from Blekinge län missing, proxied with wages from Kronobergs län.

Table 3. *(Continued)*

Year	Publication	Table/Source	Remarks
1920	See 1930.		We have used wages from 1930.
1930	SOS Lönestatistisk årsbok för Sverige 1930.	Total yearly wages by male servants in agriculture. Table 2, pp. 14–15.	
1940	SOS Lönestatistisk årsbok för Sverige 1940.	Average salaries for male day laborers in agriculture. Table 10, p. 36.	
1950	SOS Lönestatistisk årsbok för Sverige 1949.	Average salaries for male day laborers in agriculture. Table 15, p. 43.	We use wage data for 1949, disaggregated into eight regional units.
1960	Weighed average between manufacturing and private services wages.		Dyrortgrupper in the weighed series.
1970	Weighed average between manufacturing and private services wages.		Dyrortgrupper in the weighed series.
1980	Weighed average between manufacturing and private services wages.		Riksområden in the weighed series.
1990	Weighed average between manufacturing and private services wages.		
2000	Weighed average between manufacturing and private services wages.		
2007			We use three sectors only. Agriculture is part of market production of goods.

For the public services, no regional productivity differentials assumed until 2000 due to lack of reliable data. Where we do have more detailed data, the regional differences in wages for the public sector 2000 are considerably smaller than for other industries.[14] However, for the years 2000 and 2007 where we have almost perfect wage data, we do use the information we have to calculate regional wage differentials for the public sector. Table 6 lists the sources of the wage data for public services.

Table 4. Sources of the Wage Data and Remarks for Manufacturing.

Year	Publication	Table/Source	Comments
1855	See 1860.		Wages 1860 were used.
1860	Lundh, Olofsson, Schön, and Svensson (2004).	Regional data from nine regional areas, p. 47.	Province wage levels proxied by the region that was closest in geographical location.
1870	Lundh et al. (2004).	Regional data from nine regional areas, p. 47.	Province wage levels proxied by the region that was closest in geographical location.
1890	Lundh et al. (2004).	Regional data from nine regional areas, p. 47.	Province wage levels proxied by the region that was closest in geographical location.
1900	Lundh et al. (2004).	Regional data from nine regional areas, p. 47.	Province wage levels proxied by the region that was closest in geographical location.
1910	See 1900.		We have used wages from 1900.
1920	See 1930.		We have used wages from 1930.
1930	SOS Lönestatistisk årsbok för Sverige 1931.	Average yearly wage by male manufacturing workers. Table 19, p. 95.	We use wages from 1931.
1940	SOS Lönestatistisk årsbok för Sverige 1940.	Average yearly wage by male manufacturing workers. Table 34.	
1950	SOS Lönestatistisk årsbok för Sverige 1949.	Total salary per worker. Table 51.	We use 1949 wages. Wages proxied by ore- and metal-industry workers (apart from Västernorrlands and Jämtlands län, data refer to miscellaneous manufacturing workers).
1960	SOS Löner 1961, del 2.	Hour wage earnings 1961, adult male workers, men. Table 14, p. 58.	Dyrortsgrupper.
1970	SOS Löner 1971.	Average hourly wage earnings 1971, adult male workers in mining and manufacturing, 2nd quarter. Table 13, p. 126.	
1980	SOS Löner 1980, del 2	Average hourly wage earnings 1971, adult male workers in mining and manufacturing, 2nd quarter 1980. Table L.	

Table 4. (*Continued*)

Year	Publication	Table/Source	Comments
1990	SOS Löner i Sverige 1990-1991.	Salaries white collar workers private sector manufacturing, full time employees 1990. Table 9.	
2000	National accounts, www.scb.se	Production of goods, wage sum per employee.	
2007	National accounts, www.scb.se	Production of goods, wage sum per employee from the national accounts.	

Table 5. Sources of the Wage Data and Remarks for Private Services.

Year	Publication	Table/Source	Comments
1855	See 1860.		Wages 1860 were used.
1860			Weighed average of industry and agricultural wages per county.
1870			Weighed average of industry and agricultural wages per county.
1890			Weighed average of industry and agricultural wages per county.
1900			Weighed average of industry and agricultural wages per county.
1910	See 1900.		We have used wages from 1900.
1920	See 1930.		We have used wages from 1930.
1930	SOS Lönestatistisk årsbok för Sverige 1930.	Yearly average wages for male retail and storage workers by dyrort. Table 12.	Dyrorter reclassified to: A−B (=2), C−E (=3), F = 4, and G = 5.
1940	SOS Lönestatistisk årsbok för Sverige 1940.	Yearly average wages for male retail and storage workers by dyrort. Table 31.	Dyrorter reclassified to: A−B (=2), C−E (=3), F = 4, and G = 5.
1950	SOS Lönestatistisk årsbok för Sverige 1950.	Yearly median wages for male retail and storage workers by dyrort. Table 58, p. 128.	

Table 5. (*Continued*)

Year	Publication	Table/Source	Comments
1960	SOS Löner 1961.	Wages May 1961, male shop assistants 30–39 years, Table 15, p. 56.	
1970	SOS Löner 1971, del 1.	Male shop staff and drivers, hourly wages. Table 21, p. 180.	Riksområden.
1980	SOS Löner 1980, del 2.	Male shop staff, storage staff and drivers, hourly wages 2nd quarter 1980, full time employees. Table 29.	Riksområden.
1990	SOS Löner 1990.	White collar workers, monthly salaries, private sector, full-time employees. Table 9.	
2000	National accounts. www.scb.se	Production of services, wage sum per employee from the national accounts.	
2007	National accounts. www.scb.se	Production of services, wage sum per employee from the national accounts.	

Table 6. Sources of the Wage Data for Public Services.

Year	Publication	Table/Source
2000	National accounts, www.scb.se	Public sector and nonprofit organizations, wage sum per employee from the national accounts.
2007	National accounts, www.scb.se	Public sector and nonprofit organizations, wage sum per employee from the national accounts.

Essentially, this data is sufficient to estimate regional GDPs for the Swedish regions 1855–2007 according to Eq. (4). We use this equation, with one exception as we do not make use of the scalar β_j. It can be shown that with our definition of the input variables, the scalar reduces to 1.

Some Preliminary Tests

Using preliminary estimations for 1910, 1993, and 2006, we can assess the impact of the unreliable assumption problem, the sector aggregation problem, and the correlation of sector/regional structure problem on the Swedish estimations.[15] First, results in Geary and Stark (2002) as well as

Enflo et al. (2009) suggest that estimates using wage differentials as productivity proxy yield more precise estimates than using only an average national productivity measure (leaving out the w_{ij}/w_j in Eq. (4)). In the examples of Enflo et al. (2009), use of wage differentials reduces the average "mis-specification" of regional GDPs, and drastically reduces the maximum regional difference between the estimations and the official estimates (this holds true for both 1993 and 2006). Thus, accounting for regional wage differentiation drastically improves the precision of the estimates. Concerning the suggestion that a weighted average between agriculture and service wages is a reasonable proxy for regional wages in the service sector (see Geary & Stark, 2002), this will obviously hold for the case where there is some degree of voluntary labor mobility between sectors. For the Swedish case, authors have indeed argued that regional competition for labor from manufacturing sectors led to an upward pressure on agricultural wages in some regions during the industrialization process (see Söderberg & Lundgren, 1982). So far, we however have too incomplete data to systematically test the exact empirical consequences of this assumption.

When it comes to the sector aggregation problem for the Swedish estimations, results in Enflo et al. (2009) suggest that the number of industries distinguished between may have some but comparatively small implications for the aggregate results. The differences between outcomes when distinguishing between seven manufacturing industries (food, textile, mineral, metal and machinery, mining, wood, and power production) compared to using one aggregate manufacturing industry (see above) in 1910 are rather small. The difference is less than 10% for all Swedish provinces except Stockholm, which obtains a smaller value added with the seven industries disaggregation than with the one-manufacturing sector alternative. However, more differentiated sector data is not at all always better. In fact, making the estimation for economy as a whole (one "industry") instead of distinguishing between three industries yielded somewhat higher precision in the regional estimates for 2000. The convergence in productivity patterns, together with the fact that the public sector has expanded enormously since the 1960s in Sweden, suggests that such a result can however not be taken as an imperative to reduce all historical G-S estimations using one whole-economy average only.

In all, Enflo et al. (2009) find that the two conditions that causes the most significant sector aggregation problems in 1910 are (1) how services of dwellings are distributed regionally, and (2) whether forestry is separated from agriculture or not. The forestry sector strongly deviates from other parts of agriculture in Sweden with a considerably higher value added per worker. Notwithstanding this, we include the forestry in the agriculture industry (this is further discussed below). We distribute service dwellings incomes according to the population size of the region.

Concerning the sector/regional structure problem, it has already been concluded that the recommended G-S three-sector disaggregation performs generally well in comparison to specifications that rely on more disaggregated data. In their tests, Enflo et al. (2009) also discover estimation problems of more regional-specific character, that need to be addressed in order to arrive at regional theoretically and empirically sound GDP. The comparative higher labor productivity of forestry compared to agriculture might cause a regional bias in the Swedish case, as the forestry industry is unevenly distributed regionally with a large share of forestry taking place in the Northern provinces. As many wood workers however also work in the agricultural sector under conditions of mixed and seasonal farming, we prefer to treat agriculture and forestry as integrated sectors. Also under these conditions, the higher productivity of the Northern provinces is reflected in favorable wage differentials compared to the rest of the country.

Contrary to what could be expected, separation of mining and power production from manufacturing industries does not appear to make a difference for the most northern regions in Sweden in 1910. We find no indications that mining had an extraordinary high labor productivity, and power production still constituted a small part of total manufacturing value added (around 2%). However, the sensitivity of the estimations will increase the smaller the size of the region, as the risk of sector/regional structure problem will increase. Based on our results for 2000 the use of the G-S GDP estimation method for regions of less than about 150,000 inhabitants can, as a rule of thumb, not be recommended.

As the preliminary tests of this section have provided us with some confidence in using the estimation method outlined in sections three and four, but also pointed to some problematic aspects that should be considered in empirical situations, we now turn to the final estimation outcomes. The findings will be structured according to the expectations E1–E6.

THE FINAL REGIONAL GDP ESTIMATION RESULTS

According to *E1*, we expect the G-S method to yield high precision estimates for the Swedish regional GDP data 1855–2007.[16] To test this expectation, two reference points are created (2000 and 2007), where the estimations can be compared to official data from Statistics Sweden.[17] Results are displayed in Table 7. In 2000, the misallocation (i.e., error or the sum of value added attributed to the wrong region) is 5% of total GDP (first column).[18] In 2007 the error is smaller, 4% of total GDP (second column). If we instead measure at the level of the regions, the unweighted average error is around 5% of regional GDP (third and fourth columns).[19] For the vast majority of our provinces, the differences created by our estimates compared to official data are very similar to the reported differences in Geary and Stark (2002). In 2000 however, differences exceed 10% in three provinces. The least precise estimate is that of Uppsala län, which yields a 12% underestimation of regional GDP compared to the official estimates. Also in 2007 differences in three provinces exceed 10%. The least precise estimate is now that of Kalmar län (−16%). The most precise estimate for both sample years is for Skåne län.[20] In general, the G-S method applied to the Swedish data yields fairly precise estimates. However, the method may for some few individual regions mis-estimate GDP with up to 16%. To tell if trends and longer term indications in the data are at all interpretable, we should therefore need to know if errors are systematic or occur due to more or less haphazard circumstances.[21] For our comparison points, we find little systematic errors in the regional estimations. The correlation between regional errors in 2000 and 2007 is 0.08. This suggests that the measurement errors for individual provinces are at least temporary compared to the errors of other regions.

Overall, the G-S method implemented for the Swedish data yields results in line with E1. The results are of course tested for two sample years only,

Table 7. Comparison between Geary–Stark and Official Estimates for 2000 and 2007.

Misallocation, % of National GDP		Average Estimation Error, Regional Level, % of Regional GDP		Worst Estimation, Error, % of Regional GDP		Best Estimation Error, % of Regional GDP	
2000	2007	2000	2007	2000	2007	2000	2007
5%	4%	5%	5%	−12%	−16%	0%	0%
				(Uppsala)	(Kalmar)	(Skåne)	(Skåne)

Note: Correlation between regional estimation errors 2000 and 2007: 0.08.

but the differences between our G-S estimates and official province estimates are generally well within the range of those reported in the international literature. The fact that errors for individual regions seem not to be persistent and systematic over time, open up for interpretations of long-term results and trends, even if not for exact interpretations of the value of an individual province in a specific year. There are also few reasons to expect that historical estimations should be less precise than the estimations for our more contemporary reference points (2000 and 2007). Even though the wage information about the service industries is scarce in a historical perspective, we do have good historical data for agriculture. This is important, as agriculture was of course extremely dominating in a historical sense (and accounted for over 70% of labor force in 1855). In fact, the post-WWII period until 1980 could be expected to be the most problematic period for our estimations, as this period features neither the almost perfect regional wage data on the expanding service sector that exist for later years, nor does it feature the period the extreme dominance of agriculture as the earlier years, or the mediating effects on regional GDP that the expansion of the public sector later could be presumed to generate.

According to *E2* we expect, for a variety of reasons many of which have to do with regional path dependency and structural inertia, very high correlation between regional production shares in the short run. Indeed, we do find that the degree of stability in the regional system in terms of regional GDP is very large in the shorter run. If we measure the shares of national GDP that individual regions account for in each year, and then correlate the regional distribution of shares between each 10-year period (1870–1880, 1880–1890, etc.), the average correlation coefficient for the 14 combinations is 0.99.[22] According to the *E3*, we also expect high (but lower than E2) correlation between regional production shares in the long run. Indeed, if we correlate the regional distribution of national GDP shares in 1855 and 2007, the correlation is high, about 0.85. This correlation is as expected lower than the average 10-year correlations of E2.

As expected, the regional system is extremely stable over time in term of production values. This is true for shorter periods (ten years), but also to a lesser extent for very long time spans. Considering the information in our aggregate regional production data, regional production structures indeed appear to be very sticky. Even if this is in itself an interesting empirical observation, one can also regard it as a result that is favorable in terms of our method. Contrary to what we obtain here, instable regional GDP results with many spikes would suggest that the G-S method yields unreliable outcomes.

The stability of the Swedish regional system measured in terms of average correlations might however still hide incremental changes that are specific to particular growth regimes. According to *E4*, we expect some turbulence (spatial redistribution of production) in the Swedish regional system until 1920, and thereafter more stabile structures. Investigating this, we first consider the correlation of the shares of each region of national GDP in 1855, with regional shares in each consecutive year. Turning to a visual inspection of the results (Fig. 1), the correlation between the distribution of production every estimation year and the distribution in 1855 suggests three broad phases of regional development. 1855–1910 was indeed a (comparatively, NB the scale of the *y*-axis) turbulent period with a decreasing correlation with the distribution of 1855. With some variations, the correlation was then actually rather stabile until the 1980s. After this, the correlation turns downwards again, but admittedly this change is not drastic compared to the preceding years. Indeed, we do observe a greater instability of the regional system during early stages of industrialization. Changes in the distribution after this do occur, but at a much more incremental pace than in the period before 1910.

The results of Fig. 2 are even more suggestive of these findings. In Fig. 2, we plot the correlation between the regional shares of national GDP for each consecutive observation combination (1855–1860, 1860–1870, etc.). The curve also suggests an initial period of quite severe instability of the system (even though all correlations are above .9). The decisive point of stability seems to have been reached in 1920/1930.

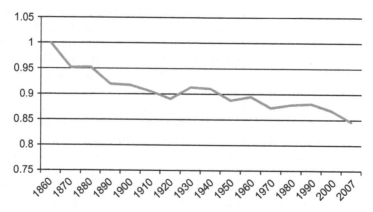

Fig. 1. Correlation between Yearly Regional Shares of National GDP and the Regional Shares in 1855.

To complement the correlations, Fig. 3 shows the coefficient of variation of regional GDP in the Swedish regional system.[23] The graph suggests that the inequality (measured by the standard deviation) in distribution of production in the regional system has increased substantially over the time

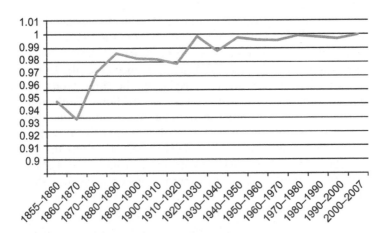

Fig. 2. Correlation between Yearly Regional Shares of National GDP between Consecutive Years of Measurement.

Fig. 3. Coefficient of Variation for Regional GDP.

period that we investigate. This is less the case if Stockholm is excluded, but the process is still visible. Visually, the graph however suggests a broadbrush periodization of more or less dramatic sequences of increasing convergence. From 1855 to 1900, the divergence in regional GDP did not increase substantially in the system. Between 1900 and 1940 however, the dispersion of production in the system increased each year combination until 1940. During the postwar period until 1980 the process once again came to a standstill, but only to diverge again from the 1980s.

The anatomy of the same process can be clearly illustrated by considering the percentages of national GDP per province (Fig. 4). Even though the names of all provinces are not displayed, the three larger provinces (including the three major urban centers of Stockholm, Gothenburg, and Malmö) can be easily distinguished. The upper most line represents Stockholm. Clearly, the increasing CVs in Fig. 4 are driven by the relative expansion of the big city regions, especially Stockholm. Over the while period 1855–2007, Stockholm increases its share from about 12% of total national GDP to about 28%. Many other regions decrease their shares, but this is of curse connected to the enormous relative expansion of Stockholm. This trend is remarkably persistent over time. Even though the redistribution of production was more pronounced during early industrialization, divergence in the system has continued to take place caused by the growth of the metropolitan areas, mainly Stockholm.

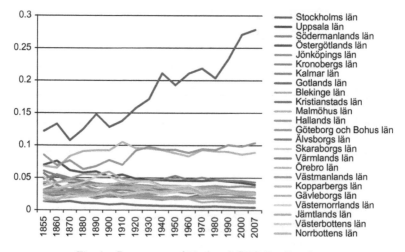

Fig. 4.   Percentage of National GDP Per Province.

Turning to the connected issue of regional growth, Fig. 5 suggests that there was also a drastic convergence in the yearly standard deviation in the growth of the provinces. The regional differences in growth were significantly larger in the beginning of the period that we study, than in the later period. This also underlines the notion of E4 with an early redistribution of production values in the system. In the early years of industrialization, some regions would show an average annual growth of 5–7%. Since 1980, the Stockholm region has been the leading region with an average annual growth between 2% and 3%.

According to *E5*, we also expect a slow convergence in GDP/capita in the Swedish regional system, primarily after 1920. Fig. 6 shows the coefficient of variation of GDP per capita in the Swedish regional system. It is quite clear from the figure that there is a trend-wise convergence over time of GDP per capita across the provinces. Also after excluding Stockholm, which might again be suspected to be an outlier in this context, the pattern overall persists. However, the early 1900s seem not to be a decisive point in this regard. Instead, the convergence trend appears to be systematically interrupted during the process of growth.

According to *E6*, the Swedish industrialization process is, compared to other countries, supposed to have benefited countryside locations to a large extent. As we saw previously, the convergence tendencies in GDP per capita have been very strong over time in the Swedish system. However we

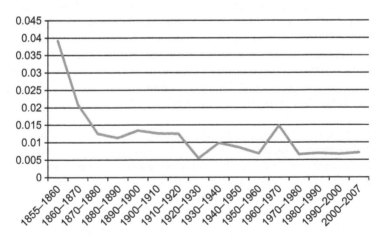

Fig. 5. Yearly Standard Deviation of the Annual Growth of Regions (Fixed Process, Annual Compound Growth Rates).

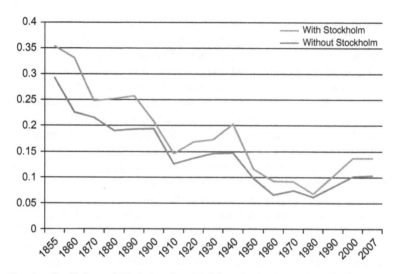

Fig. 6. Coefficient of Variation for GDP Per Capita in the Swedish Regions.

have also seen that the metropolitan areas, most notably Stockholm, has expanded drastically over time in terms of production size. In 1980, the regional differences in GDP/capita were at their lowest level since the introduction of modern statistical measurement. But this process is not only fuelled by the fact that Stockholm has become more equal in this sense, to other parts of the country (Fig. 7). The less fortunate provinces in the beginning of industrialization also converged toward the national mean. This dual process would have served to reduce regional deviations in GDP per capita. However, 1980 seems to have introduced yet another period of divergence in regional GDP per capita. With the introduction of the knowledge-driven economy, the regional differences are once again increasing.

In terms of efficiency therefore, the industrialization process indeed early benefited peripheral locations, as the GDP/capita gap in the system quickly decreased. On the other hand, this might have well to do with the migration of population to Stockholm and the other major city provinces. Even if we only have province data, it is probably safe to say that early industrialization indeed benefited peripheral locations, but in terms of scale, this process was fast taken over by the expansion of the most densely populated provinces. This conclusion is also supported in our concluding reflections below.

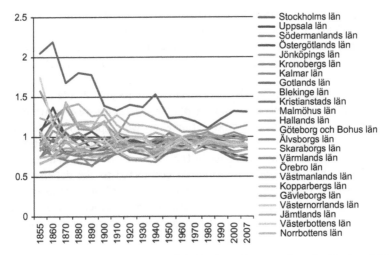

Fig. 7. GDP Per Capita in the Swedish Regions Compared to the National Mean GDP Per Capita.

Lastly, we might consider the fact that aggregate accounts of the kind above tend to obscure the development paths of individual regions. We conclude by creating a regional growth taxonomy where we take the two structural periods of growth that many of the figure above indicate (−1910 and 1910−), and study which regions have positive or negative differentials in terms of shares of regional GDP and population. For each province and year, this means that we calculate the following difference

$$D_i = \left(\frac{\text{GDP}_i}{\text{GDP}} - \frac{\text{Pop}_i}{\text{Pop}} \right) \times 100 \qquad (6)$$

Where D_i is the difference indicator, GDP_i is the GDP of region i, GDP is the national GDP, Pop_i is the population of region i, and Pop is the national population.

The D_i for a specific year and province then is the degree to which it has an "excess" share of regional GDP compared to its shares of population. This is of course similar to calculating the relative regional GDP per capita. Then we simply say that a province that has an average positive D_i in both 1855−1910 and 1910−2007 is a generally above-average performing region (on average, it always had a larger share of GDP than population). On the other hand, a province that had a negative average D_i in both 1855–1910 and 1910–2007 was a generally below-average performing region. A province that had an average D_i of above 0 in 1855–1910 but below 0 in 1910–2007 is called an early grower, and the opposite is called a late grower.[24]

This simple taxonomy yields surprisingly clear results (Table 8). The big-city provinces are the only ones that display a general above-average growth during the entire period we study. Early growers, provinces that early during industrialization had a larger share of GDP than population, are primarily provinces along the coast in the North of Sweden. The dramatic expansion of these provinces is primarily connected to the dependence on natural resources that characterized early stages of industrialization in Sweden. The rest of the provinces are categorized as general below-average performers. However, this is a heterogeneous group, since some very

Table 8.   Provinces and Their Growth Groups.

Province	Category
Stockholms län	General above-average
Uppsala län	Early growers
Södermanlands län	General below-average
Östergötlands län	Early growers
Jönköpings län	General below-average
Kronobergs län	General below-average
Kalmar län	General below-average
Gotlands län	General below-average
Blekinge län	General below-average
Kristianstads län	General below-average
Malmöhus län	General above-average
Hallands län	General below-average
Göteborg och Bohus län	General above-average
Älvsborgs län	General below-average
Skaraborgs län	General below-average
Värmlands län	General below-average
Örebro län	General below-average
Västmanlands län	General below-average
Kopparbergs län	General below-average
Gävleborgs län	Early growers
Västernorrlands län	Early growers
Jämtlands län	Early growers
Västerbottens län	General below-average
Norrbottens län	Early growers

expansive provinces (i.e., the metropolitan regions) tend to elevate the national GDP to which we refer. But especially for the countries that experienced a large migration to the United States, the D_i was very negative during the beginning of our investigated period.

CONCLUSIONS AND IMPLICATIONS

While characterized by slowly changing structures, the 150 years of regional economic development in Sweden that we analyze in this paper are marked by clearly visible turning points. The general trend is toward a more homogenous system in terms of value added per capita in the different provinces. Especially in the early stages of industrialization, convergence was fast. This lends support to the presumed existence of equilibrating forces through the infrastructure and communication networks that were established already during the later part of the 18th century. However, the development in the scale of production structures in the provinces is characterized by quite a contrasting evolution. Here, the metropolitan provinces (Stockholm, Gothenburg, and Malmö) have increased shares substantially. This is especially the case for Stockholm. The factor linking these seemingly contradicting observations is of course migration. As migration has worked to equilibrate differences in GDP per capita, so have the absolute geographical differences in production and population become more marked in Sweden. Even if early industrialization was marked by substantial turmoil, it seems to have set out development path that was perhaps only changed in the late 1980s. The structural crisis in the late 1970s seems to have marked the beginning of a new period of divergence in the knowledge learning economy, also in GDP per capita. In a historical perspective, this is a quite spectacular finding.

The estimates of regional GDP that this paper provides, open up to a whole range of novel long-term research questions. Especially interesting is the periodization of convergence and divergence in GDP per capita in the regions, and to what extent these are connected to macro developments in the wider economy. Another fruitful avenue of research could be to further investigate the relations between economic growth and migration under 150 years of regional development. Within the framework of the larger ESF project, it will also be possible to relate the Swedish experiences to a larger European context.

NOTES

1. In the paper, the term regional GDPs is used. Sometimes, the literature refers to this as GRP (Gross Regional Product).

2. The ESF-funded network initiative "Historical Economic Geography of Europe."

3. More advanced analyses of the Swedish GDP data can be found in Henning, Enflo, and Andersson (2011) and Enflo and Rosés (2012).

4. In such a theoretically informed description, only investments and changes in infrastructure can shock the stable system (apart from, of course, truly exogenous chocks such as natural disasters or wars, which in most cases indeed tend to show up during the time perspectives that we now dwell upon).

5. All equations refer to the calculations of regional GDP in a specific year.

6. We do not make any distinction between "industry" and "sector."

7. We refer to differences in labor productivity (value added per employee), which of course implicitly takes into account productivity differences stemming from a wide variety of traditional productivity sources.

8. The difference is very stable over these years. This operation does not have any implication for the calculation of regional shares of GDP, but only for the nominal figures. The large difference is due to the fact that we use GDP at factor prices from the SHNA, and market prices from Statistics Sweden.

9. For some years, the census reports population size per industry including all children, wives, and servants, even if they are not directly employed in the particular industry. However, since the census data is only used to calculate the regional shares of employees for the different industries, which we then compare to the national known total of employees in each sector from the SHNA, this does not matter for our results.

10. This is also the most detailed aggregation level where we can get consistence and decent wage data.

11. The most notable exception from this scheme is 1855, for which we have occupation level data only. We have made a different but comparable scheme to aggregate the occupations into our four sectors. This scheme can be found in Appendix A.

12. For 1855, we have had to rely on the occupations classifications due to data restrictions. The classification of occupations into sectors is found in Appendix A.

13. The resulting harmonized employment series per sector are presented in Appendix B.

14. Due to this uncertainty, we have calculated the indicators with and without public sector. This does not change the interpretation of the empirical results.

15. For 1910 we use the procedure and data outlined above. For 1993 and 2006 we estimate using the data provided in the national accounts in this preliminary test.

16. In Appendix C, the outcomes of the final GDP estimations are displayed per province. Here, aggregated GDP figures for the eight Swedish NUTS 2 regions can also be found.

17. We use 21 provinces to match the SCB data which is adjusted to the more recent administrative system. We also adjust for the difference between the factor cost and market price estimations in our different sources.

18. This is calculated as the sum of absolute differences between our estimates and the official province GDP across all regions, as share of total GDP.

19. This is calculated as the average difference between our estimates and the official province GDP for each region as share of the regional GDP.

20. One reason for this could be that Skåne has an economy that is structurally very representative of the Swedish general economy (Henning et al., 2009).

21. For example by the temporary fluctuation of value added in a region. Svensson Henning (2009) has shown that regional value added can fluctuate extensively in individual industries on an annual basis.

22. We exclude the first and last combinations as these are not 10-year periods, but the results do not change if they are included.

23. This is the (unweighted) standard deviation of regional GDP divided by the (unwieghted) mean regional GDP. A CV weighted by regional size (population) yields very similar results with a slight difference in levels. For all coefficients of variations in this paper, we have in fact also experimented with weighed version. Since the results of these are not distinguishable from the ones discussed here, we remain with the unweighted versions.

24. A multiplicative measure (i.e., when shares are divided) yields exactly the same final outcomes for the provinces.

ACKNOWLEDGMENTS

The authors gratefully acknowledge funding from the Swedish Research Council, project numbers 2008-2023 (Henning and Enflo) and from the Jan Wallander and Tom Hedelius foundation, project numbers W2009-0402:1 (Henning) and W2008-0357:1 (Enflo). Support from European Science Foundation Grant "Historical Economic Geography of Europe, 1900–2000" part of the GLOBALEURONET, is also thankfully acknowledged.

REFERENCES

Andersson, Å. E. (1978). Demografisk och ekonomisk utveckling. In Att forma regional framtid. 13 forskares syn på regionala problem. En rapport från ERU. LiberFörlag, Stockholm.

Davis, R. D., & Weinstein, D. E. (2002). Bones, bombs, and break points: The geography of economic activity. *The American Economic Review*, *92*(5), 1269–1289.

Enflo, K., & Rosés, J. (2012). *Coping with regional inequality in Sweden: Structural change, migrations and policy, 1860–2000*. European Historical Economics Society (EHES) Working Paper No. 0029.

Enflo, K., Svensson Henning, M., & Schön, L. (2009). Approximating historical GRP using productivity, labor and wage data. Experiences from Swedish estimations for 1910, 1992 and 2006. Paper presented at the XVth World Economic History Congress, Utrecht, August. Available on request from the authors.

Geary, F., & Stark, T. (2002). Examining Ireland's post-famine economic growth performance. *The Economic Journal*, *112*(482), 919—935.

Henning, M., Enflo, K., & Andersson, F. N. G. (2011). Trends and cycles in regional economic growth. How spatial differences shaped the Swedish growth experience from 1860—2009. *Explorations in Economic History*, *48*(4), 538—555.

Jörberg, L. (1972) *A history of prices in Sweden 1732—1914*. Part II. Lund: CWK Gleerup.

Krantz, O., & Schön, L. (2007). *Swedish historical national accounts 1800—2000*. Lund Studies in Economic History 41. Almqvist & Wiksell International.

Lundh, C., Olofsson, J., Schön, L., & Svensson, L. (2004). *Wage formation, labour market institutions and economic transformation in Sweden 1860—2000*. Lund Studies in Economic History 32. Almqvist & Wiksell International.

Lundmark, M., & Malmberg, A. (1988). *Industrilokalisering i Sverige — regional och strukturell förändring*. PhD thesis. Kulturgeografiska institutionen, Uppsala universitet, Uppsala.

Martin, R., & Sunley, P. (2006). Path dependency and regional economic evolution. *Journal of Economic Geography*, *6*(4), 395—437.

Neffke, F., Henning, M., & Boschma, R. (2011). How do regions diversify over time? Industry relatedness and the development of new growth paths in regions. *Economic Geography*, *87*(3), 237—265.

Neffke, F., & Svensson Henning, M. (2013). *Skill-relatedness and firm diversification*. Strategic Management Journal, *34*(3), 297—316.

Persson, J. (1997). Convergence across the Swedish counties, 1911—1993. *European Economic Review*, *41*, 1835—1853.

Schön, L. (2000). *En modern svensk ekonomisk historia*. Stockholm: SNS förlag.

Svensson Henning, M. (2009). *Industrial dynamics and regional structural change. Geographical perspectives on economic evolution*. PhD thesis. Meddelanden från Lunds universitets geografiska institution, avhandlingar CLXXXI.

Söderberg, J., & Lundgren, N.-G. (1982). *Ekonomisk och geografisk koncentration 1850-1980*. Stockholm: LiberFörlag.

Williamson, J. G. (1965). Regional inequality and the process of national development: A description of the patterns. *Economic Development and Cultural Change*, *13*(4—2), 1—84.

APPENDIX A

Table A.1.   Occupations and Sectors for 1855.

Occupation	Our Sectors
Men	
Senior clergymen (Högre prästerskap)	Public services
Military clergymen (Regementspastorer)	Public services
Other clergymen (Vice pastorer mm)	Public services
Preachers in healthcare facilities (Lasarettspredikanter mm)	Public services
Preachers on industry estates (Bruks- och huspredikanter)	Public services
Cleargymen teachers in high schools (Prästvigda lärare mm vid läroverk)	Public services
Private clergymen teachers (Prästvigda enskilda lärare)	Public services
Parish clerks (Prästvigda klockare)	Public services
Church assistants (Kyrkobetjänter)	Public services
Teachers/Church assistants (Skollärare/kyrkobetjänter)	Public services
Other elementary school teachers (Övriga folkskolelärare)	Public services
Academic teachers (Lärare vid akademier och elementärläroverk)	Public services
Other teachers in public schools (Lärare vid andra allmäna läroverk)	Public services
Private teachers (Enskilda lärare)	Public services
Royal estates (Kronobetjäning)	Public services
City white-collar staff (Städernas tjänstemän mm)	Public services
White-collar staff in mines (Tjänstemän vid bergverken)	Manufacturing
Forestry and hunting services (Skogs- och jägeribetjäning)	Agriculture
Customs (Tullbetjäning)	Public services
Physicians (Läkare mm)	Public services
Other civil white-collar staff (Övrige civile tjänstemän)	Public services
Police (Polis)	Public services
Other civilian government officials (Övrig statlig civil betjäning)	Public services
Officers army (Officerare armén)	Public services
Soldiers army (Soldater mm armén)	Public services
Officers navy (Officerare flottan)	Public services
Soldiers navy (Soldater mm flottan)	Public services
Boatswains (Båtsmän)	Public services
Musicians (Musikanter mm)	Private services
Skippers (Skeppare och ångbåtsförare)	Private services
Boat skippers (Båtskeppare)	Private services
Seamen international (Sjömän utrikes sjöfart)	Private services
Seamen domestic (Sjömän inrikes sjöfart)	Private services
Pilots (Lotsar)	Public services
Lighthouse-keepers (Fyrvaktare)	Public services
Other workers (Diverse arbetare)	−
Retired (Ur tjänst avgångne personer)	−
Private services, not agriculture (I enskild tjänst, utom jordbruket)	Private services
Leaseholders (Possessionater, arrendatorer mm)	Agriculture
Farmers (Bönder, torpare mm)	Agriculture

Table A.1. *(Continued)*

Occupation	Our Sectors
Agricultural laborers (Stattorpare)	Agriculture
Crofters (Arbetsföre backstuguhjon)	Agriculture
Gardeners (Trädgårdsmästare)	Agriculture
Fishermen (Skärbönder och fiskare)	Agriculture
Miners (Bergshantering idkande)	Manufacturing
Mill and work workers (Brukshantering idkande)	Manufacturing
Manufacture workers (Fabrikshantering idkande)	Manufacturing
Craftsmen (Hantverk idkande)	Manufacturing
Artists (Konstnärer)	Private services
Wholesaler (Grosshandlare)	Private services
Brokers (Mäklare och skeppsklarerare)	Private services
Shop-keepers (Minuthandlare)	Private services
Booksellers (Bokhandlare)	Private services
Pharmacists (Apotekare)	Private services
Innkeepers (Gästgivare mm)	Private services
Women	
Own agriculture (Lantbruk för egen räkning)	Agriculture
Own manufacturing (Bruks- eller fabriksrörelse egen räkning)	Manufacturing
Own craftsmen (Hantverk och handel egen räkning)	Manufacturing
Hustrur med särskilt näringsfång	–
Manufacture assistants (Bruks- och fabriksbiträden)	Manufacturing
Shop assistants (Hantverks- eller handelsbiträden)	Private services
I övrigt levande av sitt arbete	–
Midwifes (Barnmorskor)	Public services
Teachers in public schools (Lärarinnor i folkskolor)	Public services
Governesses and private teachers (Guvernanter och enskilda lärarinnor)	Public services
Private services (I enskild tjänst)	Agriculture

APPENDIX B: EMPLOYMENT PER SECTOR, 1860–2000

Table B.1. Employment in Agriculture, Per County.

	Employment in Agriculture														
	1860	1870	1880	1890	1900	1910	1920	1930	1940	1950	1960	1970	1980	1990	2000
Stockholms län	42,587	35,234	37,537	38,964	39,231	35,900	37,056	33,442	32,063	22,237	15,074	9,424	6,799	5,253	6,076
Uppsala län	25,907	24,119	24,312	26,198	25,293	24,645	25,939	23,906	20,600	15,059	10,270	8,627	6,934	4,914	4,033
Södermanlands län	38,607	38,339	38,346	38,220	37,220	35,490	36,364	32,574	28,569	19,268	12,792	7,928	6,337	4,362	3,654
Östergötlands län	67,111	59,549	58,554	56,748	56,138	52,972	52,391	49,185	44,483	30,674	20,186	13,180	10,376	7,491	6,761
Jönköpings län	49,559	51,214	56,308	49,310	47,866	43,172	41,758	39,845	32,636	27,290	18,958	12,326	8,939	6,709	5,276
Kronobergs län	39,984	46,633	52,349	46,580	42,529	38,021	35,350	33,138	27,608	23,201	15,401	9,300	6,592	4,730	3,359
Kalmar län	54,033	52,930	52,759	52,543	51,183	47,028	46,091	43,243	37,812	28,719	20,273	13,268	9,889	7,337	6,056
Gotlands län	12,852	13,682	12,706	14,127	14,170	13,516	13,236	13,240	10,848	9,715	7,417	5,127	4,486	3,006	2,599
Blekinge län	26,820	27,437	31,708	31,864	30,512	25,813	22,467	20,169	17,309	13,247	9,356	5,879	4,240	2,887	2,617
Kristianstads län	69,206	65,349	65,118	62,358	59,277	52,632	49,768	47,427	44,912	33,621	26,275	17,520	12,614	8,782	7,359
Malmöhus län	78,911	76,598	78,677	71,971	67,400	59,459	56,890	55,261	56,638	41,082	32,160	23,087	17,078	11,118	9,992
Hallands län	37,373	39,483	41,993	38,482	37,711	32,862	31,212	30,362	26,165	22,551	16,506	12,493	10,067	7,033	5,668
Göteborg och Bohus län	48,071	51,821	52,640	49,315	47,445	41,223	38,826	34,370	31,652	25,293	17,257	11,284	6,830	4,055	3,328
Älvs borgs län	83,512	86,323	85,785	79,953	75,730	65,739	60,458	54,904	47,322	38,688	25,577	16,995	11,563	8,009	5,456
Skaraborgs län	66,645	71,224	73,551	70,553	67,811	60,873	57,650	54,633	48,254	37,290	24,562	16,046	12,835	8,959	6,783
Värmlands län	69,109	73,795	76,637	69,849	64,942	59,443	56,145	53,094	50,317	38,160	24,760	12,989	8,696	6,090	3,914
Örebro län	42,878	47,992	46,533	43,705	42,148	37,170	35,407	32,018	28,406	19,200	13,100	8,854	1,151	4,165	3,850
Västmanlands län	29,095	28,329	30,404	30,427	32,203	29,050	27,778	24,970	20,875	15,466	10,788	7,239	5,478	3,648	3,187
Kopparbergs län	38,879	55,968	52,956	53,416	53,014	48,849	48,603	44,470	40,783	30,628	18,796	10,314	7,635	6,474	4,453
Gävleborgs län	29,156	33,959	35,128	38,896	39,601	41,464	43,366	43,484	41,476	28,484	18,966	10,524	7,742	5,846	4,400

Table B.1. (*Continued*)

Employment in Agriculture

	1860	1870	1880	1890	1900	1910	1920	1930	1940	1950	1960	1970	1980	1990	2000
Västernorrlands län	33,964	35,489	38,532	46,844	51,327	50,758	48,576	46,461	46,482	30,690	19,118	10,128	6,498	4,976	3,914
Jämtlands län	19,735	21,973	24,867	27,393	29,325	32,715	34,278	34,080	33,431	25,084	17,379	8,246	6,103	4,687	3,615
Västerbottens län	21,522	27,044	31,675	36,677	42,515	47,882	50,305	52,547	46,293	38,314	23,409	12,673	8,075	5,888	3,925
Norrbottens län	15,424	22,993	28,008	29,995	34,539	37,367	39,951	41,889	38,583	30,986	18,434	9,067	6,168	4,596	3,051

Table B.2. Employment in Industry, Per County.

Employment in Industry

	1860	1870	1880	1890	1900	1910	1920	1930	1940	1950	1960	1970	1980	1990	2000
Stockholms län	36,462	36,651	53,105	60,894	69,977	82,845	96,725	135,730	170,674	205,374	243,447	197,002	157,421	163,460	151,008
Uppsala län	7,160	8,612	12,258	11,491	13,586	13,402	15,736	19,253	19,894	25,665	27,520	30,895	24,385	27,136	23,930
Södermanlands län	9,053	11,551	14,980	15,748	20,324	19,824	23,578	29,036	35,041	44,988	51,279	49,980	43,630	36,427	30,975
Östergötlands län	21,918	27,176	32,928	30,596	33,930	35,794	39,919	48,967	56,575	71,190	75,988	74,021	66,207	59,312	52,718
Jönköpings län	7,105	10,546	14,378	13,898	22,397	24,743	30,889	38,085	42,386	56,588	62,811	63,000	62,674	54,057	59,362
Kronobergs län	4,699	7,184	10,101	8,689	11,439	12,784	16,696	19,958	19,036	25,757	30,092	31,119	31,419	28,371	26,292
Kalmar län	12,358	15,278	19,241	18,677	21,641	22,082	26,292	32,277	29,891	39,025	41,940	44,039	44,754	38,578	34,222
Gotlands län	3,604	3,215	3,421	2,964	3,709	3,738	4,497	5,802	5,489	6,366	5,234	6,189	5,008	5,619	5,349
Blekinge län	6,207	8,601	10,078	10,668	14,910	15,697	17,296	19,931	21,391	24,380	27,991	29,637	29,094	23,429	20,837
Kristianstads län	11,687	10,912	15,090	13,531	16,953	20,072	25,266	31,532	32,488	40,034	43,104	45,607	40,438	39,733	36,517
Malmöhus län	21,419	28,789	40,704	45,771	61,940	63,855	73,934	91,249	100,980	120,439	132,300	120,291	106,434	9,9864	86,110
Hallands län	4,080	5,531	6,907	7,730	11,126	12,864	14,876	19,011	20,205	27,188	28,871	32,724	31,953	31,762	29,038
Göteborgoch Bohus län	16,694	16,897	24,614	29,283	46,064	51,460	65,801	89,801	95,800	114,797	130,884	118,275	104,629	103,102	95,958
Älvs borgs län	8,169	8,739	13,044	15,986	23,634	29,344	39,620	54,775	67,692	85,409	89,867	89,446	78,096	66,636	60,216
Skaraborgs län	6,443	8,783	13,156	14,599	16,407	18,325	21,932	27,107	30,509	39,080	44,218	44,641	46,318	44,211	39,032
Värmlands län	9,446	12,996	17,087	17,740	22,725	26,580	33,446	40,955	38,165	49,047	55,317	5,0931	46,518	39,224	32,248
Örebrolän	8,540	13,253	18,827	17,879	24,645	28,792	33,269	38,541	49,045	56,653	61,734	54,119	46,062	40,931	36,789
Västmanlands län	7,550	10,748	15,300	15,713	18,611	20,060	25,446	29,043	35,112	48,169	58,021	56,673	55,686	43,396	36,238
Kopparbergs län	9,238	10,740	17,366	20,017	27,709	30,103	37,339	43,239	43,369	52,485	59,208	51,370	48,196	40,304	35,015
Gävleborgs län	10,264	13,292	22,102	29,667	38,538	33,947	39,649	49,496	42,939	54,223	56,862	54,381	51,625	42,203	37,897
Västernorrlands län	6,047	5,733	10,874	27,371	29,601	27,417	35,051	45,469	35,120	46,015	49,162	41,479	37,525	35,092	26,286
Jämtlands län	2,048	1,743	2,370	5,111	9,657	6,460	9,077	10,340	10,734	14,772	15,321	13,895	12,330	132,777	11,078
Västerbottens län	2,137	1,792	5,107	5,799	10,360	9,304	13,567	21,306	18,107	25,362	35,367	30,936	32,137	31,085	26,876
Norrbottens län	1,237	1,920	4,128	4,917	12,529	14,724	18,813	24,711	19,679	28,426	41,140	33,454	31,961	31,497	25,036

Table B.3. Employment in Services, Per County.

Employment in Series

	1860	1870	1880	1890	1900	1910	1920	1930	1940	1950	1960	1970	1980	1990	2000
Stockholms län	31,654	32,032	41,166	48,308	60,507	72,811	108,471	152,034	197,578	225,449	224,798	295,866	296,211	388,143	466,742
Uppsala län	4,775	2,365	4,279	5,110	5,294	6,504	9,808	10,938	12,281	15,087	16,374	23,079	26,601	32,088	35,383
Södermanlands län	5,687	3,327	5,363	6,149	8,795	11,087	13,895	15,002	16,435	19,589	21,798	23,639	26,682	28,111	28,254
Östergötlands län	12,220	8,036	11,453	13,015	13,971	18,921	24,431	29,124	30,603	36,045	37,714	40,432	45,236	48,021	54,741
Jönköpings län	4,349	3,070	6,106	6,238	8,485	10,291	13,804	18,342	19,170	24,850	28,192	30,547	33,000	38,107	41,737
Kronobergs län	2,626	2,451	4,064	4,292	5,585	6,801	8,221	10,100	10,058	13,139	14,397	16,609	19,730	23,497	26,184
Kalmar län	9,223	13,097	15,572	14,944	14,228	14,510	15,625	19,484	18,685	21,935	23,741	22,281	24,729	25,357	25,328
Gotlands län	3,052	3,847	3,634	2,733	2,807	2,896	3,522	4,202	4,566	5,427	5,910	5,347	6,728	6,278	6,776
Blekinge län	5,844	6,739	7,221	6,863	7,502	8,626	9,951	13,208	12,953	13,888	14,573	13,873	14,309	15,311	17,163
Kristianstads län	6,499	6,304	8,126	8,496	10,158	12,668	16,997	20,577	20,403	24,656	26,030	27,982	29,562	31,470	32,365
Malmöhus län	13,265	18,573	23,359	28,001	35,076	44,362	54,140	69,402	72,298	82,840	87,346	109,274	107,018	122,309	131,084
Hallands län	4,579	6,334	6,392	5,931	7,673	9,587	11,087	13,021	13,775	16,388	17,943	22,169	25,191	29,936	32,922
Göteborg och Bohus län	16,548	28,572	33,487	39,822	44,563	45,113	60,127	81,169	84,242	99,066	98,799	117,015	120,914	144,612	155,222
Älvsborgs län	6,491	5,546	7,526	7,866	9,509	12,212	16,211	24,204	26,493	32,605	34,849	41,380	41,270	47,178	49,379
Skaraborgs län	6,097	4,879	8,017	8,467	8,832	10,298	14,273	16,322	16,762	21,383	23,486	23,766	25,480	27,460	26,788
Värmlands län	5,643	4,129	7,100	7,717	9,399	11,650	15,653	20,000	20,738	25,562	29,977	28,231	31,038	34,385	33,372
Örebro län	4,338	4,143	7,228	7,591	9,373	11,655	16,087	21,222	20,833	24,584	27,210	28,220	27,737	31,808	34,873
Västmanlands län	4,478	2,979	4,950	5,097	6,566	7,988	11,355	11,903	13,508	18,031	20,884	25,700	26,724	32,314	32,430
Kopparbergs län	3,343	2,854	5,020	6,188	7,929	10,260	14,016	18,130	18,896	24,240	28,711	26,343	32,346	34,794	33,260
Gävleborgs län	5,682	9,340	12,702	12,598	15,852	18,480	21,425	26,596	24,418	29,196	32,967	30,751	32,648	35,037	33,459
Västernorrlands län	3,822	6,650	8,343	9,089	10,547	14,453	18,982	24,529	24,363	29,440	34,015	32,443	34,832	34,683	35,002
Jämtlands län	854	1,014	1,603	3,595	4,763	5,283	7,917	9,868	10,437	13,893	15,897	13,798	17,065	17,339	17,618
Västerbottens län	1,953	2,726	2,851	3,070	3,830	4,734	8,485	12,278	14,061	18,336	24,035	24,609	29,363	31,738	32,184
Norrbottens län	1,561	2,603	2,572	2,591	6,390	9,319	13,335	18,022	16,558	21,514	27,219	26,524	34,002	34,811	32,851

Table B.4. Employment in Public Services, Per County.

Employment in Public Services

	1860	1870	1880	1890	1900	1910	1920	1930	1940	1950	1960	1970	1980	1990	2000
Stockholms län	8,408	7,231	9,126	12,002	13,016	21,369	32,117	37,047	73,548	83,040	117,973	177,140	241,360	246,142	212,121
Uppsala län	1,686	2,151	2,568	2,847	2,770	3,029	3,509	4,126	6,535	8,539	11,639	24,228	35,335	39,839	38,963
Södermanlands län	1,772	2,471	2,937	3,079	2,692	2,897	3,064	4,198	6,404	7,413	10,375	21,105	28,755	31,996	28,262
Östergötlands län	3,148	4,360	4,902	5,364	5,607	4,906	5,913	7,045	11,235	12,325	16,413	31,187	48,859	55,020	45,067
Jönköpings län	2,424	3,315	3,899	4,142	3,392	3,953	4,283	5,087	8,471	8,979	12,176	22,431	32,708	37,573	35,320
Kronobergs län	1,738	2,492	2,671	2,848	2,909	2,249	2,357	2,763	4,336	4,474	6,202	12,645	1,8731	21,336	19,719
Kalmar län	2,406	3,274	3,454	3,374	4,337	2,904	3,339	4,071	6,167	6,802	9,022	17,617	24,412	28,848	26,351
Gotlands län	695	793	938	839	863	1,250	1,277	1,299	2,443	2,465	3,059	5,288	7,684	8,194	7,680
Blekinge län	3,305	3,400	3,485	4,236	3,218	7,188	9,078	8,747	8,536	6,653	7,480	12,855	18,090	19,951	17,864
Kristianstads län	2,727	2,988	3,581	3,624	3,414	3,364	4,045	4,990	8,188	8,946	11,235	20,570	29,468	34,679	31,894
Malmöhus län	3,947	4,834	6,337	7,581	7,216	8,843	12,325	14,466	24,708	25,833	36,670	67,431	95,113	102,140	90,714
Hallands län	805	1,158	1,391	1,403	2,175	1,995	2,476	2,924	4,601	5,050	6,746	13,823	22,664	29,511	28,748
Göteborg och Bohus län	3,093	3,529	4,602	5,373	6,546	7,354	10,656	12,921	22,112	25,168	36,199	60,800	93,124	102,997	93,227
Älvsborgs län	2,524	3,881	4,640	4,820	4,372	4,080	4,549	5,373	9,319	10,213	15,728	28,688	41,705	51,039	47,075
Skaraborgs län	2,680	4,094	5,029	5,291	3,908	4,410	4,133	5,075	7,922	8,002	10,126	19,274	29,639	34,833	28,114
Värmlands län	1,998	2,654	3,121	3,175	4,399	3,168	3,882	5,006	7,633	8,835	12,281	21,066	32,049	37,235	31,458
Örebro län	1,244	1,741	2,180	2,403	3,289	2,599	3,224	3,985	6,553	7,556	11,202	23,268	30,932	36,880	31,672
Västmanlands län	1,742	2,065	2,469	2,832	2,494	2,501	2,833	3,100	5,002	6,333	9,880	19,624	28,421	30,478	26,718
Kopparbergs län	1,559	1,955	2,340	2,576	2,853	2,602	3,764	4,896	6,336	7,737	11,285	20,067	30,366	36,664	32,336
Gävleborgs län	1,714	2,090	2,757	3,213	4,261	3,026	3,909	4,798	7,672	8,436	11,504	20,849	32,071	37,316	31,592
Västernorrlands län	863	1,140	1,423	1,739	3,756	2,843	4,005	5,165	8,369	10,315	13,558	21,829	31,877	35,557	29,903
Jämtlands län	837	948	1,105	1,242	1,750	1,596	2,340	2,993	5,157	5,382	6,967	10,978	17,326	19,921	16,820
Västerbottens län	594	976	1,066	1,215	2,026	1,789	2,342	3,304	6,631	7,281	10,455	20,030	31,844	37,191	34,362
Norrbottens län	556	907	1,029	1,169	2,072	2,862	4,122	5,307	7,728	10,000	13,865	23,205	35,070	38,978	32,508

APPENDIX C

Table C.1. Estimated Regional GDPs for Swedish Provinces (län) 1855–2007.

National Data	1855	1860	1870	1880	1890	1900	1910	1920	1930	1940	1950	1960	1970	1980	1990	2000	2007
Swedish GDP (nominal)	793	764	926	1,260	1,380	2,147	3,192	12,670	10,138	14,096	31,516	69,914	165,382	504,553	1,283,479	1,991,364	2,683,447
Swedish GDP (1910/1912 price lvl)	842	960	1,206	1,465	1,664	2,359	3,182	4,104	5,630	7,126	10,660	14,990	24,730	30,383	37,512	45,532	
Percentages of national GDP	1855	1860	1870	1880	1890	1900	1910	1920	1930	1940	1950	1960	1970	1980	1990	2000	2007
Stockholm län	12.17%	13.29%	10.76%	12.48%	14.83%	12.82%	13.78%	15.75%	17.14%	21.12%	19.29%	21.08%	21.85%	20.36%	23.34%	27.09%	27.84%
Uppsala län	2.63%	3.30%	2.41%	2.44%	2.16%	2.10%	2.10%	2.25%	2.08%	1.99%	1.96%	1.97%	2.43%	2.49%	2.57%	2.54%	2.57%
Södermanlands län	3.14%	3.90%	3.02%	3.16%	3.17%	2.99%	3.15%	2.92%	2.71%	2.88%	2.89%	2.94%	2.99%	2.92%	2.64%	2.33%	2.41%
Östergötlands län	6.98%	7.60%	6.15%	5.79%	5.97%	5.18%	5.50%	4.87%	4.68%	4.67%	4.59%	4.59%	4.55%	4.69%	4.46%	4.24%	3.94%
Jönköpings län	3.05%	3.31%	3.17%	3.90%	3.17%	3.09%	3.57%	3.12%	3.14%	3.23%	3.80%	3.48%	3.64%	3.75%	3.61%	3.69%	3.61%
Kronobergs län	2.22%	2.25%	2.60%	2.71%	2.40%	2.17%	2.29%	1.91%	1.78%	1.62%	1.82%	1.83%	1.95%	2.09%	2.03%	2.02%	1.92%
Kalmar län	5.66%	4.26%	4.60%	4.36%	4.04%	3.77%	3.42%	3.30%	3.15%	2.72%	2.88%	2.65%	2.70%	2.81%	2.56%	2.29%	2.48%
Gotlands län	1.32%	1.22%	1.38%	1.08%	1.03%	0.87%	0.97%	0.77%	0.73%	0.68%	0.67%	0.60%	0.55%	0.61%	0.53%	0.46%	0.43%
Blekinge län	3.16%	2.52%	2.60%	2.58%	2.46%	2.42%	2.73%	2.30%	2.15%	2.03%	1.71%	1.79%	1.80%	1.83%	1.60%	1.53%	1.42%
Kristianstads län	4.02%	5.34%	4.22%	4.01%	3.83%	3.58%	4.01%	3.52%	3.34%	3.11%	3.12%	2.93%	3.08%	3.03%	2.90%	2.90%	2.77%
Malmöhus län	6.80%	6.54%	8.33%	9.08%	9.22%	9.24%	10.53%	9.55%	9.52%	9.27%	8.81%	8.33%	9.30%	9.10%	9.03%	8.62%	8.90%
Hallands län	2.64%	2.65%	2.94%	2.31%	1.80%	2.23%	2.32%	2.16%	2.05%	1.89%	2.13%	1.94%	2.29%	2.47%	2.57%	2.31%	2.46%
Göteborg och Bohus län	8.52%	6.92%	7.66%	6.31%	6.79%	7.74%	7.00%	9.19%	9.78%	9.33%	9.33%	8.86%	9.42%	9.30%	10.07%	9.83%	10.38%
Älvsborgs län	6.04%	5.32%	4.76%	4.28%	3.72%	4.04%	4.11%	4.34%	4.60%	4.78%	5.32%	4.73%	5.06%	4.73%	4.56%	4.55%	4.31%
Skaraborgs län	3.79%	4.28%	4.50%	4.63%	3.87%	3.58%	3.66%	3.05%	2.85%	2.87%	3.09%	2.82%	2.87%	3.07%	2.89%	2.80%	2.71%
Värmlands län	4.81%	5.50%	4.94%	4.49%	4.13%	3.94%	3.82%	3.91%	3.80%	3.50%	3.59%	3.65%	3.20%	3.29%	2.98%	2.72%	2.60%
Örebro län	2.91%	3.04%	3.76%	3.32%	3.10%	3.37%	3.39%	3.63%	3.52%	3.75%	3.50%	3.49%	3.34%	3.01%	2.95%	2.91%	2.72%
Västmanlands län	2.26%	2.90%	2.73%	2.98%	2.73%	2.89%	2.58%	2.63%	2.38%	2.59%	2.80%	3.08%	3.26%	3.31%	2.95%	2.83%	2.59%
Kopparbergs län	2.96%	3.17%	4.00%	3.80%	3.98%	3.92%	4.35%	3.86%	3.66%	3.48%	3.59%	3.58%	3.14%	3.34%	3.01%	2.83%	2.70%
Gävleborgs län	4.31%	4.19%	4.85%	5.55%	5.46%	5.92%	4.84%	4.59%	4.55%	3.83%	3.82%	3.65%	3.37%	3.51%	3.13%	2.81%	2.71%
Västernorrlands län	5.16%	3.45%	3.79%	4.27%	5.14%	5.29%	4.30%	4.43%	4.42%	3.62%	3.60%	3.80%	2.99%	3.11%	2.86%	2.50%	2.40%
Jämtlands län	1.38%	1.82%	1.95%	2.14%	2.30%	2.61%	1.89%	1.99%	1.79%	1.81%	1.71%	1.77%	1.23%	1.38%	1.32%	1.16%	1.16%
Västerbottens län	2.25%	1.76%	2.24%	2.05%	2.25%	2.70%	2.34%	2.68%	2.83%	2.45%	2.83%	3.07%	2.40%	2.77%	2.67%	2.52%	2.54%
Norrbottens län	1.83%	1.47%	2.63%	2.27%	2.43%	3.55%	3.35%	3.29%	3.37%	2.79%	3.16%	3.37%	2.60%	3.04%	2.78%	2.51%	2.42%
Percentages of National GDP Per NUTS Region	1855	1860	1870	1880	1890	1900	1910	1920	1930	1940	1950	1960	1970	1980	1990	2000	2007
SE11 Stockholm	12.17%	13.29%	10.76%	12.48%	14.83%	12.82%	13.78%	15.75%	17.14%	21.12%	19.29%	21.08%	21.85%	20.36%	23.34%	27.09%	27.84%
SE12 Ö Mellansverige	17.91%	20.73%	18.07%	17.69%	17.13%	16.53%	16.72%	16.31%	15.36%	15.87%	15.73%	16.07%	16.58%	16.42%	15.57%	14.87%	14.24%
SE21 Småland med öarna	12.24%	11.04%	11.75%	12.05%	10.64%	9.90%	10.24%	9.10%	8.80%	8.24%	9.17%	9.05%	8.84%	9.26%	8.73%	8.47%	8.45%
SE22 Sydsverige	13.98%	14.40%	15.15%	15.67%	15.52%	15.24%	17.27%	15.36%	15.01%	14.41%	13.64%	13.05%	14.18%	13.95%	13.53%	13.05%	13.09%
SE23 Västsverige	20.99%	19.16%	19.86%	17.53%	16.18%	17.59%	17.09%	18.74%	19.27%	18.87%	19.88%	18.35%	19.64%	19.56%	20.09%	19.50%	19.87%
SE31 N Mellansverige	12.08%	12.86%	13.80%	13.83%	13.58%	13.79%	13.01%	12.36%	12.01%	10.80%	11.00%	10.88%	9.70%	10.14%	9.12%	8.35%	8.01%
SE32 Mellersta Norrland	6.54%	5.27%	5.74%	6.42%	7.45%	7.89%	6.19%	6.41%	6.21%	5.44%	5.31%	5.58%	4.22%	4.49%	4.17%	3.66%	3.55%
SE33 Övr Norrland	4.09%	3.24%	4.87%	4.32%	4.68%	6.25%	5.69%	5.97%	6.20%	5.24%	5.98%	6.44%	5.00%	5.81%	5.45%	5.02%	4.96%

Source: SHNA and own calculations.

Table C.2. Relative Regional GDP Per Capita, National Average = 1.

Regional GDP/Capita, Index National Average = 1	1855	1860	1870	1880	1890	1900	1910	1920	1930	1940	1950	1960	1970	1980	1990	2000	2007
Stockholms län	2.05	2.19	1.68	1.80	1.78	1.39	1.33	1.40	1.37	1.53	1.23	1.24	1.19	1.11	1.22	1.32	1.31
Uppsala län	1.05	1.37	1.00	1.00	0.85	0.87	0.91	0.97	0.92	0.92	0.89	0.88	0.90	0.85	0.82	0.77	0.73
Södermanlands län	0.92	1.19	0.93	0.98	0.98	0.92	0.97	0.91	0.88	0.95	0.95	0.97	0.97	0.96	0.89	0.81	0.83
Östergötlands län	1.10	1.22	1.01	0.99	1.07	0.95	1.03	0.94	0.93	0.94	0.93	0.96	0.96	0.99	0.95	0.92	0.86
Jönköpings län	0.67	0.75	0.74	0.91	0.78	0.78	0.92	0.81	0.83	0.85	0.99	0.91	0.96	1.03	1.01	1.05	0.99
Kronobers län	0.56	0.57	0.68	0.73	0.71	0.70	0.80	0.71	0.70	0.68	0.81	0.86	0.95	1.00	0.98	1.02	0.97
Kalmar län	0.97	0.74	0.82	0.81	0.83	0.85	0.83	0.84	0.84	0.76	0.86	0.84	0.90	0.97	0.91	0.86	0.98
Gotlands län	1.03	0.94	1.06	0.90	0.96	0.84	0.97	0.81	0.78	0.74	0.79	0.83	0.83	0.91	0.80	0.72	0.70
Blekinge län	1.03	0.83	0.86	0.86	0.83	0.85	1.01	0.92	0.91	0.89	0.83	0.93	0.95	0.99	0.91	0.91	0.86
Kristianstads län	0.75	0.98	0.79	0.79	0.83	0.84	0.97	0.86	0.83	0.80	0.85	0.86	0.94	0.90	0.86	0.89	0.86
Malmöhus län	0.92	0.89	1.10	1.19	1.20	1.16	1.27	1.16	1.15	1.11	1.07	1.00	1.04	1.02	1.00	0.91	0.91
Hallands län	0.87	0.85	0.96	0.78	0.63	0.81	0.87	0.86	0.84	0.79	0.92	0.85	0.96	0.89	0.87	0.75	0.78
Göteborg och Bohus län	1.58	1.25	1.37	1.10	1.09	1.18	1.01	1.28	1.31	1.22	1.18	1.06	1.06	1.09	1.17	1.10	1.14
Älvsborgs län	0.86	0.76	0.71	0.68	0.65	0.74	0.79	0.85	0.90	0.93	1.04	0.95	1.01	0.92	0.89	0.91	0.87
Skaraborgs län	0.66	0.74	0.77	0.82	0.75	0.76	0.84	0.74	0.72	0.76	0.88	0.85	0.90	0.95	0.90	0.92	0.97
Värmlands län	0.75	0.86	0.79	0.76	0.78	0.80	0.81	0.86	0.86	0.83	0.90	0.94	0.91	0.96	0.91	0.88	0.87
Örebro län	0.74	0.77	0.93	0.83	0.81	0.89	0.90	0.98	0.99	1.05	1.00	1.00	0.98	0.91	0.93	0.94	0.91
Västmanlands län	0.83	1.08	1.00	1.06	0.95	1.00	0.92	0.92	0.90	0.98	0.97	0.99	1.01	1.06	0.98	0.98	0.96
Kopparbergs län	0.68	0.73	0.95	0.91	0.97	0.92	1.03	0.90	0.90	0.89	0.95	0.94	0.91	0.97	0.90	0.90	0.90
Gävleborgs län	1.24	1.19	1.37	1.42	1.26	1.28	1.05	1.01	1.00	0.89	0.94	0.93	0.93	0.99	0.93	0.89	0.90
Västernorrlands län	1.74	1.14	1.17	1.15	1.18	1.17	0.95	0.99	0.98	0.84	0.89	1.00	0.88	0.96	0.94	0.90	0.90
Jämtlands län	0.90	1.14	1.15	1.17	1.10	1.20	0.88	0.88	0.82	0.83	0.83	0.95	0.79	0.85	0.83	0.80	0.84
Västerbottens län	1.08	0.84	1.02	0.88	0.88	0.96	0.80	0.87	0.85	0.71	0.86	0.96	0.83	0.94	0.91	0.87	0.90
Norrbottens län	1.05	0.82	1.44	1.14	1.11	1.35	1.15	1.06	1.04	0.82	0.92	0.97	0.82	0.95	0.90	0.87	0.89

POLITICAL ECONOMIC LIMITS TO THE FED'S GOAL OF A COMMON NATIONAL BANK MONEY: THE PAR CLEARING CONTROVERSY REVISITED

John A. James and David F. Weiman

ABSTRACT

The increased use of checks in nonlocal payments at the end of the nine-teenth century presented problems for their clearing and collection. Checks were required to be paid in full (at par) only when presented directly to the drawn-upon bank at its counter. Consequently, many, primarily rural or small-town, banks began to charge remittance fees on checks not presented for collection in person. Such fees and the alleged circuitous routing of checks in the process of collection to avoid them were widely criticized defects of the pre-Federal Reserve payments system. As the new Federal Reserve established its own system for check clearing and collection, it also took as an implicit mandate the promotion of universal par clearing and collection. The result was a bitter struggle with non-par banks, the numbers of which initially shrunk dramatically but then rebounded. A 1923 Supreme Court decision ended the Fed's

Research in Economic History, Volume 30, 91–134

Copyright © 2014 by Emerald Group Publishing Limited
ISSN: 0363-3268/doi:10.1108/S0363-326820140000030002

active (or coercive) pursuit of universal par clearing, and non-par bank-ing persisted thereafter for decades. Not until the Monetary Control Act of 1980 was universal par clearing and true monetary union, in which standard means of payment are accepted at par everywhere, achieved.

Keywords: Non-par banking; payments system; monetary union; check clearing and collection; Federal Reserve

JEL classifications: N22; E58; G21

INTRODUCTION

True monetary union was a long time in coming in the United States, almost 200 years. Let us be clear here as to what we mean by "true," distin-guishing between a monetary and a payments system union. The power to create the former was authorized to the federal government by Article I, Sections 8 and 10, of the Constitution and implemented in the Coinage Act of 1792 which established the dollar as the national unit of account, the value of which was set in terms of fixed amounts of gold and silver specie (see Weiman, 2006).[1] However, this alone did not ensure a fully integrated payments system in which readily acceptable means of payment were received at full value (in other words, at par) in different locations. Many or most of the benefits deriving from a monetary union or common cur-rency area are at the micro level, such as price transparency or facilitating price comparisons (De Grauwe, 2012, pp. 54–55). But the major such direct benefit, the elimination of transactions costs from converting one local currency into another, is more properly associated with a standar-dized payments instrument and network rather than just a common unit of account. A complete national payments union at par in fact was not achieved until 1980 with the Monetary Control Act.

From early on the U.S. mint produced specie coins, which were accept-able everywhere at par. Nevertheless they were relatively little used in inter-city or interstate commerce because of the expense and risk in shipping them. Rather, such payments were generally accomplished through the use of a paper "credit instrument" of some sort – state bank notes, bills of exchange, or bank drafts, all of which generally did not exchange at par across locations. The Civil War and the passage of the National Currency (Banking) Acts, 1863–1865, marked an important step toward a more inte-grated payments system and monetary union, creating a uniform national paper currency, national bank notes, issued by federally chartered banks, which circulated at par throughout the country, regardless of the point of issue, replacing the heterogeneous mass of state bank notes circulating at various rates of discount. Although lighter than specie, paper currency still was risky and inconvenient to ship to settle retail intercity or interregional transactions. In the period after the Civil War checks, which earlier had not generally circulated beyond city limits, began to displace bank drafts as the standard nonlocal means of payment and by the turn of the century had become the virtually universal method of payment in long-distance wholesale trade. These nonlocal checks presented a major complication in the evolution of the payments system (James & Weiman, 2010). Unlike drafts which usually had been cleared and settled in some common financial center where banks maintained correspondent accounts, checks by common law need to be presented at the drawn-upon bank's counter for settlement, so that there were then thousands of potential settlement locations spread across the country. If settlement occurred through other procedures the paying bank could charge a remittance fee, so that the check depositor received less than the full value of the check in payment.

The second major step toward a national monetary or payments union was the Federal Reserve's efforts in its early years at promoting universal par clearing of checks, by this time the preferred and dominant method of nonlocal payment, so that depositors received the full value of their check in payment without deduction.[2] This turned out to be a vigorously contested policy. "Probably no subject in the entire history of banking has been the cause of more heated controversy than has the par check collection and absorption of exchange controversies" (Miller, 1949, p. 1), "one of the bitterest in all the banking history of the United States" (Tippetts, 1924, 1926).[3] It is on the par clearing controversy and non-par banking that this paper focuses. The second section describes the evolution of the payments system between the Second Bank of the United States and the Federal Reserve. The third and fourth sections focus on the Fed's efforts to promote par clearing and collection of checks, while the fifth considers those banks which resisted the Fed's efforts. The sixth section concludes.

THE PRE-FED SYSTEM

After the demise of the Second Bank of the United States, independent banks developed two types of private networks to facilitate interbank transactions. At the local level during the 1850s banks in New York, Boston,

Philadelphia, and Baltimore began to form clearing associations for the clearing and collection of local checks (Cannon, 1910; Gorton & Mullineaux, 1987). At the nonlocal level interregional integration of the system of clearing and collecting financial obligations could not be internalized along Chandlerian (1977) lines through the formation of large-scale enterprises, due to the prohibition against interstate branch banking. Making payments at a distance posed a difficult problem in a country characterized predominately by independent unit banks with no central monetary authority or integrated nationwide banking system (see Knodell, 1998). It could have been accomplished by shipping specie to the payee, but a system of intercity payments involving the physical transfer of cash to settle every transaction would have been a costly one indeed. Most intercity financial transactions instead involved the use of a bank credit instrument of some type — bank notes, later supplanted by the use of drafts (Colwell, 1860, pp. 135, 190, 262, 447).

The spatial gaps in the payments system between local clearing houses and between city and country banks were filled by the development of the correspondent banking system. "Country" banks began routinely to maintain reserve balances in commercial centers, notably Boston and New York, first for the redemption of note issues (see Myers, 1931; Weber, 2003), later for the sale of drafts. The bank draft, a check drawn by one bank against funds deposited in another (financial center) bank authorizing payment to a named individual, became the intercity or interregional payments instrument of choice. Local banks then could sell their customers who needed to make a payment in a distant city a draft drawn on their account with a correspondent bank there, obviating the immediate need to ship cash.

By mid-century a tiered system of bank correspondents with New York as a national center mediating interregional payments had begun to emerge (Bodenhorn, 2000, pp. 192–198). The emergence of New York as the preeminent commercial center meant that maintaining a New York correspondent became increasingly important for interior banks. Almost 600 out of 700 incorporated U.S. banks by that time maintained New York accounts (Myers, 1931, p. 115). New York funds became the readily acceptable means of payment everywhere because so many agents made payments there. Drafts or other credit instruments payable in New York City drawn on the local bank's correspondent account there consequently became the most common medium for settling debts not just between interior cities and New York, but even between agents in different communities. The hierarchical reserve structure established by the National Banking

Acts, distinguishing between central reserve cities (national financial center — New York), reserve cities (regional financial centers — Boston, Philadelphia, San Francisco, etc.), and country banks reflected and reinforced the correspondent banking networks in place.

As the draft developed as a general means of nonlocal payment, so also did the correspondent banking system mature, being two sides of the same coin. This in turn allowed for a quite efficient system of essentially net collective settlement of nonlocal payments — transactions between parties whose banks shared the same city correspondent could be settled as an intrabank "on us" transfer of funds; those between parties whose banks had different correspondents in the same financial center involved only a transfer of funds within the local clearinghouse, greatly reducing the necessary shipment of reserves (Garbade & Silber, 1979, pp. 5–6; Goodfriend, 1991, p. 11).

After the Civil War however such payment arrangements began to change. To be sure, the National Banking Acts created a uniform national paper currency (national bank notes) backed by U.S. government bonds which circulated at par or face value (Redenius, 2007), but the use of currency, even in local transactions, was on the wane. It was undermined by the diffusion of deposit banking which had been primarily confined to eastern urban areas in the antebellum period. Banks in the postbellum period were increasingly becoming primarily banks of deposit rather than banks of issue (see James, 1978, pp. 22–27) — the overall ratio of deposits in commercial banks to currency rose from 1.50 in 1870 to 2.03 in 1880, then more than doubled the 1870 value to 3.22 in 1890, and more than doubled again to 6.67 by 1910 (Carter et al., 2006, Vol. 3, p. 604). State-chartered banks which had appeared to have been down and out in 1865 as a result of the tax on state bank note issues imposed by the National Banking Acts gained a new lease on life. The revival of state banking, invigorated in part by liberalized incorporation laws (James, 1978, pp. 29–36), picked up considerably in the 1880s and with it the increased use of checks in payments.

Unlike the antebellum precedent however, checks around this time came to be used in nonlocal as well as local transactions. Their diffusion was not looked upon with favor by many bankers. Mr. Channing Whitney of Adrian, MI in 1881 judged it a "great evil. We depend quite largely upon our New York exchange to meet the current expenses of the banks, and we find that merchants send forward their checks to Eastern points, which are received there by Eastern banks and credited at par to the merchants having deposits therein, and then return to the Western Bank, being again credited at par, we find that to a great extent legitimate sources of

the revenues of the banks, which, of course, is small, are being cut off"
(p. 23).[4] Discussions of out-of-town check collections began to appear on
agendas and programs of state bankers' association meetings (e.g., Blye,
1885; Hammond, 1890). David Kinley (1910, pp. 123, 196–199), the leading contemporary authority on the payments system, estimated by the turn
of the twentieth century checks had become the "preponderatingly method
of payment" in both local and long-distance trade, accounting for about
95 percent of wholesale trade transactions.[5]

Checks offered distinct advantages to bank customers, as compared with
drafts, in making nonlocal payments. For one thing, the use of checks was
clearly more convenient for payers, who avoided the transactions costs (the
trip to the bank) and fees of purchasing drafts. Moreover, with the purchase of a draft the payer's account was debited immediately, while with a
check it was not debited until the check was collected. At the same time
however, the increased use of checks for out-of-town payments imposed
significant costs on the payees and their banks. Unlike a draft, the collection and clearing of individual checks involved additional time, risk, and
transactions costs. In particular, banks under common law were not
obligated to redeem checks promptly or at par, unless they were presented
for collection at their office. Settlement procedures remained relatively
unchanged. It was still generally accomplished by the issue of a draft on a
financial center, usually New York, in interregional transactions. New
York remained "the clearing house of the country" in O. M. W. Sprague's
words (1910, p. 126). But clearing and collection became more complicated.
Rather than most collections being focused in a central locale, New York,
as under the draft system, collection points became much more dispersed.
Indeed there were now as many potential collection points as there were
banks, thousands or tens of thousands.[6]

With the greater frequency of checks in long-distance trade, banks
devoted increasing resources to their transit department and became more
attentive to their collection costs. Advocates of scientific management
urged bankers to adopt more systematic methods of cost accounting, which
would yield estimates of the profitability of their business accounts.
Obviously, collection costs varied with the individual characteristics of
banks and their customers. Still, these procedures revealed systemic factors,
those which uniformly affected all banks at a given location and so gauge
the center's nodality in the payments system.

Standard procedures divided collection costs into three distinct components: service and exchange charges, and the costs associated with lags in
receipts (Kent, 1900; Spahr, 1926, pp. 72, 109–117). The first two items

encompass the very real expenditure of resources on shipments in the circu-lation of checks and legal tender or its equivalent. To dispatch out-of-town checks for collection, banks incurred direct costs of clerical labor, materi-als, and postage, as well as a portion of their overhead expenses on office space and supervisory personnel. If necessary to settle their accounts, banks could ship legal tender and recorded these transport costs under the cate-gory of "exchange."

It was considered potential negligence for a bank to collect checks by sending them directly to the paying bank through the mail. The bank upon which the check was drawn became then the agent for obtaining payment from itself and could, for example, take its time in remitting payment. The paying bank was also allowed to deduct a fee, an "exchange charge," or "remittance fee" to defray the costs of transmitting the funds to the collect-ing bank (Spahr, 1926, p. 104).[7] The actual costs incurred in fact were often quite minimal with settlement usually accomplished by the issue of a draft drawn on a money center banks rather than the physical shipment of cash. This was non-par banking, in which the collecting bank received less than the face value of the check in payment. Check depositors could argue that any such charges be absorbed by the bank and their account be credited at par because of the negligence of the bank in its collecting practices.

To avoid the negligence issue, collecting banks pursued a number of strategies. For example, they might instead mail the check to a bank near the paying bank, and that bank could then present the check at the counter for payment in full.[8] Numerous banks advertised their collection services for their nearby area in trade periodicals at the time. There was a charge for this service also however, a "presentment fee," again in principle to compensate for remitting the funds to the collecting bank (see, e.g., Federal Reserve Bank of Richmond, 1926, p. 383).[9] But since there might have been some competition in the market for collecting locally checks which had been deposited with out-of-town banks, such charges were prob-ably lower than that exacted by the paying bank for collecting on itself, which of course had monopoly power over paying its own checks. These exchange charges, remittance, and presentment fees offered the paying bank a way to recoup revenue lost due to decreased sales of drafts. Indeed Spahr (1926, p. 103) suggested that bankers often found that they could charge collecting banks more and with less compunction than they could charge their own customers for the sale of drafts.

To escape such charges, banks often employed the correspondent bank-ing system to establish reciprocal or mutual par clearing relationships with distant banks. For example, some banks would agree to collect checks drawn on themselves and on banks in a nearby area at par for specific other banks if they agreed to do the same in their territory. Similarly, two banks might agree to carry balances with each other earning no interest ("double-headed" accounts) to have their items collected at par in their respective districts. Or, city banks might have credited items sent to them by country correspondents at par, absorbing whatever collection costs on them that were necessary. The beneficiary country bank however was required to maintain a sufficiently large balance with its city correspondent at zero or low interest rates to justify the absorption of such collection costs.[10] Similarly, country banks might choose to maintain correspondent accounts with particular money center banks to have checks passing through the latter drawn on banks in the area directed to the former for collection (in this case earning some sort of presentment fee) (Spahr, 1926, p. 101). To avoid explicit exchange charges in collection, checks could have passed from bank to bank to bank rather than directly routed to or near the paying bank. Thus, a bank into which an out-of-town check had been deposited would consult its list of correspondent banks which offered par collection and send it in the direction of the paying bank or to a bank which might have a par clearing relationship with the paying bank. In turn, if the receiving bank in the first step did not have a par clearing relationship with the paying bank, it would pass the check on to a third (correspondent) bank, and so forth.

Banks, on the other hand, were also sensitive to the very real costs of funds idled in the process of collections, the "float." During the period between the deposit of out-of-town checks and their redemption in legal tender or reserves, banks carried these assets as "cash items" on their balance sheets. Although highly liquid, their inventory of receivables did not count as legal reserves and so could not support the creation of additional loans and deposits. Rather, they represented interest-free loans to payers and their banks. A longer period of collection, accordingly, increased the opportunity cost of collections, equal to the foregone interest from holding excess "potential" reserves. In many cases, banks offered their customers immediate credit upon the deposit of "foreign" checks, and so bore the expense of additional interest payments. In particular, competition for retail business was said to have sometimes (often?) forced collecting banks to absorb such costs themselves rather than passing them on to their customers who had deposited the check originally which was credited at par (Spahr, 1926, p. 113). Competition also forced many banks to give immediate credit to the customer who had deposited the check and the right to draw against it even though the paying bank had not yet remitted.[11] Many bankers were quite distressed at "what is now so often done, [having to] place at once in credit everything and anything at face value, without discount or charge," glumly concluding that "the banks themselves and alone are responsible for the existing state of things" (Blye, 1885, p. 135). The collecting banks thus bore the direct collection costs, the float (of uncertain duration), and also the risk that the item might ultimately be returned due to lack of funds in the drawing account.

In order to avoid remittance charges, checks in the process of collection may have been passed from bank to bank depending on mutual par clearing relationships, rather than following efficient paths. Such indirect routing to avoid remittance charges was widely criticized in the pre-Fed period (e.g., Cannon, 1910; Hallock, 1903), and some notorious cases were frequently cited. Without detailing the precise route here, there was the case of a check deposited in a Hoboken, NJ bank drawn on a Sag Harbor, NY bank which passed through 11 banks and was in transit 11 days, traveling some 1,500 miles, to avoid remittance charges in collecting on the bank about 100 miles away (Cannon, 1910, pp. 70–73; Hallock, 1903, pp. 19–22; Spahr, 1926, pp. 105–106). One more example. Hallock (1903, p. 24) cited the case of Harrison and Eureka Springs, Arkansas, adjacent towns on the same railroad. The Harrison bank could collect at par checks sent through Wichita, Kansas. So checks deposited in Harrison drawn on Eureka Springs were sent first to Wichita, then to St. Louis, from there to Springfield, Missouri, and finally to Eureka Springs.

This indirect routing of out-of-town checks in the process of collection was generally held to have been the "greatest evil" (Spahr, 1926, p. 103) of the *ancien régime*, and the view it had been a widespread practice became the standard characterization of this period (e.g., Duprey & Nelson, 1986; U.S. House Committee on Banking, Finance, and Urban Affairs, 1983, pp. 348–349, 1080). More recently writers from the Federal Reserve Bank of Richmond however have entered the fray to defend the pre-Fed system (Lacker, Walker, & Weinberg, 1999; Weinberg, 1997). Their argument basically is that private payment networks would have configured themselves efficiently or optimally in line with the usual flow of commerce. Thus, the odd circuitously routed check was just an exception to the normal pattern of payments. After an "irregular" check had been deposited in a bank, the choice became one between sending the check directly toward the paying bank and incurring presentment or remittance fees or else including the check in a bundle of other checks routed to a correspondent in the expectation that it would in turn route the check toward its destination. The marginal cost of including one more check in such a bundle was about zero.

Indeed, "it is possible that presentment fees reinforced network efficiency by reducing the incentive for individual banks to bypass the network" (Weinberg, 1997, p. 39). Results were not always satisfactory since "some mistaken routing choices were inevitable in a decentralized system with thousand of banks," but the proper cost comparison facing the collecting bank was "between the *expected* cost of sending the check along to the next correspondent bank (including the cost of sending it to subsequent correspondents) and the cost of a more direct route ... The fact that some items ended up following routes that look excessively costly ex post does not mean that routing choices were inefficient *ex ante*" (Lacker et al., 1999, p. 21).

They allege that the widespread criticism of the system at the time was orchestrated by city bankers, since it was typically they who paid the presentment fees while country bankers were the ones who reaped them (Anderson, 1916, p. 125; see also Summers & Gilbert, 1996, p. 4). It was then really a dispute about the allocation of costs within the check collection system rather than about their aggregate level (Lacker et al., 1999, p. 22). Some empirical support for this position has been offered by Chang, Danilevsky, Evans, and Garcia-Swartz (2008) who examined the remittance records of the State National Bank of Bloomington, Illinois for 1910. They found that nonlocal check clearing and collection was normally an orderly and efficient process. While not denying that there could have been some circuitous routings with checks wandering around the country, they conclude that such cases were "the exception rather than the norm" (p. 457).[12]

In any case, after an out-of-town check had been deposited in it by one of its customers the collecting bank sometimes, perhaps often, had relatively little idea as to what value of funds would be remitted and how long the collection process would be.[13] Virtually from the beginning of the widespread diffusion of nonlocal checks in the 1880s, there was discontent with the system for their clearing and collection which had developed, and thus proposals for reform were offered.[14] These grumblings and suggestions were fairly regularly enunciated at conventions of American Bankers' Association or of state organizations and in contributions to *Bankers' Magazine*. Some proposed statewide (e.g., Blye, 1885), regional, or national clearinghouses and collection agencies (e.g., Hammond, 1890). The Boston Clearing House foreign department is an example of this model. Others focused on establishing uniform exchange charges to make sure that banks didn't compete against each other in collection costs and that they passed them on to depositors rather than absorbing them. The New York Clearing House plan exemplifies this approach. We describe both of these below.

Antebellum New England had experience with regional clearing of bank notes for over three decades under the Suffolk system (Bodenhorn, 2002). After the Civil War there had been two abortive attempts at regional clearing for country checks – in 1877 and 1883 (Hallock, 1903, pp. 50–51) – but it was finally achieved in 1899 with the establishment of the foreign department of the Boston Clearing House. Member banks presented out-of-town checks which had been deposited with them to the clearinghouse, where they were sorted. Checks drawn on each out-of-town bank were packaged together and mailed to the issuing bank. Each bank then would by return mail send a draft drawn on its Boston (or New York) correspondent or currency[15] to cover the amount at par. Since it took two nights to obtain most remittances, the clearinghouse manager settled with the presenting city banks on the second morning in the regular intracity clearing process (Hallock, 1903, pp. 49–111 describes the mechanics in detail; see also Cannon, 1910, pp. 259–275; Spahr, 1926, pp. 126–128).[16]

Although some 97 percent of New England checks were collected at par, around 3 percent (unsurprisingly) were not. Non-par remittance was concentrated among those banks the most distant from Boston – northern Maine (Aroostock county), the White Mountains of New Hampshire, parts of Vermont, and the southwest corner of Connecticut – 72 out of the 624 New England total. The Clearing House receiving short remittances from these banks after four months began to charge for collecting such checks – 10 cents per $100, with no charge less than 10 cents – which in turn were passed on to the depositor of the check. While collecting banks and depositors bore these costs, the non-par banks themselves enjoyed the benefits of a free collection extending over most of New England because they had the use of the entire free list without penalty (Hallock, 1903, pp. 60–62).

On August 13, 1901, the Association voted to have checks drawn on New England banks which did not remit at par collected by express companies, which would present directly the checks at the issuing bank's counter. Over the next something less than three months the clearinghouse collected $3,544,813 on non-par checks by express. In retaliation, 58 of the non-par banks settled in silver coin rather than by drafts. Some $2,313,250 in silver coins was ordered and transmitted to the paying banks from the sub-treasuries of Boston and New York at government expense and then shipped to the Boston Clearing House. Express charges incurred by the government came to $2,700, and the Clearing House in turn paid $8,500 to express the silver to Boston, a sum which was charged to "general expense." These costs, much greater than had been anticipated, led the Clearing House to drop the plan of direct presentment and return to the former arrangement of charging member banks for collecting non-par items, which in turn were passed on to their customers (Hallock, 1903, pp. 63–66). Other strategies had been proposed to deal with non-par banks. One was simply to return the non-par check uncollected to the depositor. Non-par banks then would have been faced with having to explain why their customers' checks were not acceptable to banks in Boston and throughout New England. Another was to charge non-par banks for collecting through the clearinghouse just as those banks charged it for collecting their own items, in other words reciprocity. In effect there would have been no free list in New England for non-par banks (Hallock, 1903, pp. 61–63). Neither of these plans were adopted.[17]

The Boston system did lower collection costs and decrease collection times – it reduced by around 80 percent the number of daily collection letters sent from Boston to New England country banks and instead of remitting on a weekly or biweekly basis country banks made daily remittances of a single payment (Duprey & Nelson, 1986, p. 22). It thus served as the basis for (some) emulation. In 1905 the Kansas City, MO Clearing House organized a foreign or country clearing department similar to that in Boston, covering initially 300 or so of the "most expensive" points and later extended to include all of the Kansas City hinterland. Member banks were obliged to clear all items drawn on banks in that territory which would have cost 10 cents per $100 or more if they had been sent directly through the clearinghouse. Such an arrangement exploited some economies of bulk shipment but did not necessarily promote par clearing. In 1908 Atlanta banks organized the Georgia collection department (later extended to Florida and Alabama), again taking advantage of economies in bulk shipment saving on postage and clerical costs. By 1916, 14 city clearinghouses had country or foreign departments including Oklahoma City, Nashville, Chattanooga, Richmond, and Louisville (Watkins, 1929, p. 108).

The focus of the New York Clearing House was national instead of regional and on collection costs rather than on presentment fees, aiming to standardize collection charges and make sure that the collecting banks didn't bear them. Also in 1899 it attempted to deal with the torrent of "foreign" checks by dividing the country into distinct zones for the purpose of assessing collection (or exchange) charges.[18] For banks in New York and the metropolitan region and in larger metropolitan centers, member banks could use their discretion in assessing charges on the collection of checks. The rest of the country was divided into zones where banks were obliged to charge 1/10 to 1/4 percentage points on collections with none less than 10 cents. At some points the charge was discretionary. The first violation incurred a fine of $5,000; the second, the possibility of expulsion from the clearinghouse.[19] Based on an internal survey conducted in May 1912, over 70 percent of the collections business involved banks at "discretionary" points, while less than 5 percent were on the "1/4" points.

For each discretionary point, the clearinghouse report provides information on the average daily collection business, the average period of collection, and information about the extent of par clearing and collection charges. At one extreme Philadelphia and Boston banks accounted for just over 40 percent of the checks sent for daily collection. The dense volume of transactions and geographic proximity limited the collection period to only 3.5 days, and as a result most New York banks cleared these checks at par. At the other extreme checks sent to the west coast — Los Angeles, San Francisco, and Seattle — totaled just over $100,000 (or less than 1 percent of the daily collections) and took almost two weeks for final settlement. Most New York banks charged collection fees on these transactions, which ranged from 0.08 percent for San Francisco to 0.14 percent for Seattle.

The graphs in Figs. 1 and 2 show more systematically the variation between the density of interactions (as measured by the log of the daily

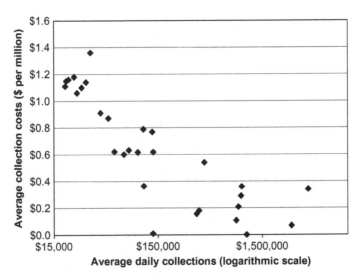

Fig. 1. Average Collection Costs of New York Clearing House Association Banks on Nonlocal Checks by City or Location of the Paying Bank, May 1912. *Source*: New York Clearing House Association, "Report of the Committee on Inland Exchange to the Clearing House Committee," November 4, 1912.

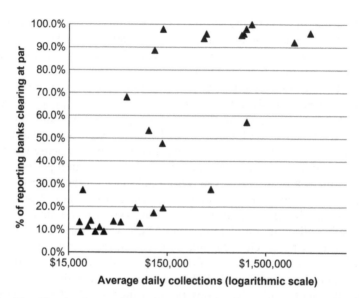

Fig. 2. Par Clearing between New York Clearing House Association Banks and Banks in Distant Centers – Locations, May 1912. *Source*: See Fig. 1.

volume of collections) and the average collection period and the extent of par clearing by New York banks. The collection period clearly increases with the distance from New York, as evidenced by the additional days to collect checks on cities in the south and west. Still, the collection period for banks in the New York metropolitan region was actually greater than that for banks in Baltimore, Boston, and Philadelphia. A system of par clearing had in effect been established that embraced the metropolitan region but also nearby metropolitan centers.

Finally (but chronologically first) there was the case of Sedalia, Missouri, fifth largest city in the state, population 15,231 in 1900, well-known as a center of railroads as well as of vice and prostitution.[20] After the local clearinghouse (of five banks) was established in 1893, a clearing area with a radius of some 40 miles around the town, encompassing some 15 towns all linked by rail to Sedalia emerged. Each of the 22 out-of-town banks maintained a correspondent account with a Sedalia bank. They would mail checks drawn on banks in the area to their city correspondent, where their account would be immediately credited at par. The items then were cleared through the clearinghouse. The paying banks' accounts were debited, and the checks sent back (in a single shipment of all which had been presented for payment that day) by mail from the clearinghouse (Hallock, 1903, pp. 43–47).[21] The Sedalia plan did explicitly involve par clearing, in which out-of-town checks were directly debited from their correspondent account. But such a scheme did not prove popular elsewhere, on the grounds that the country bank would not know how much was in its city correspondent account (unlike with bank drafts) at any particular time and did not have the opportunity to examine the items before their being charged against it.

In the years preceding the passage of the Federal Reserve Act a bit of progress had been made toward rationalizing and standardizing intercity check clearing and collection. The Boston regional scheme had spread to Kansas City and Atlanta. But on the other hand, the New York plan of fixed collection rates, undoubtedly in violation of the antitrust acts in any case, had devolved into one in which the great majority of charges were discretionary. And the Sedalia model, the only which guaranteed par clearing, was limited geographically and little emulated. All in all, according to Spahr (1926, pp. 121, 123), "The general tone of the discussion [of country clearings and collections] was one of despair of any effectual remedy. Plan after plan fell by the wayside" (see also Miller, 1949, pp. 13–14).

ENTER THE FEDERAL RESERVE

Notwithstanding the perceived inefficiencies of the existing system of check clearing and collection, improving it was not a fundamental priority of the Federal Reserve Act, which aimed to provide an elastic currency. Although the contours of the Act had been under discussion and debate for a year or so, a provision for reserve banks to provide check collection services did not appear in the proposed legislation until toward the end of 1913. Section 13 of the final Federal Reserve Act described the items which might be accepted on deposit by Federal Reserve banks. Included were "checks and drafts upon solvent member banks, payable upon presentation." Section 16 authorized the Federal Reserve Board to require district banks to act as a clearing house for member banks with the further proviso that checks and drafts drawn on member banks be accepted at par.[22] Stevens (1996, 1998) argues that the motivation here was to make reserve balances useful to member banks, the collection system creating a "glue" (his term) to tie member banks to the new central bank. Member bank deposits, which paid no interest, held at district banks could be used as clearing balances, thereby displacing correspondent accounts.

Each district bank was to act as essentially a regional clearing house for intra-district payments.[23] Interdistrict clearing and settlement was the province of the Gold Settlement Fund under the control of the Federal Reserve Board, established in May 1915. Each district bank was required to deposit at least $1,000,000 in gold or its equivalent with the nearest Sub-Treasury. Initially settlement was weekly. At the close of business on Wednesdays each district bank was required to telegraph to the Board amounts due to other district banks at that time. Daily settlement began July 1, 1918. Until June 1918 communication had been done on commercial telegraph wires. At that time the Fed inaugurated a leased wire system to be used exclusively by the Federal Reserve system. Member banks as well had access to the leased wire network (the original "fed wire") free of charge (Spahr, 1926, pp. 291–329).

Now to intra-district clearing and settlement. But first, before a system-wide policy was developed, some district banks had devised their own. Two districts, St. Louis (number 8) and Kansas City (number 10) obtained permission to institute a system of compulsory clearing.[24] In Boston the district bank was first elected a limited member of the Boston Clearing House with clearing house settlements accomplished by checks drawn on the reserve bank. Then on July 15, 1916, the Federal Reserve Bank of Boston took over the Boston Clearing House (which became a department in the new bank) and began clearing and collecting checks drawn on New England, establishing a par clearing region, something not quite within the grasp of the earlier Boston Clearing House scheme (Spahr, 1926, pp. 168–169).

Participation in the original system of check clearing and collection begun in 1915 was voluntary. District banks would receive from cooperating member banks checks drawn upon other cooperating member banks at par. The receiving bank's account was credited immediately while the paying bank's account was debited immediately. Cooperating banks remitted at par even if the Fed returned the check to the paying bank through the mail. The level of participation proved to be disappointing. Outside the St. Louis and Kansas City districts only about 1,150 member banks signed on, or less than 20 percent. "In the main, comparatively small advance was made in rendering effective the provisions of the law which provided for the standardization of exchange and clearance practices" (Spahr, 1926, p. 173; see also Anderson, 1916, p. 129). Gilbert (1998, p. 136) attributed the poor showing of the voluntary system to network effects. While many banks might have favored such a system in principle, its practical appeal depended on how many other banks participated. After only a relatively small number of banks opted in initially, participation then became less attractive. Why give up revenue from presentment fees if it allowed you to make par presentments to only a limited number of banks?[25]

The Board decided to replace the voluntary system with a compulsory one which took effect on July 15, 1916. Well, not totally compulsory. Member banks could choose whether to collect items through the Federal Reserve system or else to send them as before for collection through their regular correspondents. Member banks were allowed to send to the Fed checks drawn on other member banks (in their own district or in others). The compulsory element lay in requiring all member banks to pay "without deduction" all checks drawn upon them which were presented by Federal Reserve banks. And presentment through the mail was considered equivalent to presentment in person at the counter. Member banks could charge remittance or presentment fees in general as long as they didn't charge the Fed. The Fed also accepted for collection checks drawn on nonmember banks if they agreed to remit at par to the Federal Reserve bank of the district in which they were located. The Board regularly published a par list of nonmember banks upon which checks could be collected. If physical remittance of currency was necessary the shipping costs were absorbed by the Federal Reserve.

The earlier scheme of giving immediate credit for items to be collected was replaced by one of "deferred availability." Items submitted would be counted in the collecting bank's reserve at the Fed according to a schedule which reflected the average time necessary to collect them based on mail times.[26] The Fed carried the float for any collections which took longer than the published time schedules, so the time for being credited for items in process of collection became completely predictable.[27] Service charges for the collection of checks were initially imposed, ranging from 0.9 cents per item for Boston to 2.0 cents for San Francisco with 1½ cents per item being the most common figure. They was gradually reduced in steps to zero by June 15, 1918.

Earlier, some nonmember banks had already had access to the Fed collection system through their member bank correspondents, because district banks were required to receive items sent to them with no discrimination made between those simply bearing the endorsement of a member banks and those bearing the endorsement both of a nonmember and a member bank. An amended Section 13 (as of June 21, 1917) formalized the relationship with nonmember banks. It gave Federal Reserve banks the power to receive checks and drafts not only from member banks but also from non-member banks as well. Nonmember banks and trust companies were allowed to clear and collect checks through the Federal Reserve as long as they agreed to remit at par to Fed for items drawn upon themselves and maintained sufficient clearing balances with the Fed.[28] After the compulsory system was instituted Federal Reserve banks quickly became major processors or collectors of checks. The value of checks processed by Federal Reserve banks, which had amounted to 14.7 percent of the total handled by major private clearinghouses in 1917, rose to over 50 percent by 1926 and to 65 percent in 1934.[29] Something of a division of labor developed as city banks often found it more expeditious to clear local checks through the local clearinghouse but to send their out-of-town items to the Federal Reserve banks because of the latter's advantages in being able to send checks for collection through the mail, receiving payment at par, and crediting accounts at standardized times.

THE PAR CLEARING CONTROVERSY

First of all, we take "par clearing," "par collection," and "par remittance" as synonyms. By this we mean that the value of a check is paid to the collecting bank by the paying bank (not necessarily precluding charges to bank customers however) in full without deduction. In other words, there are no remittance charges.[30] Universal par clearing was not mentioned in the original Federal Reserve Act. Even so, from the beginning the Fed insisted that member banks pay at par on items collected from them.[31] From early on as well the Fed foresaw a regime in which par clearing was universal, or almost so, in its words "a national enterprise for the convenience of the public and the promotion of commerce" (Preston, 1920, p. 590). Thus, the Board wrote in its *Third Annual Report* (1916, p. 10), in view of the disadvantage a given bank would face if checks drawn on its competitors circulated at par and the possible reduction in the necessary level of clearing reserves, "It is believed that in the near future checks upon practically all banks in the United States can be collected at par by Federal Reserve banks." As a step toward that goal in December 1916, an amendment to Section 16 was proposed to allow nonmember banks to collect through the Fed as long as they paid their own checks at par and kept a clearing balance with the reserve banks (In its February 1917 *Bulletin* the Board wrote "we hope that within 90 days the check clearing system will be comprehensive and all embracing" (p. 80).)

That was not to be however. The American Bankers Association, among others, lobbied vigorously for banks' rights to charge presentment fees, even to Federal Reserve banks. The result was an amendment submitted by Senator Hardwick of Georgia which would have allowed both member and nonmember banks to make "reasonable charges, but in no case to exceed 10 cents per $100 ... for collection or payment of checks and drafts." The Senate approved the bill including the Hardwick amendment, and it went to conference committee, with President Wilson weighing in that he regarded the amendment "as most unfortunate and as almost destructive of the function of the Federal Reserve banks as a clearing house for member banks" (quoted in Vest, 1940, p. 91; Wyatt, 1944, p. 375). Unable to strike the amendment, the House conferees led by Carter Glass inserted the phrase "to be determined and regulated by the Federal Reserve Board" after "reasonable charges" and added the provision "but no such charges shall be made against Federal Reserve Banks." The revised bill passed both houses with the import that charging presentment fees to the Federal Reserve was now prohibited by law, totally contrary of course to the original intent of the Hardwick amendment. The position that Federal Reserve could not pay remittance fees on checks to be collected was reaffirmed by the Attorney General in 1918 (March 21) (Wyatt, 1944, pp. 372–379).

The Hardwick amendment might have been a compromise between the need or desire for many banks to recoup or maintain some revenue from collection charges on the one hand and the desire for a more standardized or predictable system of collections on the other. H. Parker Willis (1923, p. 1061), for example, conceded that a charge of no more than 1/10 of 1 percent was "very modest" (in W. P. G. Harding's words) as compared with rates which many banks had charged in the past. "In some ways this would have been a great advance over the condition which had existed prior to the adoption of the Federal Reserve Act, inasmuch as it would have forbidden the exorbitant rates of exchange [sic] which had come to prevail in a great many parts of the country." But Federal Reserve opposition to the proposal was unyielding because "it would have tended largely to destroy the Federal Reserve clearing system itself." The rationale for the Fed's clearing and collection was "far deeper and more important than any consideration of exchange charges. Par clearance was necessary in order to direct the stream of checks and drafts to the reserve banks and thus to keep the reserve balances there constantly living and changing, thus preventing them from becoming mere dead sums of cash held simply because required by law ... The larger the basis of items cleared through reserve banks, the more effective and perfect the clearance" (p. 1062).

Did the advantages of the new "compulsory" system which then offered nonmember banks shorter and predictable collection times and a reduction in necessary clearing balances in exchange for agreeing to remittance at par lead to a massive voluntary embrace of the Fed's clearing and collection system? Not exactly. For one thing, nonmember banks could still clear and collect their items received drawn upon member or nonmember banks on the par list through the Fed via their correspondent banks which were members without directly joining the system themselves. In other words, they could continue to charge remittance fees on collections of checks drawn upon them while at the same collecting their items received at par through the Fed (Miller, 1949, p. 22; Preston, 1920, p. 584). In lieu of a widespread voluntary stampede to par remittance, district Federal Reserve banks then began to make direct efforts to encourage or coerce nonmember banks to join the par list. The Boston bank, as we noted, achieved universal par clearing in its district virtually from the inception, something not quite reached by the Boston Clearing House. Other district banks employed education and persuasion. The Richmond bank (1926, pp. 411–413), for one, "partly by correspondence and partly by personal visits of qualified representatives," pointed out the advantages of the system and tried to induce them to "cooperate by agreeing to remit at par in acceptable funds." Nevertheless, the number of nonmember banks on its par list increased only from 264 in January 1918 to 351 in December 1918. Another strategy was inducing nonmember banks to sign on if their neighbors in immediate competition signed on also. Thereby, West Virginia became a whole-par state on February 1, 1920 and Virginia on April 1, 1920.

Talk alone, however, often proved not to have been quite enough. An alternative strategy, à la the Suffolk system, was direct presentment by an agent of the Fed at the paying bank's counter of items to be collected at par (see Magee, 1923). To "clean up" its district and achieve universal par clearing there during 1918 the New York district bank "found it necessary for a considerable time to collect checks on something less than a hundred nonmember banks by means of express companies." At a December 1918 meeting Federal Reserve officials concluded that every effort should be made to increase the number of banks on the par list, and as a result the numbers of par list banks swelled over 1,919 (Preston, 1920, p. 572). Fig. 3 shows monthly totals of nonmember banks on and off the par list between 1917 and May 1924. Starting from rough parity at the end of 1918 (10,409 nonmember banks on the par list and 10,198 incorporated nonmember banks not on the par list as of December 15), over the course of the year the par list totals swelled to 15,851 while the not-on-par-list total fell to

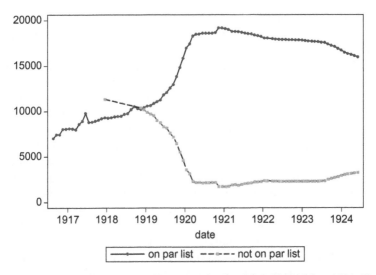

Fig. 3. Nonmember Banks on and not on the Par List, 1917–May 1924 (End of Year Figures). *Source*: Board of Governors of the Federal Reserve System (1943), *Banking and Monetary Statistics*, pp. 54–55.

4,609. By the end of 1920 nonmember banks not on the par list amounted to less than 10 percent of nonmember banks on the list (1,732 and 19,172 respectively) with universal par clearing prevailing in 9 of the 12 Federal Reserve districts.[32] The *Federal Reserve Bulletin* reported the figures for par and non-par banks by district every month.

   These burgeoning numbers might however overstate the extent of sincere conversion to par clearing and collection. While earlier the par list represented the names of banks which had agreed to remit at par, over this period it is also said to have included names of banks to which the Fed had decided to collect at par by direct presentation at the counter. In any case, either the threat of or the implementation of the policy of direct presentment of items to be collected to non-par banks generally proved quite effective, so that according to the Board "as a rule such steps were not necessary for any length of time." In the case of the Richmond district November 15, 1920 was named the date after which checks would be collected by presentation in North Carolina. Four hundred and seventy-eight banks immediately jumped to the par list, but 24 required further persuasion. Similarly, in other states in the district just on the verge of universal par clearing a final nudge was necessary as well – in West Virginia to 8 banks; in Virginia to 24 "personal presentation of checks had to be made, sometimes once, sometimes oftener" (Spahr, 1926, pp. 244–245; see also Tippetts, 1924, p. 635).

The drive toward universal par clearing stalled, and the number of banks not on the par list after two years of steady declines began to rise in 1921. As was the case with the Suffolk system almost a century earlier, the practice of direct presentation of items to be collected created considerable animosity toward the Fed.[33] Many banks took umbrage at being required to pay without deduction on items presented even though the Fed bore any necessary remittance costs. Some thought when checks were presented for payment "in a manner contrary to custom," that is in large quantities for cash on the spot, it violated the implicit contract between payers and collectors. Direct presentment of checks at the counter by the Fed was often referred to as an "embarrassment" (e.g., U.S. House Committee on Banking and Currency Committee, 1920, p. 27).[34] Others believed that "acts lawful in themselves [presentment] may be committed for unlawful and vicious purposes and are then unlawful" (Spahr, 1926, p. 238). Resistence to the Fed ranged from lack of cooperation in rendering payment[35] to more collective forms of political organization. Notable among the latter was the National and State Bankers' Protective Association formed in 1920 and headquartered in Atlanta. That year it claimed a membership of 15,000 of the 21,000 in the American Bankers' Association (Miller, 1949, p. 25; see also Preston, 1920, pp. 577–578).

The first legislative success for non-par banking came in Mississippi. A law was passed March 6, 1920 to prevent Federal Reserve banks from collecting checks drawn on banks in the state (both national and state) at par in order to provide for the "solvency, protection, and safety of the banking institutions of Mississippi." When "cash items" were presented paying banks "shall continue to make such charge as fixed by custom ... one-tenth of one percent of the total amount ... And not less than 10 cents on any one such transaction." Similar laws followed quickly in Louisiana, South Dakota, Georgia, Alabama, North Carolina, Tennessee, and Florida. In some, such as Mississippi and Florida, the charges were mandatory; in others, discretionary (Federal Reserve Bank of Richmond, 1926, pp. 419–421). At the federal level in that same year bills following the proscriptions of the National and State Bankers' Protective Association that both member and nonmember banks be allowed to charge remittance fees no larger than 10 cents on $100 (the McFadden and the Steagall bills) were considered by the House Committee on Banking and Currency, but no action was taken.

Another, and ultimately decisive, front in the struggle against universal par clearing was litigation.[36] One of the first cases started with the Federal Reserve Bank of Atlanta's letter to nonmember banks in its district on December 23,1919 which noted "while, as stated, the Federal Reserve Act does not permit us to pay exchange for the remittance of bank checks and drafts payable upon presentation, we can incur any cost that is necessary in order to carry out the purpose of the Act, and we would very much regret to be forced to adopt methods of collection that would prove embarrassing, annoying and expensive to you." The Country Bankers' Association of Georgia filed a petition to enjoin the Fed from acting on its plans (*American Bank and Trust Co., et al. v. Federal Reserve Bank of Atlanta, et al.*). The case made its way from District Court through the Fifth District Circuit Court of Appeals up to the Supreme Court where it was remanded to District Court for trial. After rising to the Supreme Court for a second time, the opinion rendered by Justice Brandeis on June 11, 1923 held that Federal Reserve banks indeed might collect checks at par by direct presentation at the counter as long as they don't accumulate checks with the intention of coercing or embarrassing the paying bank.

Similar disputes played out between the San Francisco district bank and an Oregon state bank and between the Cleveland district bank and a Kentucky bank with similar resolutions, that the Federal Reserve banks could not use oppressive or coercive tactics in collections.[37] The case of *Farmers and Merchants Bank of Monroe, North Carolina, et al. v. Federal Reserve Bank of Richmond, Virginia* however was conclusive. A 1921 North Carolina law allowed paying state banks there to charge remittance fees of no more than 1/8 percent with a minimum of 10 cents per item and to settle by means of a draft drawn on a correspondent account rather than cash at the counter. The Richmond bank returned checks as dishonored when the paying bank refused full settlement in cash at the counter. The Supreme Court reversed the decision of the North Carolina Supreme Court which declared the law unconstitutional and decided in favor of the non-par state banks. The June 11, 1923 opinion again written by Justice Brandeis noted that the North Carolina statute "merely" removed the "absolute" legal requirement of the common law that a check presented at the counter must be paid in cash rather than through issuing a draft. The Court went out to argue that Section 13 of the Federal Reserve Act was only permissive. The Fed was not required to receive checks for collection ("Any Federal Reserve bank *may* receive from any of its member banks..."). Furthermore, the Act did not mandate universal par clearance and collection of checks. There was nothing in the Act from which such an obligation might have been inferred. Thus, states might constitutionally pass laws which took away from Federal Reserve banks the right to collect checks at par in cash with direct presentment which had been its principal tool in promoting universal par clearing.

After these decisions the Federal Reserve abandoned its push to achieve universal par clearing. Instead, the policy became one of having nothing to do with non-par banks. Regulation J of 1924 provided that no Federal Reserve bank would "receive on deposit or for collection" any check drawn on a nonmember which could not be collected at par. Such checks had to be cleared and collected through private channels (Tippetts, 1924, pp. 644–646).[38]

NON-PAR BANKS

The concerted efforts after 1917 to expand the par list had decreased the share of non-par banks in total commercial banks to just 5.75 percent by the end of 1920. Such a figure however includes member banks, which had no choice but to be on the par list. Considering only nonmember banks, those who had some choice as to whether to be on the par list or not, that non-par share in 1920 becomes 8.4 percent. This figure however is low in fact in view of the Fed's alleged practice of putting some banks on the par list (grudgingly) even though collections were done by direct presentment by express companies or agents (as long as they paid at par) as noted earlier. Fig. 3 shows clearly that 1920 was the high-water mark of par clearing. The number of par list banks then began to drift downward, and those not on the par list began to rise, particularly in and after 1923 with the Supreme Court decisions.[39] By the end of the decade non-par banks made up more than one-quarter of all nonmember banks (three times the 1920 level). Indeed the share continued to rise over the 1930s as the numbers of non-par banks shrank less than did those of par-list nonmember banks, reaching a peak of 36 percent in 1942.

There had therefore been a lot of non-par banks around, although they were by no means uniformly dispersed. Universal par clearing prevailed in the Northeast (Boston and New York districts from the earliest data, December 31, 1918; Philadelphia from a year later). In the Cleveland and San Francisco districts there were only very small numbers of non-par banks. But in 10 states in 1925 a majority of nonmember banks had been non-par, the high having been Mississippi with 92 percent (and by 1947 the number of such states had only fallen to nine (Miller, 1949, p. 130).

How large were these fees? In the *Second Annual Report of the Federal Reserve Board* (1916, pp. 169, 217–218, 234, 244, 274, 287, 300, 322, 342, 353, 386) each regional bank reported on remittance fees charged in its district. They ranged between 1/20 of 1 percent and 3/10 of 1 percent with many averaging around 1/10 or 1/8 of 1 percent. Higher rates prevailed in the South and Great Plains – 1/6 of 1 percent average in Atlanta, 1/5 of 1 percent in Dallas, 3/10 of 1 percent in Kansas City. No district noted any change in the fees charged, which had been maintained at those levels "for many years," after the introduction of the Fed except in the Kansas City district which witnessed a "material reduction." Fifty years later Jessup (1967, p. 3) characterized the prevailing rate as 1/10 of 1 percent with a minimum of 10 cents, while the Federal Reserve Bank of Minneapolis cited a range between five cents and one dollar depending on the size of the check (1966, p. 3).

Income from presentment or remittance fees must have been significant enough to non-par banks that they were willing to forgo any potential cost savings from participating in par clearing and collection in order to preserve it.[40] The *First Annual Report of the* Federal Reserve Board (1915, p. 168) observed that "broadly speaking, the smaller the bank the larger the percentage of its earnings derived from exchange." Indeed, the Federal Reserve Bank of Richmond (1926, p. 391) claimed that "in many instances throughout the South the exchange revenue of the small or country bank constituted considerably more than half of the bank's income."[41] And non-par banks were generally rather small. On December 31, 1938 deposits of non-par banks (which constituted 18 percent of all commercial banks) amounted to only 2 percent of total deposits, exclusive of interbank deposits (Vest, 1940, p. 94).[42]

Under the Federal Reserve regime there was no longer an issue of allocating clearing and collection costs between paying bank and collecting bank since the Fed covered all remittance costs. After October 1917 it provided stamped envelopes with collection letters for return remittances as well as stood ready to absorb "the cost of postage, insurance, and expressage in connection with shipments of currency in settlement of clearing balances" for nonmember maintaining clearing accounts (as well as for member banks) (*Fifth Annual Report of the Federal Reserve Board*, 1918, p. 77). Presentment fees charged after this time therefore have often been taken as a clear indication of monopoly power (e.g., Stevens, 1998; see also Spahr, 1926, p. 236).[43]

Local monopoly power furthermore was said to have allowed these banks to survive in an environment of widespread par clearing and collection. Would not payee discontent at remittance charges exacted on the collection of non-par checks, for example receiving $999 for a $1,000 check, have induced payers or depositors to move their business to par list banks? Three postwar studies of non-par banking (Kreps for North Carolina (1959), Jessup for the nation as a whole (1967), Dudley for Louisiana (1970)) all agreed that non-par banks were generally located in small, rural, one-bank towns. Jessup (1967, p. 25) found that, as of the end of 1964, 77 percent of non-par banks were in one-bank towns and 18 percent more were located in towns which had only another non-par bank. Only 5 percent of non-par banks faced local competition from a par list bank.[44] Non-par banks also tried to make sure that remittance charges were paid by outsiders rather than locals. No presentment fees were charged on local checks (drawn on the same bank) or on other nearby non-par banks (each agreed to accept checks drawn on the other at par). And not all outsiders paid the fees either. Checks written by large local depositors (say an automobile dealership) to outsiders were often honored at par to avoid losing the account to a par bank. Special checks for that depositor were printed with an indication that they were collectible at par (Jessup, 1967, pp. 74–75).[45]

Other costs however were involved in maintaining an extensive payments network in addition to just direct clearing costs. In particular there was the question of providing access to that network for people in very small towns and rural locations. As noted above, exchange and remittance fees were an important revenue source for many banks in such low population density locations. Without this income many banks in small towns probably would not have been viable. Thus, to enable access to the check clearing and collection system for many small town customers their banks needed to charge remittance fees.[46] William Baxter in an influential article (1983) argued that in payments networks characterized by joint costs and interdependent demand ("a transaction involves a joint demand by payor and payee for method of payment and on the supply side the cooperation of two banks.") side payments or interchange fees between financial institutions (in which the price the buyer pays is more than the sum the seller receives) could be necessary to achieve equilibrium.[47] Remittance fees, which in effect supported a more geographically extensive or comprehensive payments network than otherwise would have been possible, might be considered as such an interchange fee. However, "the role of the interchange fee in the process of check clearance, a commercial context in which an unregulated market solution might have been expected to work reasonably well and to yield instructive results, was aborted and continues to be suppressed by a mixture of subsidies and coercion by the Federal Reserve System" (1983, p. 571).[48]

Baxter went on to observe that in an environment with many agents negotiation over fees for each transaction would be inefficient. Thus, efficiency would dictate some standard practice collectively determined interchange fees. That of course did not happen in this case. Individual banks set their own remittance charges and indeed often set different charges to different payees. Those charges were born by recipients of non-par checks, primarily out-of-towners residing in larger cities (see above), who did also benefit from the system by being able to do business with and receive payments from small town customers more easily and expeditiously. That does not deny however that they also may have been paying some exactions due to local monopoly power. In any case the patchwork of different charges and practices in a payments system with substantial numbers of non-par banks probably did not make for the most efficient payments system. But it did however allow for a more extensive national payments system, one covering more ground, than probably would have prevailed under universal par clearing.

Although arguably a reasonable argument for the early years of the Fed, this rationale for non-par clearing, expanding access, and enabling banking services to be provided to communities where stand-alone banking would not otherwise have been viable, should have faded as access to other banking institutions increased in those areas.[49] One factor at work which undermined the position of post-Fed non-par banks virtually from their beginning was the diffusion of the automobile. The car of course expanded the distance over which bank customers might have traveled easily and quickly and made for more convenient access to banking services in nearby towns. Similarly, increasing population density over time made for a more competitive banking environment as well.[50] Thus, as time progressed the access argument for non-par banking became less relevant and the monopoly characterization becomes increasingly plausible and pertinent.[51] That said, non-par banking proved quite persistent. To be sure, its position did erode, but over a long period, half a century.

Finally here, consider the subsequent history of non-par banks. From their peak in 1925 with 3,970 banks in 42 states[52] the total had fallen to just 7 in 1 state (Louisiana) by 1979, the last year before they were

abolished. In general, we don't know precisely what happened to them –
whether they converted to par banks or whether they closed. Fig. 4 shows
the number of non-par banks from 1934 (we start here after the disruptions
of the Great Depression, there having been 2,643 at the end of 1934)
through their demise in 1980. Over time non-par banks became increasingly
concentrated in the South and the Great Plains. But note that the erosion
in numbers was more in steps than at relatively uniform rate of decline –
roughly steady over the later 1930s, sharp drop in the 1940s, rather gradual
decline in the 1950s and early 1960s, sharp drop in the late 1960s and early
1970s.

Figs. 5 and 6 show non-par bank totals for selected states over time.
First of all in Fig. 5 we see the numbers in North and South Carolina drift-
ing down gradually over time, consistent with competition from par banks
reducing their numbers. In Louisiana the decline over the late 1960s and
early 1970s is to be sure steeper, but not discontinuous. In contrast, consider the states in Fig. 6. There we see abrupt, discontinuous drops in the
number of non-par banks to zero – in 1949 in Wisconsin; 1968 in
Minnesota; 1971 in South Dakota; 1970 in Georgia. Such charges were not
the result of market forces, but instead were due to legal changes, states
passing laws prohibiting non-par banking.

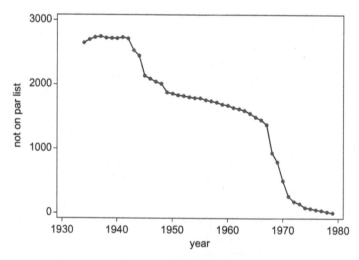

Fig. 4. Banks Not on the Par List, 1934–1979 (End of Year Figures). *Source*:
Board of Governors of the Federal Reserve System, *Annual Reports*, 1934–1979.

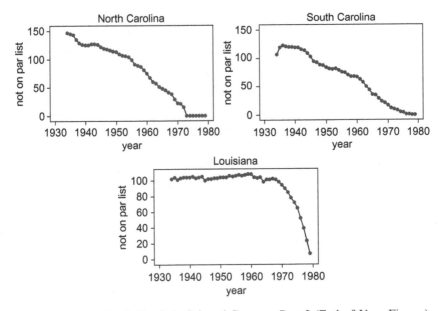

Fig. 5. Non-par Bank Totals in Selected States – Part I (End of Year Figures). *Source*: Board of Governors of the Federal Reserve System, *Annual Reports*, 1934–1979.

Indeed, a majority of the decline in non-par bank numbers from 1934 to 1979 (53 percent) may be attributed to discontinuous drops in numbers to zero due to changes in state non-par banking laws in 14 states. They came in two waves or groupings – in the Midwest in the 1940s[53] and in the South and Great Plains in the late 1960s and early 1970s.[54] Taking away these two periods of mass extinctions, non-par banking looked quite robust for many years. Indeed, it was not until the 1960s that the tide seemed to turn against non-par banking. In 1964 the executive council of the American Bankers Association adopted a resolution that all checks in the United States be cleared at par. The next year the Board of Governors recommended legislation to Congress that would require universal par clearance (but it didn't pass) (Federal Reserve Bank of Minneapolis, 1966, pp. 1, 8). Toward the end of the decade the second wave of prohibiting legislation began. In some states, such as the Dakotas and Georgia, numbers of non-par banks did not turn down until the 1960s, but in Minnesota they held up right until the end.

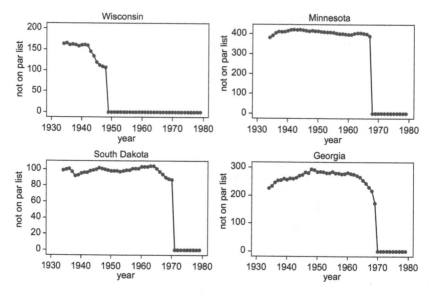

Fig. 6. Non-par Bank Totals in Selected States – Part II (End of Year Figures). *Source*: Board of Governors of the Federal Reserve System, *Annual Reports*, 1934–1979.

SUMMARY AND CONCLUSIONS

The push for universal par clearing and collection of checks marked an important step toward a true and comprehensive U.S. monetary union, one in which bank deposits, like official currency, were recognized and accepted at par or full face value throughout the country. Vigorous and concerted opposition by primarily small-town state bankers however stalled the Fed's efforts in the early 1920s. Thereafter non-par banking proved to be remarkably resilient, for decades. Its ultimate demise was due primarily to legislation (state and then last and least, federal in 1980) rather than Federal Reserve pressure or market forces. Without such legislation, it still might be being practiced today.

After lying dormant for decades, the "par clearing controversy" was revived by Baxter (1983) and Lacker et al. (1999). Because of demand externalities, they observe, the distribution of the costs and benefits of the check payments network is essentially "indeterminate" (Baxter, 1983). Viewed from the equivalent perspective of a two-sided market, the demand for network services depends not just on the overall level of costs but on the price structure, which comprises a fixed membership or access fee and a variable usage rate (Rochet & Tirole, 2006). For example, banks could pay a fixed rate such as a compensating or excess reserve balance to a central clearing agent, a usage fee in the form of exchange charges to the paying bank, or some combination of the two.

The Fed's insistence on "universal par clearing" corresponds to a price structure with a fixed access fee only, a mandatory clearing balance in a regional reserve bank. In other words, it would realize a primary goal of the 1913 banking reform – centralizing the reserves and (par) settlement transactions of all check-issuing banks (Laughlin, 1912, pp. 21–22). Under this arrangement the Fed can earn sufficient "seigniorage" revenues to underwrite the formation and operation of its interbank network including possible short-run losses from the timely direct presentment of checks on holdouts (McAndrews, 1998b, pp. 318–321). In other words, only a public institution like the Fed could credibly threaten to enforce par clearing among all check-issuing banks.

Though the Fed's policy deprived banks of revenues from payments services (i.e., usage fees), it yielded potential benefits as well: economies in remitting checks and funds and in excess reserves tied up in clearing balances and the float (Gilbert, 2000; James & Weiman, 2010). The success of the Boston clearinghouse's foreign department, which embraced virtually all New England banks by the early 1900s, illustrates how this tradeoff could pay off.[55] In an economically diversified and developed region like New England, banks mediated large, steady volumes of intra-regional check payments. Because of their dense *mutual* interactions, charging each other "exchange" only multiplied transactions costs and yielded little *net* revenue. Moreover, banks could profit from their larger excess reserves either by making additional loans locally or placing these funds in the Boston money market.[56]

Many "country banks," especially in the South and Great Plains, regarded mandatory par clearing as "a polite suggestion and invitation ... to commit suicide" (Federal Reserve Bank of Atlanta Archives, 1916b). Writing to the Fed's New Orleans branch, the head of a Mississippi national bank explained why the economic logic of par clearing did not apply to his case (Federal Reserve Bank of Atlanta Archives, 1916a). His bank would lose an estimated $7–$8 thousand annually in exchange revenues, which he might have mentioned were derived largely from remittances to New York banks. At the same time, it had few opportunities to loan out the additional excess reserves except to New York correspondents for the standard two percent interest rate on bankers' balances (James, 1976). His plight was in fact endemic to banks in peripheral regions like the Cotton

South, which faced systemic seasonal constraints on their lending and borrowing. Put more generally, it implies that the Fed's plan for a common national bank money, like the National Banking Acts design of a common national currency, was poorly adapted to more sparsely settled regions dominated by a single export sector (Redenius & Weiman, 2011; Rockoff, 2003).

Instead of abolishing exchange rates, a Florida state banker suggested that the Fed "rectify exorbitant charges" by country banks (Federal Reserve Bank of Atlanta Archives, 1916b). He was in effect proposing a modified version of the Hardwick amendment, which in its original form could undermine the Fed's goal of fashioning a truly centralized check clearing and settlement system. From the two-sided market perspective, this compromise implies a tiered pricing plan not unlike the tiered capital and reserve requirements of the National Banking Acts. Banks in more developed regions would still have to comply with the Fed's par clearing mandate, which would establish a par zone embracing the largest banks and the vast majority of check transactions. Country banks on the periphery could charge exchange rates up to a fixed level, say 1/10 percent. This plan would have institutionalized transfers from money center to peripheral banks and so achieve a more traditional goal of the American banking system, maximal access to local banking.[57]

In more recent years, despite the demise of non-par banking, non-par payments networks have proliferated. In contrast to checks, credit and debit cards are not subject to direct presentment requirements. The conditions under which payments are settled therefore are determined by private contracts. In credit card networks, this typically involves an interchange fee so that the sum the merchant or seller receives is less than that which the buyer or purchaser pays. ATM networks are similarly non-par payments arrangements, and the issues of non-par banking play out here in rather familiar form. Again there are interchange fees between banks. In addition, and controversially, there are often surcharges paid to the owner of the ATM. On the one hand, these fees might reflect exactions of local monopoly power. On the other, they might encourage more widespread deployment of ATM machines and hence greater access for customers (McAndrews, 1998a; Hannan, Kiser, Prager, & McAndrews, 2003).

NOTES

1. This monetary union however was not an unmixed blessing in view of Hugh Rockoff's argument (2003) that the United States did not become an optimal currency area until the 1930s.

2. Strictly speaking, clearing involves the transmission of a payment order to the buyer's intermediary, its verification and approval, and calculation of interbank payments obligations, while settlement involves the reverse delivery of good funds to seller's account. So the issue here in what follows is really about collection and settlement at par, but "par clearing" is the term which has traditionally been used and we stick to it here.

3. In addition to public policy forums (e.g., Harding, 1920; U.S. House Committee on Banking and Currency Committee, 1920) the issue attracted considerable academic interest at the time as well (e.g., Harding, 1920; Preston, 1920; Spahr, 1926; Tippetts, 1923, 1924, 1926, 1929; Willis, 1923).

4. Mr. Charles Jenkins (1884, pp. 57–58) too was indignant at the practice of "remitting in checks instead of by bank drafts collectible in New York" and urged "men of business, if they wish to avoid threatened inconvenience and expense, to insist, as far as possible, that their country correspondents substitute bank drafts on New York for their own checks , in making future remittances." He then went to suggest darkly: "If there is no abatement of the abuse, the banks might properly adopt the other remedial measures which have been suggested for their protection, and for the general safely, convenience, and advantage of the business of the country."

5. There is some dispute about the precise timing of the diffusion – the Federal Reserve Bank of Richmond (1926, p. 380), for example, dated the transition a bit earlier, to the early 1890s – but the consensus seems that the transition had been essentially accomplished by the end of the century.

6. A. W. Blye, Receiver of the Middletown National Bank (NY), was one of the unhappy ones (1885, p. 135). "There is no good reason to be given why parties desiring to transmit money to other places should not now, as heretofore in the distant past, conform to the same rule as at that time prevailed [i.e., drafts], and the banks derive a legitimate income from having the facilities to provide for such transfer accommodations, and also escape the annoyance and expense of having to collect checks upon every bank in a State, together, as is often the case, with those upon banks in other States."

7. The fact that often these terms were used synonymously, although they do not mean the same thing, is an imprecision that has muddied the discussion of this issue considerably (e.g., Jessup, 1967, p. 3; Wyatt, 1944, p. 366). Exchange charges reflected the price in local dollars of a dollar in a distant location and were widely quoted in newspapers and trade periodicals. The leased telegraph wire system of the Fed in 1918 enabled costless (to member banks) transfers of reserve deposits, and the Gold Settlement Fund facilitated settlement of interregional (interdistrict) payments imbalances. Stevens (1998, p. 7) however argued that the decisive factor in eliminating exchange charges was the Board's ability to manipulate the relative sizes of district banks' reserve base. In 1918, domestic exchange rates settled essentially to par and by two years later they were no longer reported in the press (Garbade & Silber, 1979, p. 15; Gilbert, 1998, p. 136). Remittance or presentment fees, charges by the paying bank for settling a check drawn on it, however were not driven to zero, and it is upon them that this paper focuses. See Stevens (1998) and Miller (1949, pp. 2–3).

8. In cases however when other local banks were judged "undesirable as collecting agents" many banks decided that it was better to send their checks directly to the paying bank and risk any negligence complications. "Although legally unsound the practice soon became rather widespread" (Spahr, 1926, pp. 178–179).

9. Mr. E. S. Butts of Vicksburg, Mississippi, for example, observed: "There is scarcely a bank in the North or East or West where the collections originate that is not flooded with applications from banks in other parts of the country to send them collections. It is a struggle morn, noon, and night between those five banks [in Vicksburg] to see who gets the Kansas City collections, the St. Louis collections, the Cincinnati collections, and the New York and the Boston collections ... I am trying to get every collection I can ... ." And the compensation for such collections should be sufficient. Mr. Thompson of Tacoma, WA claimed, "If our collection man wants to run a mile or two and has to go and present a paper two or three times, we are not going to rest with ten cents exchange; we are going to charge what it is worth" (Hammond, 1890, pp. 112, 114).

10. But all correspondent banks may not have been this calculating. The Federal Reserve Bank of Richmond (1926, p. 389) noted that there had been "unintelligent competition" in which a number of banks carrying interbank accounts "through ignorance or through the reckless desire to show large figures in their statements have been willing to do a considerable amount of this business at a loss to themselves."

11. James G. Cannon (1910, p. 60) observed that "this practice is quite general." The granting of immediate credit for items in the process of collection extended to correspondent bank relationships as well. Thus, a bank might send its out-of-town checks to be collected to its city correspondent and count those then as increased reserve balances immediately. "This was one of the most serious defects of the banking system before the establishment of the Federal Reserve System" (Federal Reserve Bank of Richmond, 1926, p. 384).

12. To underscore the point, the average transit time in shipping checks from New York to banks throughout the country was roughly comparable under the mature correspondent banking and Federal Reserve clearing-collection systems (James & Weiman, 2010, pp. 257–258).

13. In many cases, a more important component of total collection time than the transit time of a check to the paying bank was the latter's schedule of making remittances. According to one New York "bank clerk" (Shreve, 1898) they varied from semi-weekly up to monthly payments. Boston banks, for example, offered "more favorable" terms than Philadelphia banks – semi-weekly settlements with more rapid turnaround on "large amounts" as compared to only weekly payments. Within New York state the frequency of banks' remittances covered the gamut.

14. Indeed toward the end of the decade *Rhodes' Journal of Banking* offered a prize for the best paper on the subject, which elicited a number of submissions "but most of them were wide of the mark, putting out various pet hobbies, etc." (Hammond, 1890, p. 111).

15. Almost 90 percent of the remittances were drafts on Boston banks (Spahr, 1926, p. 128).

16. B. J. Shreve (1898, p. 226), bank clerk writing in *Bankers' Magazine* the year before this plan went into effect, argued that a country clearinghouse was "hardly a feasible scheme" since "nearly all out-of-town banks" make a profit from handling country checks and "they are not likely to surrender any part of such profit for the benefit of a central bank in their locality."

17. The pioneer in the clearing and collection of country checks was the London Clearing House which began such operations in 1858. Country bankers would send in one letter all the items to be presented for collection to their London agents, being confined to only ones drawn on banks in England and Wales, one night's mail from London. There they were presented at the Clearing House to the agents of the drawn-upon country banks. The clearing banks mailed the items received back to the issuing banks. Those banks in turn, after examining the checks drawn, mailed instructions to debit their account for the total. Final settlement occurred two days after clearing. Even though the same common law applied in England as in the United States about check presentment, there there was virtually universal remittance at par. The checks of banks charging a "commission" or exchange for remittance were not handled by the London Clearing House. "The greater number, however, of the banks which had until that time charged these commissions, voluntarily and very considerably ceased to do so, when it was pointed out to them how much inconvenience was caused by the practice" (Hallock, 1903, pp. 27–39; see also Barnett, 1884).

18. See the New York Clearing House Association Archives, "Report of the Committee on Inland Exchanges to the Clearing House Committee" (November 4, 1912), and "Brief Submitted to the Hon. George Wickersham, Attorney-General of the United States, in Behalf of the New York Clearing House Association" (February 6, 1911).

19. Another plan to institute uniform collection charges in New York had been proposed some 14 years before (Blye, 1885, p. 136). A similar plan had been put into effect in St. Louis in 1895 (Hallock, 1903, pp. 112–131; Spahr, 1926, pp. 110–111, 126). Spahr (1926, p. 123) reported a lack of uniformity in charges even within the same bank, much less across banks. "The large dealer whose account was sought by the banks had no difficulty in using his bank as an agent to collect at par the out-of-town checks which he accepted in payment. On the other had, the holder of the less desirable account was more likely to be charge something."

20. It was characterized by the *St. Louis Post-Dispatch* as the "Sodom and Gomorrah of the nineteenth century."

21. In some other locations such as Lancaster, PA as well as some towns in Connecticut, New Jersey, and Illinois, banks followed the Sedalia model for collections in the immediate hinterland (Cannon, 1910, pp. 61–63; Spahr, 1926, pp. 128–130).

22. Stevens (1996) describes and analyzes the positions and attitudes of the Founding Fathers of the Fed in some detail. "Few of them claimed any responsibility for, or even awareness of, the payments services franchise in the Act" (p. 10). See also Wyatt (1944, pp. 367–372). However the reform proposed by the National Monetary Commission, the establishment of a National Reserve Association, was designed not just to prevent the breakdown of the payments system during panics, but also was to "become the most important part of the machinery for making settlements between different parts of the country ... in the regular course of its operations," offering a "unified method of handling checks" which, along with free currency shipping, "would be able to exert such pressure as might be needed to secure prompt remittance at par" (Sprague, 1911, pp. 836–839). It should be noted

here however that such provisions have also not elicited much interest by most later chroniclers of the early history of the Fed. Neither in Meltzer's voluminous history of the Fed (2003) nor in Friedman and Schwartz's *Monetary History of the United States* (1963) are the check clearing and collection provisions even mentioned, much less the later par clearing controversy. Nevertheless the Federal Reserve Board in its Annual Report (Federal Reserve Board, 1915–1925, p. 14) regarded the organization of these clearing functions as "one of the most important responsibilities with which it is charged under the Act."

23. Unlike city clearinghouses which practiced multilateral net settlement however, reserve banks operated gross settlement systems in which they collected the total amount each owed for items that had been presented and paid the gross amount due to each bank for items that had been deposited.

24. After the voluntary clearing system was instituted (see below) and member banks in the St. Louis were given the option of withdrawing from the compulsory plan, Spahr (1926, p. 168) reported only 20 percent chose to do so. In the Kansas City district member banks were not given the option of withdrawing.

25. Other objections to this system included: (1) under the old regime banks could count as reserves checks as soon as they had been sent out for collection while checks sent to them by collecting banks were not deducted until received, thereby benefitting from the float; (2) the immediate debiting of items made it more difficult for banks to manage their reserve positions, often creating overdrafts in their accounts.

26. For example, within its district the Federal Reserve Bank of Richmond gave credit on items as follows: checks drawn upon banks in Richmond – immediate credit at Richmond; checks drawn upon banks in Maryland – two days after receipt; checks drawn upon banks in North Carolina – three days after receipt. And so forth (Federal Reserve Bank of Richmond, 1926, p. 399). Outside its district, the New York bank gave credit from one day after receipt for checks drawn on banks in major Eastern cities up to eight days for checks drawn on nonmajor Western locations (five for Los Angeles and San Francisco banks) (Spahr, 1926, pp. 184–185).

27. As of 1924 the float amounted to about 10 percent of the value of uncollected items. Much of this was due, it was said, to the New York and Philadelphia district banks putting remote banks on a two-day crediting schedule while it generally took at least three days (Spahr, 1926, pp. 183–184).

28. Participation was a tougher sell to nonmember banks. To the extent that there were still non-par points on which to collect correspondent banks were still needed, and those banks usually paid interest on clearing deposits held with them in contrast to the Federal Reserve which paid none and counted toward legal reserve requirements. Moreover city correspondents often accepted checks for immediate credit thus carrying the float (Preston, 1920, p. 583).

29. To be more precise, the comparison is with checks cleared through around 200 clearinghouses across the country, including all major cities. Thus, the figures do not reflect all private check clearings around the country, but close (Garvy, 1959).

30. Note that the service charges originally exacted by the Federal Reserve represented compensation for costs incurred by the collecting bank and thus were not

inconsistent with par clearing. According to Section 16 of the Act, "Nothing herein contained shall be construed as prohibiting a member bank from charging its actual expense incurred in collecting and remitting funds."

31. Even though the extent of the original network was limited, the commitment of the Fed, or at least Carter Glass, to the principle of par clearing and collection was strong. In the wake of the Pujo Committee hearings, Glass argued his bill would "put an end to the flagrant abuse involved in excessive charges for collections and exchange ... Naturally thousands of banks deriving large profits from the practice of charging constructive interest upon checks in transit and very arbitrary charges for collections and for exchanges exhibited great distaste to this provision of the bill. They vigorously protested to members against the inclusion of this prohibition and thus the effort to remove this tax burden upon the business of the country was contested with the utmost pertinacity. *However, those of us in the House who sought to tear down these tollgates upon the highways of commerce prevailed* [sic]" (quoted in Wyatt, 1944, pp. 370–371). Opposition to par clearing during the formulation of the Act is chronicled in Willis (1923, pp. 399–402).

32. The holdouts were in the Richmond, Atlanta, and St. Louis districts (in seven Southeastern states – Tennessee, South Carolina, Louisiana, Mississippi, Alabama, Georgia, and Florida).

33. The extent and intensity of opposition to the Federal Reserve among small-town bankers expressed at the 1920 *Hearings on Par Collection of Checks* held by the House Committee on Banking and Currency (see also Preston, 1920, pp. 580–581) was palpable – in addition to the testimony, page after page of objections sent in by bankers not present were offered (pp. 105–113), as well as surveys presented by state banking commissioners and banking association officials showing three-quarters of banks in North Dakota opposed (p. 22), 1 out of 367 responses in Kentucky favoring par clearing (p. 77), 63 out of 255 Virginia state and national banks supporting it (pp. 86–87). The one city banker to testify was Mr. C. B. Claiborne, vice president of the Whitney National Bank in New Orleans who was "convinced that there is not any man in this country, who has not socialism in his system, that would not come to the conclusion that we are entitled to make a charge [remittance fee]" (p. 41).

34. That practice, "an undisputed legal right to ask for payment over the counter" (p. 5), is defended to Congress by a Board member in Harding (1920). As for large sums presented, several district banks reported holding items for collection from paying banks until they amounted at least $100 in order to reduce direct presentment costs (pp. 32–36).

35. Forms of less than accommodating behavior ranged from counting out payments in as slow and deliberate manner as possible, and providing payment in silver and other coins difficult and expensive to transport (remember the case of the Boston Clearing House), to tendering "bills wadded and mixed up with other currency." At times the American Express Company refused to serve as presentment agents because of trouble involved in making collections (Miller, 1949, p. 24; Spahr, 1926, p. 250). For one specific example, see the protracted struggle with the recalcitrant Cones State Bank of Pierce, Nebraska (Preston, 1920, pp. 574–575).

36. The following discussion of some major cases is rather terse. More detailed discussions and descriptions are available in Murchison (1923), Tippetts (1926,

1929), Spahr (1926, pp. 256–286), Wyatt (1944, pp. 380–396), and Miller (1949, pp. 28–40).

37. *Brookings State Bank v. Federal Reserve Bank of San Francisco*; *Farmers and Merchants Bank of Catlettsburg, Ky. v. Federal Reserve Bank of Cleveland, Ohio.*

38. But we are not quite done yet with issues of non-par banking which resurfaced a decade later in the "absorption-of-exchange controversy." The Banking Act of 1933 prohibited member banks from paying interest on demand deposits "directly or indirectly." The issue became whether if banks absorb remittance fees incurred in the collection of non-par checks rather than passing them on to depositors that constituted implicit interest payments. This dispute between the Federal Reserve (yes) and the FDIC (no), involving also a series of Congressional hearings, lasted until 1945 when the Board of Governors instituted the "$2 rule" (abolished briefly in 1960 and then restored that same year). Member banks were allowed to absorb remittance fees "in amounts aggregating not more than $2.00 for any one depositor in any calendar month ..." Nonmember banks were free to absorb such charges (Jessup, 1967, pp. 15–18; Miller, 1949, pp. 41–70, 101–124; Vest, 1940, pp. 95–96). And in the 1960s the Board of Governors revived the idea of Congress legislating universal par clearing, but to no avail (Federal Reserve Bank of Minneapolis, 1966, p. 8).

39. Between 1920 and 1925 the number of non-par banks more than doubled, from 1,755 to 3,970, the high point terms of numbers (but not in terms of shares).

40. For a later date (1964), Jessup used data compiled by the FDIC (Jessup, 1967, pp. 47–56, 111) to examine the earnings structure of non-par banks. Presentment fees totals were not reported directly but rather lumped into "other service charges, commissions, fees, and collection and exchange charges," so we're talking upper bounds here (a more detailed survey of a 25 percent sample of nonmember banks showed "exchange charges" made up around 85 percent of that composite income entry in Southern states but only 60 percent for Midwestern/Great Plains non-par banks). In any case, across 14 non-par banking states that revenue category averaged 9.1 percent of "total current operating revenue," with 51 percent of non-par banks reporting 5–10 percent averages and just 3 percent, averages of 20 percent or more. A similar study for 1942 found "other service charges ..." averaging 19 percent of total revenue for non-par banks in 27 states. So connecting the dots suggests the further one goes back in time the more relatively important "exchange earnings" were.

41. Vest (1940, p. 95) noted that "in recent years not a few banks have withdrawn from membership in the Federal Reserve System giving as their reason their desire to increase their earnings by charging exchange on checks."

42. Only 13 of those non-par banks were located in towns with populations greater than 25,000 (Vest, 1940, p. 94). Interestingly or not, Jessup (1967, p. 3) found that on December 31, 1965 the 1,492 non-par banks in the U.S. (about 10 percent of total numbers) accounted again for the same 2 percent of total bank deposits.

43. However, in his model Baxter (see next paragraph) took banks in the payments system to have behaved competitively (1983, p. 554). Lacker et al. (1999, p. 20) pointed to the manner in which common costs were shared so that "presentment fees that are 'excessive' ... are not necessarily evidence of monopoly power."

44. Just to add a bit more here, in 1968 Louisiana only 16 of non-par banking communities had (1960) populations greater than 5,000, and 53 of the 87 were one-bank towns (Dudley, 1970, p. 20). Baxter (1983, pp. 565–566) noted that the case in which non-par and par banks shared the same market was "inherently unstable." If there had been a par bank in the area checks drawn on the non-par bank could have been forwarded to the par bank for collection by direct presentation at the counter (with payment at par). Thus, "conversion from nonpar to par of any one bank in any area usually led to the conversion of all in the area." See also Jessup (1967, p. 81).

45. It was proposed by some at the time that loss of income from remittance fees could have been made up by service charges imposed on local customers' checking accounts (Preston, 1920, pp. 582–583).

46. Were there alternative institutional arrangements that could have provided banking services to these out-of-the-way locations? Extensive branch banking, for example, might have allowed offices in towns too small to support their own bank. Perhaps, but initially at least they do not seem to have necessarily been that substitutable. In 1925, for example, while statewide branch banking was allowed in states such as Georgia, North Carolina, and South Carolina, they also had substantial numbers of non-par banks (Southworth, 1928, p. 22). But by the early 1960s Jessup (1967, pp. 57–62) found that the numbers of non-par banks shrank the most in states which allowed statewide branching as they were absorbed into branch networks.

47. As has been outlined earlier, Weinberg (1997) and Lacker et al. (1999, pp. 18–22) pursue a similar theme in their defense of the pre-Fed *ancien régime* clearing system.

48. Baxter's paper was the genesis of the burgeoning literature on interchange fees in credit card networks which we shall not consider here.

49. Local customers generally preferred using par rather than non-par banks even though it was outsiders rather than they who paid the charges of the latter (as the Federal Reserve Board had argued originally) (Jessup, 1967, pp. 74–75).

50. Consonant with these trends, the rationale for non-par banking, generating sufficient revenue to maintain banking services in small towns, diminished also. See footnote 40.

51. What were the social costs of monopoly power exercised by non-par banks? Since non-par banks were excluded from the Fed's check clearing and collection system, economies of scale in clearing that were realized were somewhat less than there might have been (although to be sure non-par banks themselves and presumedly the size of their clearings were much smaller than par list banks). Non-par banks had to continue to clear through private networks as in the pre-Fed period. Such networks were still in place since most nonmember banks cleared through correspondent networks rather than through the Fed. Gilbert (2000, pp. 140–146) has shown that the Fed's collection services allowed participating banks to operate with lower cash (to total asset) ratios. So the amount of idle cash in the banking system might have increased (but only compared to the counterfactual case in which non-par banks would have joined the Fed's clearing and collection network). Furthermore, recipients of non-par checks, taking presentment fees as another cost of doing business, might have passed such charges on to their customers in the form of higher prices

(Federal Reserve Bank of Minneapolis, 1966, p. 8; Jessup, 1967, pp. 83–84; Preston, 1920, p. 581; Tippetts, 1924, p. 630). Similarly, if the collecting bank had absorbed the charges, they might have been passed on to that bank's customers.

52. Par clearing states at that time included the whole Northeast plus Ohio, Oregon, California, Idaho, Utah, and Nevada.

53. Iowa was the first state to enact a law prohibiting exchange or remittance charges in 1943 and was followed by Nebraska in 1945 and Wisconsin in 1949. In Iowa and Nebraska at least no banks were said to have failed because of the law, with the revenue made up by the imposition of service charges on the drawers of checks. In Michigan and Montana remittance charges were voluntarily abolished through the state bankers' association. However similar legislative initiatives in Minnesota and the Dakotas stalled as well as in Georgia, Kansas, Missouri, Tennessee, Texas, and Washington (Federal Reserve Bank of Minneapolis, 1966, pp. 6–7; Miller, 1949, pp. 78–87, 91).

54. Minnesota, 1968; Missouri, 1969; North Dakota, 1971; South Dakota, 1971; Florida, 1967; Mississippi, 1970; Georgia, 1970; Tennessee, 1971; Alabama, 1971; Arkansas, 1974 (Rossman, 1971, p. 152).

55. Not coincidentally, these conditions are analogous to those for an "optimum" currency region (McKinnon, 1963; Mundell, 1961).

56. In addition to an active call loan market, Boston clearinghouse banks organized a "corner" market to trade their excess reserves (Cannon, 1910, pp. 247–252).

57. See Hammond (1970, p. 142). This proposal would in effect institutionalize a strategic pricing policy under network externalities (Farrell & Saloner, 1986, pp. 950–951; Katz & Shapiro, 1986, pp. 833–834).

ACKNOWLEDGMENTS

An earlier version of this paper was presented at the Instead of the Fed conference held at George Mason University in November, 2013. We would like to thank Chris Hanes , James McAndrews, and Hugh Rockoff for their useful comments and assume responsibility for any remaining errors. James also thanks the Bankard Fund for Political Economy for financial assistance.

REFERENCES

Anderson, G. B. (1916). Some phases of the new check collection system. *Annals of the American Academy of Political and Social Science*, 63(1), 122–131.

Barnett, R. W. (1884). The system of country clearing. *Proceedings of the Convention of the American Bankers' Association*, 81–88.

Baxter, William F. (1983). Bank interchange of transactional paper: Legal and economic perspectives. *Journal of Law and Economics*, 26(3), 541–588.

Blye, A. W. (1885). Collection of country checks. *Proceedings of the Convention of the American Bankers' Association*, 135–140.

Board of Governors of the Federal Reserve System. (1943). *Banking and monetary statistics.* Washington, DC: Board of Governors of the Federal Reserve System.

Bodenhorn, H. (2000). *A history of banking in Antebellum America.* New York, NY: Cambridge University Press.

Bodenhorn, H. (2002). Making the little guy pay: Payments-system networks, cross-subsidization, and the collapse of the Suffolk system. *Journal of Economic History*, *62*(1), 147–169.

Cannon, J. G. (1910). *Clearing houses, National Monetary Commission.* Washington, DC: Government Printing Office.

Carter, S., Gartner, S., Haines, M., Olmstead, A., Sutch, R., & Wright, G. (2006). *Historical statistics of the United States, millennial edition.* New York, NY: Cambridge University Press.

Chandler, A. D. Jr. (1977). *The visible hand.* Cambridge, MA: Belknap Press.

Chang, H., Danilevsky, M., Evans, D. S., & Garcia-Swartz, D. D. (2008). The economics of market coordination for the pre-Fed check-clearing system: A peek into the Bloomington (IL) node. *Explorations in Economic History*, *45*(4), 445–461.

Colwell, S. (1860). *The ways and means of payments: A full analysis of the credit system with its various modes of adjustment.* Philadelphia, PA: J.B. Lippincott & Co.

De Grauwe, P. (2012). *Economics of monetary union* (9th ed.). Oxford: Oxford University Press.

Dudley, D. A. (1970). *Nonpar banking in Louisiana.* New Orleans, LA: Division of Business and Economic Research, Louisiana State University in New Orleans.

Duprey, J. N., & Nelson, C. W. (1986). A visible hand: The Fed's involvement in the check payments system. *Federal Reserve Bank of Minneapolis Quarterly Review*, *10*(2), 18–29.

Farrell, J., & Saloner, G. (1986). Innovation, product preannouncements, and predation. *American Economic Review*, *76*(5), 940–955.

Federal Reserve Bank of Atlanta Archives. (1916a). *FRB history: Early 1900s correspondence.* *"Merchants National Bank (Vicksburg, Mississippi) to Marcus Walker, Managing Director, New Orleans Branch, May 18, 1916".* Atlanta, GA: Federal Reserve Bank of Atlanta.

Federal Reserve Bank of Atlanta Archives. (1916b). *FRB history: Early 1900s correspondence.* *"R. F. E. Cooke, Leesburg State Bank, Leesburg, Florida to Joseph McCord, Governor, Federal Reserve Bank of Atlanta, June 14, 1916".* Atlanta, GA: Federal Reserve Bank of Atlanta.

Federal Reserve Bank of Minneapolis. (1966). Nonpar banking: Near the end of an era? *Federal Reserve Bank of Minneapolis Monthly Review*, *21*(5), 3–8.

Federal Reserve Bank of Richmond. (1926). Collections. In I. Wright (Ed.), *Readings in money, credit and banking principles* (pp. 377–430). New York, NY: Harper and Brothers.

Federal Reserve Board. (1915–1925). *Annual reports.* Washington, DC: Government Printing Office.

Federal Reserve Board. (1915–1940). *Federal Reserve Bulletin.* Washington, DC: Government Printing Office.

Friedman, M., & Schwartz, A. (1963). *A monetary history of the United States.* Princeton, NJ: Princeton University Press.

Garbade, K. D., & Silber, W. L. (1979). The payments system and domestic exchange rates: Technological versus institutional change. *Journal of Monetary Economics*, 5(1), 1–22.

Garvy, G. (1959). *Debits and clearing statistics and their use*. Washington, DC: Board of Governors of the Federal Reserve System.

Gilbert, R. A. (1998). Did the Fed's founding improve the efficiency of the U.S. payments system? *Federal Reserve Bank of St. Louis Review*, 80(3), 121–142.

Gilbert, R. A. (2000). The advent of the Federal Reserve and the efficiency of the payments system: The collection of checks, 1915–1930. *Explorations in Economic History*, 37(2), 121–148.

Goodfriend, M. (1991). Money, credit, banking, and payments system policy. *Federal Reserve Bank of Richmond Economic Review*, 77(1), 7–23.

Gorton, G., & Mullineaux, D. (1987). The joint production of confidence: Endogenous regulation and nineteenth century commercial-bank clearinghouses. *Journal of Money, Credit, and Banking*, 19(4), 457–468.

Hallock, J. C. (1903). *Clearing out-of-town checks in England and the United States*. St. Louis, MO: Author.

Hammond, B. (1970). *Sovereignty and an empty purse: Banks and politics in the civil war*. Princeton, NJ: Princeton University Press.

Hammond, C. W. (1890). Clearings of country collections. *Proceedings of the Convention of the American Bankers' Association*, 106–111.

Hannan, T. H., Kiser, E. K., Prager, R. A., & McAndrews, J. J. (2003). To surcharge or not to surcharge: An empirical investigation of ATM pricing. *Review of Economics and Statistics*, 85(4), 990–1002.

Harding, W. P. G. (1920). State banks in the Federal Reserve System. Senate Document No. 184, 66th Congress, 2nd Session.

James, J. A. (1976). A note on interest paid on New York bankers' balances in the postbellum period. *Business History Review*, 50(2), 198–202.

James, J. A. (1978). *Money and capital markets in Postbellum America*. Princeton, NJ: Princeton University Press.

James, J. A., & Weiman, D. F. (2010). From drafts to checks: The evolution of correspondent banking networks and the transformation of the modern U.S. payments system, 1850–1914. *Journal of Money, Credit, and Banking*, 42(2/3), 237–265.

Jenkins, C. (1884). The collection of country checks. *Proceedings of the Convention of the American Bankers' Association*, 56–58.

Jessup, P. F. (1967). *The theory and practice of nonpar banking*. Evanston, IL: Northwestern University Press.

Katz, M. L., & Shapiro, C. (1986). Technology adoption in the presence of network externalities. *Journal of Political Economy*, 94(4), 822–841.

Kent, R. (1900). The elements of cost in collecting out-of-town checks. *Bankers' Magazine*, 61, 738–739.

Kinley, D. (1910). *The use of credit instruments in payments in the United States, National Monetary Commission*. Washington, DC: Government Printing Office.

Knodell, J. (1998). The demise of central banking and the domestic exchanges: Evidence from antebellum Ohio. *Journal of Economic History*, 58(3), 714–730.

Kreps, C. H. Jr. (1959). Characteristics of nonpar banks: A case study. *Southern Economic Journal*, 26(1), 44–49.

Lacker, J. M., Walker, J. D., & Weinberg, J. A. (1999). The Fed's entry into check clearing reconsidered. *Federal Reserve Bank of Richmond Economic Quarterly, 85*(2), 1–31.

Laughlin, J. L. (1912). *Banking reform*. Chicago, IL: National Citizens' League.

Magee, J. D. (1923). Historical analogy to the fight against par check collection. *Journal of Political Economy, 31*(3), 433–445.

McAndrews, J. (1998a). ATM surcharges. *Federal Reserve Bank of New York Current Issues in Economics and Finance, 4*(4), 1–6.

McAndrews, J. (1998b). Direct presentment regulation in payments. *Research in Economics, 52*(3), 311–326.

McKinnon, R. I. (1963). Optimum currency areas. *American Economic Review, 53*(4), 717–725.

Meltzer, A. (2003). *A history of the Federal Reserve*. Chicago, IL: University of Chicago Press.

Miller, M. C. (1949). *The par check collection and absorption of exchange controversies*. Cambridge, MA: Bankers Publishing Co.

Mundell, R. A. (1961). A theory of optimum currency areas. *American Economic Review, 51*(4), 657–665.

Murchison, C. T. (1923). Par clearance of checks. *North Carolina Law Review, 1*(3), 133–152.

Myers, M. G. (1931). *The New York money market, Volume 1: Origins and development*. New York, NY: Columbia University Press.

Preston, H. H. (1920). The Federal Reserve Banks' system of par collections. *Journal of Political Economy, 28*(7), 565–590.

Redenius, S. (2007). Designing a national currency: Antebellum payments networks and the structure of the national banking system. *Financial History Review, 14*(2), 207–228.

Redenius, S. A., & Weiman, D. F. (2011). Banking on the periphery: The cotton south, systemic seasonality, and the limits of national banking reform. In P. W. Rhode, J. L. Rosenbloom, & D. F. Weiman (Eds.), *Economic evolution and revolution in historical time* (pp. 214–242). Stanford, CA: Stanford University Press.

Rochet, J.-C., & Tirole, J. (2006). Two-sided markets: A progress report. *The RAND Journal of Economics, 37*(3), 645–667.

Rockoff, H. (2003). How long did it take the United States to become an optimal currency area? In F. H. Capie & G. E. Wood (Eds.), *Monetary unions: Theory, history, public choice* (pp. 70–103). London: Routledge.

Rossman, J. E. Jr. (1971). Southern banks take cue from economic growth. *Federal Reserve Bank of Atlanta Monthly Review, 8*, 151–155.

Shreve, B. J. (1898). Country checks and country bank accounts. *Bankers' Magazine, 56*, 221–231.

Southworth, S. D. (1928). *Branch banking in the United States*. New York, NY: McGraw-Hill.

Spahr, W. E. (1926). *The clearing and collection of checks*. New York, NY: Bankers Publishing Co.

Sprague, O. M. W. (1911). The reserve association and the improvement of methods of making payments between the banks. *Journal of Political Economy, 19*(10), 831–840.

Sprague, O. M. W. (1910). *History of crises under the national banking system, National Monetary Commission*. Washington, DC: Government Printing Office.

Stevens, E. (1996). *The founders' intentions: Sources of the payment services franchise of the Federal Reserve banks*. Financial Services Working Paper No. 03-96, Federal Reserve Bank of Cleveland.

Stevens, E. (1998). *Non-par banking: Competition and monopoly in markets for payments services.* Federal Reserve Bank of Cleveland Working Paper No. 9817.

Summers, B. J., & Gibert, R. A. (1996). Clearing and settlement of U.S. dollar payments: Back to the future? *Federal Reserve Bank of St. Louis Review, 78*(5), 3–27.

Tippetts, C. S. (1923). State bank withdrawals from the Federal Reserve System. *American Economic Review, 13*(3), 401–410.

Tippetts, C. S. (1924). The par remittance controversy. *American Economic Review, 14*(4), 629–648.

Tippetts, C. S. (1926). The end of the par collection litigation. *American Economic Review, 16*(4), 610–621.

Tippetts, C. S. (1929). *State banks and the Federal Reserve System.* New York, NY: D. Van Nostrand Co.

U.S. House Committee on Banking and Currency. (1920). *Hearing on par collection of checks* [H.R. 12379], 66th Congress, 2nd Session. Washington, DC: Government Printing Office.

U.S. House Committee on Banking, Finance, and Urban Affairs. (1983). *Joint hearings on the role of the Federal Reserve in check clearing and the nation's payments system.* Banking Committee Serial No. 98-36, 98th Congress, 1st Session. Washington, DC: Government Printing Office.

Vest, G. B. (1940). The par collection system of the Federal Reserve banks. *Federal Reserve Bulletin, 26*(2), 89–96.

Watkins, L. L. (1929). *Bankers' balances.* New York, NY: McGraw-Hill.

Weber, W. E. (2003). Interbank payments relationships in the antebellum United States: Evidence from Pennsylvania. *Journal of Monetary Economics, 50*(2), 455–474.

Weiman, D. F. (2006). Introduction to the special issue on the formation of an US monetary union. *Financial History Review, 13*(1), 11–17.

Weinberg, J. A. (1997). The organization of private payment networks. *Federal Reserve Bank of Richmond Economic Quarterly, 83*(2), 25–43.

Willis, H. P. (1923). *The Federal Reserve System.* New York, NY: Ronald Press Co.

Wyatt, W. (1944). The par clearance controversy. *Virginia Law Review, 30*(3), 361–397.

THE ANTHROPOMETRIC HISTORY OF NATIVE AMERICANS, C.1820–1890

John Komlos and Leonard Carlson

ABSTRACT

We analyze heights of Indian scouts in the U.S. army born between ca. 1825 and 1875. Their average height of ca. 170 cm (67 in.) confirms that natives were tall compared to Europeans but were nearly the shortest among the rural populations in the New World. The trend in their height describes a slightly inverted "U" shape with an increase between those born 1820–1834 and 1835–1839 of ca. 1.8 cm (0.7 in.) (p = 0.000) and a subsequent slight decline after the Civil War. This implies that they were able to maintain and perhaps even improve their nutritional status through the Civil War, though harder times followed for those born thereafter. We also recalculate the heights of Native Americans in the Boas sample and find that the Plains Indians were shorter than most rural Americans. The trend in the height of Indians in the Boas sample is similar to that of the scouts.

Keywords: Physical stature; native Americans; Antebellum; height; biological living standards; welfare

JEL classifications: N00; N31

Research in Economic History, Volume 30, 135–161
Copyright © 2014 by Emerald Group Publishing Limited
All rights of reproduction in any form reserved
ISSN: 0363-3268/doi:10.1108/S0363-326820140000030003

INTRODUCTION

Our knowledge of the material conditions of Native Americans in the 19th century is quite limited because of the scarcity of evidence. To be sure, we do know that there was a massive disruption of their way of life and a large decline in population following European contact. The North American Indian population (not just in the United States) declined from 1,894,350 in a.d. 1500 to 530,000 in 1900 due to epidemics and other factors (Ubelaker, 1988). Since 1900 native population has rebounded and exceeds its level in 1500.

Available evidence on their physical stature, however, does enable us to gain at least a glimpse of one important aspect of their biological welfare in the course of much of the 19th century. Human height is a widely used synthetic indicator of nutritional status, malnutrition, and biological living standards in many different settings, including but not limited to underdeveloped economies, in historical contexts, and in circumstances in which economic indicators are either unreliable or scarce as among slaves or Native Americans (Steckel, 1995). Physical stature is positively correlated with net nutrition – the balance between the quantity and quality of nutrient intake and the demands on those resources by the human organism for growth, metabolic maintenance, work, and for resistance to diseases. Of course, individual heights depend as much on genetic potential as on nutrition, but at the population level environmental factors play a very substantial role in determining adult height (Bogin, 1999). Hence, height of a population is eminently suitable to ascertaining the nutritional and epidemiological circumstances in which that population lived prior to reaching adulthood.

We analyze a newly collected data set on the height of Native American scouts in the U.S. army. Our paper is organized as follows: in the second section we discuss prior estimates of the height of Native Americans; in the third section we explain the regression technique we use in order to estimate mean of samples in which the height distributions are biased, that is, are not normally distributed; in the fourth section we focus on the history of Indian scouts in the U.S. army; in the fifth section we present the newly discovered data; in the sixth section we report the results of the analysis of these data; in the seventh section we discuss our findings; in the eighth section we connect with the history of Native Americans in light of our findings; and in the ninth section we conclude.

PRIOR ESTIMATES OF THE HEIGHT OF THE NATIVE POPULATION OF NORTH AMERICA

The main source on the height of North American natives hitherto analyzed was collected by the prominent anthropologist Franz Boas at the end of the 19th century (Boas, 1895; Jantz, 1995). Boas published the height distributions by tribe without noticing, however, that the samples were obviously biased insofar as the distributions were not symmetric as expected: there were almost always too few men in the sample left of the mean (or mode) (1895, p. 372). This is particularly evident among the Sioux and Crow, two tribes with the largest sample sizes which biased the averages in an upwardly direction (Figs. 1 and 2). While a random sample of heights is always and

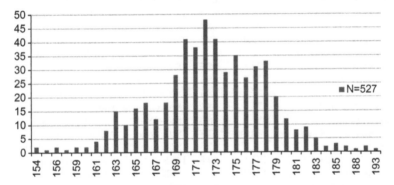

Fig. 1. Height (cm) Distribution of Sioux Men.

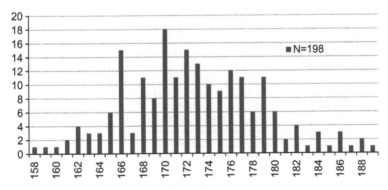

Fig. 2. Height (cm) Distribution of Crow Men.

everywhere normally distributed, the height samples of both of these tribes clearly suffer from a shortfall below c. 170 cm.

Although Jantz did state quite explicitly that "Boas' samples of Native Americans cannot be regarded as random samples ..." (1995), Steckel and Prince analyzed the Boas data set as though it were a random sample, concluding that the Plains Indians were the tallest populations in the world with a mean height of 172.6 cm (68 in.) (Table 1, row 10) (Steckel, 2010,

Table 1. Height of Males c. mid-19th Century.

	Group	Centimeter	Inches	Date, Type	Source
1	U.S. elite	175.0	68.9	1860s	Sunder (2007)
2	Tennessee, white	174.5	68.7	1850s convicts	Sunder (2004)
3	Georgia, farmers	174.3	68.6	1850s convicts	Komlos and Coclanis (1997)
4	Texas, white	174.0	68.5	1860s convicts	Carson (2009)
5	Australia	173.9	68.5	1860s	Whitwell, de Souza and Nicholas (1997)
6	Union army soldiers	173.5	68.3	1840s farmers	A'Hearn (1998)
7	Crow (Boas sample)[a]	173.1	68.1	1840–1880	Steckel and Prince (2001)
8	Sioux (Boas sample)[a]	172.9	68.1	1840–1880	Steckel and Prince (2001)
9	Tennessee, blacks	172.7	68.0	1850s convicts	Sunder (2004)
10	Plains Indians	172.6	68.0	1840–1880	Steckel and Prince (2001)
11	Union army soldiers	172.2	67.8	1840s urban	A'Hearn (1998)
12	Georgia, blacks	172.2	67.8	1840 convicts	Komlos and Coclanis (1997)
13	Ohio Nat'l Guard	172.1	67.8	1860s	Steckel and Haurin (1994)
14	Texas, black	171.9	67.7	1860s	Carson (2009)
15	West Point cadets	171.6	67.6	1860s	Komlos (1987)
16	Maryland, free black	170.7	67.2	1830s rural	Komlos (1992)
17	Plains Indians[b]	170.6	67.2	1840–1880	Own calculations
18	Georgia, black	170.6	67.2	1850s	Komlos and Coclanis (1997)
19	Sioux (Boas sample)[c]	170.2	67.1	1840–1880	Own calculations
20	U.S. cavalry	170.2	67.0	1860s	Zehetmayer (2011)
21	Indians (Boas sample)[a]	170.0	66.9	1840–1880	Own calculations
22	Indian scouts	170.0	66.9	1860s	This sample
23	Indians (Boas sample)[d]	169.6	66.8	1840–1880	Own calculations
24	African Americans	169.4	66.7	1860s farmers	Carson (2008)
25	Philadelphia	169.2	66.6	1840s	Cuff (2005)
26	Austria	166.0	65.4	1870s	Komlos (2007b)

[a]Non-normal distribution indicates sample selection bias.
[b]Estimated from the Boas sample restricted to the 8 plains tribes analyzed by Steckel and Prince using restricted truncated regression with lower limit of 170 cm for the Sioux and Crow tribes.
[c]Mean calculated with constrained truncated regression with lower limit of 170 cm.
[d]Estimated using restricted truncated regression with lower limit of 170 cm for the Sioux and Crow tribes.

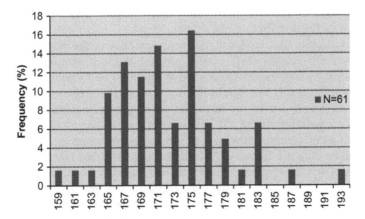

Fig. 3. Height (cm) Distribution of Arapaho Men.

p. 267; Steckel & Prince, 2001, p. 289; Prince & Steckel, 2003, p. 367). As a consequence of the sampling biases, this estimate is certainly too high (Table 1, row 17). Of the c. 1,700 observations that stem from tribes with a mean height above 170 cm, nearly two-thirds were from tribes whose height distribution did not pass the test of normality.[1] If one excludes these tribes from the Boas averages, the mean height becomes 169.6 cm (66.8 in.) or about 3.0 cm (1.2 in.) below the Steckel–Prince estimates (Table 1, row 23). Of the eight tribes they included in their analysis 72% were from the Sioux and Crow with biased samples, but the height distribution of many of the others are also similarly distorted[2] (Fig. 3). In other words, the mean height of Boas sample has to be calculated using techniques that account for the distorted nature of the sample: truncated regression, which has not been used up to now.

TRUNCATED REGRESSION

Statistical analysis of height data from nonrandom samples is facilitated considerably by the biological law that height is approximately normally distributed within a population, and its standard deviation is practically constant, that is, has a narrow range between ca. 6 cm and 7 cm among males and between ca. 5.3 cm and 6.5 cm among females even though mean heights can vary by as much as 20 cm within a population over time (Cole, 2003; Komlos & Baur, 2004).[3] Consequently, variations in a population's nutritional status affect mean heights, and not the form or dispersion of the distribution.

Height samples are frequently not representative of the population from which they are drawn, that is, they are not random samples. Thus, the Boas sample as well as the scout sample about to be examined are hardly unique in this regard. The height distributions drawn from many historical military records (prior to the introduction of universal conscription) typically have a shortfall in the left tail − fewer than expected observations − insofar as most armies imposed a minimum height requirement (Komlos, 2004). Thus, data are frequently available only for those individuals whose height exceeded the minimum height requirement (τ). In such cases, sample means and variances are biased estimators of the underlying population parameters, as are the coefficients of independent variables estimated by ordinary least squares regression (Komlos, 2003; Komlos & A'Hearn, 2004).

Suppose that we observe the latent normal random variable Y^* with mean μ and variance σ^2: $y* = \mu + \varepsilon, \varepsilon \sim N(0, \sigma^2)$ only if $y^* \geq \tau$. Thus, sample Y is: $y = \mu + \varepsilon$ if $y \geq \tau$; y missing otherwise. We observe y only if $\mu + \varepsilon \geq \tau$, or $\varepsilon \geq \mu - \tau$. Thus, conditional on being in the sample, $E(\varepsilon) \neq 0$, and is not normally distributed. Parametric methods for estimating μ build on the normal distribution of heights, enabling us to use the normal density as the likelihood function for (untruncated) heights. In the case of truncation, the area under the curve no longer integrates to unity without the lower tail. To correct for this, we can divide by the probability of being in the sample, that is, $\Pr(y > \tau)$. This is the standard way to model conditional probability as it normalizes the area under the curve to unity. The probability density function (pdf) of a truncated normal random variable is

$$f(y) = \frac{\frac{1}{\sigma}\phi\left(\frac{y-\mu}{\sigma}\right)}{1 - \Phi\left(\frac{\tau-\mu}{\sigma}\right)} \quad \text{if } y \geq \tau; \; f(y) = 0 \quad \text{if } y < \tau \tag{1}$$

where Φ denotes the standard normal pdf (Ruud, 2000, chapter 28; Greene, 1993, chapter 22). The log likelihood function of Eq. (1) can be formed and the parameter values that maximize it can be calculated using numerical methods. This maximum likelihood (ML) estimator has the usual ML properties of consistency, and asymptotic efficiency.

However, experience with actual samples demonstrated that the ML estimates can vary implausibly over time or cross-sectionally. This inference is based on the fact that there are biological limits to the variability in the physical stature of a population in the short run. The variability turns out to be particularly pronounced if sample sizes are small, if τ is close to the mode, or perhaps even to the right of it, or if it has been incorrectly identified. For this reason, it has been demonstrated that truncated regression is often more accurate if the standard deviation of the sample height distribution is simultaneously constrained to be the modern value (among men) of ca. 6.86 cm (2.7 in.). The constrained truncated regression estimator with sigma thus constrained is frequently more reliable and has greater precision (A'Hearn, 2004). As a consequence, we run the truncated regressions[4] two ways: (a) allowing the program to determine the standard deviation of the height distribution freely, and (b) constraining the standard deviations to be 6.86 cm. We refer to the former estimates as unconstrained and to the latter one as constrained.

INDIAN SCOUTS IN THE U.S. ARMY

When Congress authorized a force of 1,000 Indian scouts in 1866, the U.S. army began for the first time to formally include Indians in the military (Dunlay, 1982, p. 44). The use of scouts was the continuation of a long history of Indians serving as auxiliary troops or as allies fighting alongside American or other nations' soldiers against enemy tribes. The years 1866–1890 marked the end of warfare between Indians and the United States. Most of the roughly 270,000 Indians in the United States at that date were at peace[5] (Utley, 1973, p. 5).

Why were Indians willing to serve in the army or ally themselves with the American forces? Typically Indians saw themselves first as members of families, then clans, then a tribe, but they often saw members of other tribes as different from themselves and with good reason. Enemy tribes often raided for horses or slaves from neighbors; there were battles over territory, and revenge raids to retaliate for murdered relatives (Utley, 1973, p. 5). Thus, serving with the American army did not necessarily create a moral dilemma for Indian scouts. Hostile Indians' mobility and familiarity with the terrain made guerilla warfare effective and it sometimes required large numbers of troops to confront relatively small numbers of fighters. In such warfare, Indian scouts provided vital services as guides and interpreters.

After 1866 the army was often assigned the task of confining Indian tribes to defined lands "reserved" for Indians – reservations. Typically this was done by signing a treaty, with a tribe ceding tribal territory in return for the right to a reduced territory and goods to be provided by the federal government. For plains tribes in this era there was continuing pressure on the key resource – the bison herds. By the late 1870s the bison herds had largely been depleted and most plains tribes depended upon food issued by the government and lived in encampments near the agency. Even after they were defeated and confined to reservations, however, bands of Indians would occasionally leave the reservation and were then subject to capture by the army who would return them. Battles in this period often represented last ditch stands by Indians who did not want to move to a reservation.[6]

While fighting in the northern plains and Rocky Mountain States was greatly diminished after 1880, fighting continued in the southwestern territories of Arizona, New Mexico, and Texas until 1886 with the surrender of the Apache warriors led by the leader known to whites as Geronimo. General George Crook, perhaps the most able of the military leaders fighting in the West, found it essential to recruit Apaches to fight the hostile members of the same tribe (Utley, 1973, p. 378). The continued warfare in the Southwest is probably why Arizona is the most common state of origin for scouts in the sample about to be analyzed.

DATA ON INDIAN SCOUTS

By the 19th century most military in economically advanced countries (including the United States) recorded the height of soldiers in order to have a physical description in case of desertion and in order to document that the soldier met the height requirements. Height requirements were imposed inasmuch as short men were at a disadvantage in hand-to-hand combat and exceptionally tall men were not suitable for the cavalry on account of the high center of gravity. In order to estimate the height of Native American men, data on the height of scouts were extracted from the National Archives ($N = 12,999$) (Table 2).[7] Information available includes height, age, state of birth, date of enlistment, and occupation prior to enlistment. Indians were eminently suitable as scouts because they knew the local terrain the best. The minimum and maximum height requirement to be eligible to be in the U.S. military also applied to scouts.[8] We do not know about other possible requirements, but assume that within the acceptable range of heights the men were a random sample from their respective population. The distribution of adult heights is perfectly normal

Table 2. Characteristics of the Indian Scout Sample.

	Full Sample		Working Sample	
	N	%	N	%
Ages				
17–18	232	1.8	144	1.8
19–20	737	5.7	435	5.3
21	1,055	8.1	658	8.0
22–24	2,476	19.0	1,564	19.1
25–49	8,302	63.9	5,285	64.6
>49	166	1.3	92	1.1
Missing	31	0.2	0	0.0
Total	12,999	100.0	8,178	100.0
Occupation				
Chief	35	0.3	14	0.2
Farmer	845	6.5	540	6.6
Herder	124	1.0	83	1.0
Hunter	1,366	10.5	813	9.9
Rancher	209	1.6	159	1.9
Scout	5,860	45.1	3,558	43.5
Other	4,560	35.1	3,008	36.8
State of birth				
Arizona	5854	45.0	3,876	47.4
Arkansas	158	1.2	103	1.3
Dakota	1,964	15.1	1,449	17.7
Idaho	100	0.8	73	0.9
Indian Territory	727	5.6	437	5.3
Minnesota	122	0.9	82	1.0
Montana	635	4.9	363	4.4
Nebraska	665	5.1	491	6.0
New Mexico	530	4.1	362	4.4
Oregon	177	1.4	112	1.4
Texas	296	2.3	197	2.4
United States	130	1.0	68	0.8
Wyoming	258	2.0	176	2.2
Other U.S. states	617	4.7	389	4.8
Mexico	708	5.4	0	0.0
Other foreign states	58	0.4	0	0.0
Date of birth				
<1830	227	1.7	224	2.7
1830s	985	7.6	879	10.7
1840s	3,394	26.1	2,082	25.5
1850s	5,129	39.5	2,947	36.0
1860s	2,798	21.5	1,846	22.6
>1869	447	3.4	200	2.4
Missing	19	0.1	0	0.0

Note: This table includes those who were excluded because they were shorter than the minimum height requirement.
Source: National Archives and Records Administration (1798–1914).

between the range of 66–75 in. Outside of this range there does appear to be an obvious shortfall[9] (Fig. 4). The fact that the distributions are normal enables us to use truncated regression in order to correct for the height restrictions. The use of truncated regression enables us to infer the height of the general population of Indian men from that of the scouts.

A few of the observations were obviously inaccurate or hastily recorded and were excluded from the working data set. These 247 scouts did not have their name recorded as did the others, but were given numbers instead, which gives the impression that their information might not have been carefully recorded.[10] This impression was reinforced by the fact that the height values were uniformly repeated for these persons (almost always at 68 in.) implying that the records were not based on actual measurements. We also excluded those who were born outside of the U.S. Scouts who were between the ages of 21 and 49 (inclusive) are considered adults and those older were also excluded in the analysis. Youth – those aged 19–20 – were also included in one of the models.

We first examined the height distributions by recruitment year (annually) in order to ascertain the minimum height requirements; we found that for some years the distributions are far from normally distributed – even above the minimum height requirement. This implies that the measurements were done carelessly in those years with too many observations in the 68 in. bin. Hence, the data for those years were excluded from further analysis.[11] It became clear that very tall scouts were also fewer in number than expected. The minimum and maximum height requirements were

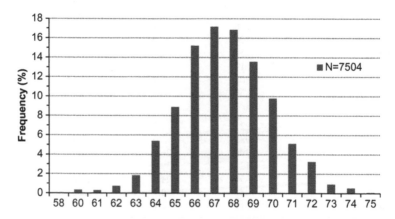

Fig. 4. Height (Inches) Distribution of Scouts.

determined by enlistment year annually,[12] because of the obvious substantial variation in the apparent recruiting practices. The minimum and maximum height requirements do not pose an insurmountable problem, though, because the use of truncated regression compensates for these deficiencies of the sample. After excluding those outside of the acceptable range of height requirements, the size of the working adult data set becomes 6,524; with the inclusion of youth the sample size is 6,899. The main analysis pertains to U.S.-born adult Indian men. We then supplement the data to include youth and compare the results to those obtained from the Boas sample.

RESULTS

The regressions control for the state of provenance as well as for the occupation of the scouts to the extent these are available (Table 3). In Fig. 5 we show a more detailed depiction of the trends of the heights of the scouts than in Table 3 (10 instead of 7 periods). There are few statistically significant spatial variations: scouts from Montana are consistently shorter than average while those from the Midwest are consistently taller (Fig. 6). However, none of the estimated coefficients of the occupation variables is consistently significant.[13]

The estimated time trend indicates the following pattern (Fig. 5 and Table 3): (1) there was a marked (and statistically significant) increase in height among those born in the second half of the 1830s. The increase in height between those born 1820–1834 and 1835–1839 was ca. 1.8 cm (0.7 in.)[14] ($p = 0.000$); (2) after the 1830s there was very little change in height, though a shallow maximum seems to have been reached around the 1860 birth cohorts; the increase in this period was an insignificant ¼ in. (0.6 cm); (3) this was followed by a statistically insignificant diminution in height of about ¼ in. (0.6 cm) among the 1870s birth cohort; (4) the constrained and unconstrained estimates are very close to one another and track each other well; the average gap between them is a mere 0.4 cm (0.15 in.) with the constrained estimates being consistently smaller; (5) the inclusion of the youth makes very little difference (these results are not reported in the graph); (6) the estimates obtained on the basis of the Boas sample fit into this general pattern extremely well both in terms of levels as well as the trend ($N = 4,430$). The estimated level of their height is on average ¼ in. (0.6 cm) below the (constrained) estimates of the scouts and run

JOHN KOMLOS AND LEONARD CARLSON

Table 3. Truncated Regression. Dependent Variable: Height (Inches) of Indian Scouts.

	Robust		Robust		Robust	
	Coefficient	Standard Error	Coefficient	Standard Error	Coefficient	Standard Error
Birth cohort						
1820–1834	**−0.91**	0.19	**−0.89**	0.18	**−0.86**	0.19
1835–1839	−0.19	0.18	−0.24	0.16	−0.14	0.18
1840–1844	−0.12	0.15	−0.16	0.14	−0.07	0.15
1845–1849	−0.06	0.13	−0.11	0.12	−0.02	0.13
1850–1854	−0.22	0.12	**−0.27**	0.11	−0.07	0.12
1855–1869	Reference		Reference		Reference	
>1870	−0.22	0.40	−0.18	0.36	−0.07	0.34
Provenance						
Arizona	0.15	0.13	0.12	0.12	0.15	0.13
Arkansas	0.07	0.38	0.08	0.35	0.10	0.37
Indian Territory	0.11	0.21	0.08	0.19	0.16	0.20
Dakota	Reference		Reference		Reference	
Montana	**−0.60**	0.28	**−0.52**	0.25	**−0.57**	0.27
Midwest	**0.60**	0.31	**0.56**	0.29	**0.69**	0.30
Nebraska	0.14	0.22	0.16	0.20	0.18	0.21
New Mexico	0.27	0.23	0.25	0.21	0.25	0.22
Other	0.58	Coefficient	0.49	0.40	0.52	0.40
South	0.25	0.26	0.21	0.24	0.31	0.25
West	0.00	0.23	0.00	0.21	−0.02	0.22
Wyoming	0.12	0.30	0.03	0.28	−0.26	0.28
Occupation						
Farmer	−0.12	0.17	−0.12	0.16	−0.16	0.17
Hunter	0.26	0.14	**0.27**	0.13	0.19	0.14
Herder	0.67	0.38	0.59	0.35	**0.74**	0.36
Rancher	0.29	0.33	0.32	0.30	0.47	0.31
Other	Reference		Reference		Reference	
Age						
age19					−0.10	0.33
age20					−0.17	0.22
Adult	Adults only		Adults only		Reference	
Constant	**66.96**	0.12	**67.13**	0.11	**66.91**	0.12
N	6524		6524		6899	
Method	Constrained		Unconstrained		Constrained	
Sigma	2.68		2.43		2.68	
Wald χ^2	45.00		49.42		47.43	
Prob $> \chi^2$	0.002		0.000		0.002	

Note: Coefficients significant at the 5% level are in bold type.

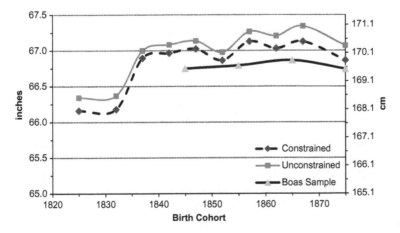

Fig. 5.   Estimated Height of Indian Men.

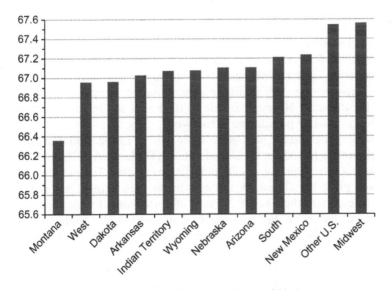

Fig. 6.   Height of Scouts by State of Birth.

parallel to it. The trend estimated on the basis of the Boas sample also has a slightly inverted "U" shape even if it is statistically insignificant; the method of estimation was to use truncated regression in which 170 cm (67 in.) was the lower limit at which shortfall begins for the Crow and

Sioux. If we confine the analysis to the 8 tribes on which Steckel and Prince concentrated, the estimated mean height becomes 170.6 cm (67.2 in.) or 2 cm (0.8 in.) below the Steckel and Prince estimate (Table 1, line 17).

DISCUSSION

The correspondence of the estimated average height of the army scouts with that of the civilians in the Boas sample is quite remarkable both in their levels and trends. The Indians (Table 1, rows 21 and 23) were about as tall as the white American-born cavalrymen (row 20). This is somewhat misleading, however, because the whites are representative of the U.S. population at large with 10% of that sample born in New England and 43% urban, whereas the Indians were mostly from the West and none was urban. This makes a considerable difference insofar as rural populations were much taller during that period. This is also the reason why the white cavalrymen appear to be shorter than the other men reported in Table 1. None of the other samples are representative of the population at large in the post-Civil War era. Rather, they either pertain to elite income groups, or refer to an earlier birth cohort or are regionally limited.[15] The white cavalrymen are the only spatially representative sample for the United States for the time. Hence, it is safe to infer that the Indians were shorter than the rural white population in the West.

However, the Indian men were quite tall in international comparison throughout the period under consideration (Table 1). At 170 cm (66.9 in.) they were taller than European populations (Table 1, rows 22 and 24). However, given the abundant nutrients in the New World, it is not appropriate to compare their height to that of Europeans. Given the rural and agricultural nature of Indian society, it is also inappropriate to compare their stature to the U.S. average either, insofar as a considerable proportion of the white population lived in towns whose dwellers were considerably shorter than average. Hence, it is more appropriate to compare Indian heights to groups that were similarly engaged in rural occupations such as U.S. farmers. Such a comparison with most of the available data indicates that the Native Americans tended to be near the bottom end of the U.S. rural height distribution (Table 1).[16] This is also true for Indian women in the Boas sample: they were shorter than most rural Americans (Table 4). The only shorter group among men was African Americans after emancipation (Table 1, row 24). The men were even shorter than the free African

Table 4.   Height of Females c. mid-19th Century.

	Group	Centimeter	Inches	Date, Type	Source
1	U.S. elite	163.6	64.4	1860s	Sunder (2007)
2	Georgia, white	163.3	64.3	Convicts	Komlos and Coclanis (1997)
3	Georgia, blacks	161.4	63.6	Convicts	Komlos and Coclanis (1997)
4	Texas, white	161.1	63.4	Convicts	Carson, African American
5	Texas, black	161.1	63.4	Convicts	Carson, African American
6	Sioux (Boas sample)	160.6	63.2	1870s	Steckel and Prince (2001)
7	Tennessee	160.0	63.0	Convicts	Sunder (2004)
8	Crow	159.1	62.6	1870s	Steckel and Prince (2001)
9	Maryland, black	158.0	62.2	1840s rural	Komlos (1992)
10	English, rural	156.8	61.8	c.1800 convicts	Nicholas and Oxley (1993)
11	Indians (Boas sample)	156.7	61.7	1860s	Own calculations
12	Irish	155.4	61.2	c.1800 convicts	Nicholas and Oxley (1993)
13	Maryland, black	155.4	61.2	1840s urban	Komlos (1992)
14	English, urban	154.3	60.8	c.1800 convicts	Nicholas and Oxley (1993)

Americans in Maryland, who were certainly at the bottom of the socioeco-
nomic distribution. The Plains Indians were not the tallest by any means
(Table 1, row 17) as argued in Steckel (2010); they were about as tall as the
free blacks of Maryland (Table 1, row 16). One can plausibly infer from
this evidence that the nutritional status and biological standard of living of
Native Americans was on average closer to those of the poorer segments of
the U.S. rural population. Their main advantage compared to the urban
population was the lower disease incidence due to the lower population
density as well as the propinquity to nutrients.

The unique slightly concave trend in both the scout and Boas samples
implies that there was probably some improvement in their nutritional status in spite of their military defeat and subsequent tribulations. The con-
stancy and perhaps even slight increase in height of the scouts in the late
1830s also implies that they did not experience the "Antebellum Puzzle" as
did most of the white population. That puzzle refers to the shrinking of the
average height of the American population in a prosperous period of economic expansion during the pre-Civil War decades. The explanation of
declining size at a time when incomes were growing has been controversial.
While some scholars suggested that the decline was due to an increase in
the incidence of diseases, others argued that the nutritional intake of the
population declined, because of a diminution in calorie and protein intake
associated with the rise in the absolute and relative food prices (Komlos,
1987). The estimated trend of the height of Indians corroborates other

findings which showed that there were groups in the society whose height did not decline at all or even increased among the cohorts born in the late 1830s. These groups were typically those who either did not purchase their food in the market, such as slaves and self-sufficient farmers, or who had sufficient income to compensate for the increase in food prices. Thus, the heights of the economic elites were also unaffected by the increases in food prices. They had sufficient income to retain their nutritional status, while the slaves were paid efficiency wages in nutrients so that they, too, remained protected from the rise in food prices. Similarly, the Indians were not buying nutrients so that agricultural prices would not have affected their nutritional status either. This is another indication that the Antebellum Puzzle was primarily anchored in the agricultural economy rather than in changes in the disease environment, insofar as diseases would not have spared these dissimilar social groups within the population: the very rich as well as the most unfortunate.

Since scouts were drawn from a variety of tribes, we look at different parts of the country in order to illuminate the above results. As discussed in what follows, there are reasons to believe that these years were hard for Indians in general. At the risk of oversimplifying (since each tribe has a unique history), we can divide the West into different regions and consider what was happening in each. These are the northern Great Plains, Oklahoma, and the Indian Territory, the southern Great Plains, the Southwest, and the Great Basin, and Pacific Northwest.

With respect to anthropometric history, the most studied group of 19th-century American Indians are the Plains Indians (Prince, 1995). Steckel (2010) and Hämäläinen (2003) show that while plains tribes adapted many similar cultural elements, some tribes were more successful than others. According to Hämäläinen (2003, p. 430), "Horses did bring new possibilities, prosperity, and power to Plains Indians, but they also brought destabilization, dispossession, and destruction. The transformational power of horses was simply too vast." Prince (1995) finds a pattern of rising heights among the Plains Sioux (combining the Yankton and Teton (Lakota) branches of the tribe) from 1820 to1880, similar to the one found here, except his data do not show a downward turn in heights in the 1870s, as does this sample. Hämäläinen argues that the Lakota were exceptionally successful among plains tribes. The traditional explanation for their success in challenging white settlers and the federal government is a large population "and organizational capability." In addition, Hämäläinen argues that the "Lakota also became so dominant because they succeeded ... [at] finding a functional equilibrium among horse numbers, ecological constraints, and economic, cultural, and military imperatives" (p. 859).

Other tribes were not doing as well. For example, the Crow tribe was further west and was fully equestrian (no longer lived in fixed villages) by the 1820s, but the tribe was at war with many other tribes over horses and territory. As a result, the Crow were more often on the edge of starvation than were the Sioux and ended up allying themselves with the American army in wars with other tribes. Tribes in the extreme North, such as the Blackfeet, were constrained by poorer weather and at times lacked adequate grass to get their horses through the winter alive (Hämäläinen, 2003, pp. 852−853). Tribes that combined fixed settlements and agriculture with hunting, such as the Pawnee and Osage, remained at risk for raids by the mounted plains tribes in the 1850s (Hämäläinen, 2003, pp. 856−858).

The post-Civil War period saw the accelerated destruction of the bison herds and a rapid decline in the ability of the northern plains tribes to sustain themselves. "By 1877, after only a few fights with the U.S. army, all northern tribes were confined on reservations on both sides of the forty-ninth parallel [the border with Canada]" (Hämäläinen, 2003, p. 853). After that date, battles on the plains consisted of desperate fights by small groups of warriors leaving the reservations. Once they were on reservations, Indians began to achieve modest success as farmers (Carlson, 1981, 1992).

NOTES ON THE HISTORY OF NATIVE AMERICANS

The results presented here conclude that broadly speaking, there was a slight improvement in the biological standard of living of Indian scouts from the 1830s through the American Civil War, followed by a decline thereafter. Scouts were drawn from a variety of tribes in different parts of the country, who would have had unique nutritional experiences. As shown in what follows there are ample reasons to believe that tribes in different parts of the country would have found the 1830s more difficult than the subsequent decades.

The Indian Territory (Oklahoma)

In the second quarter of the nineteenth century the dominant policy towards Indians in the United States is known as the Removal Policy.

Many tribes in the East were pressured to sign treaties exchanging their land in the East for new lands west of the Mississippi River. This was seen as a way to open Indian lands to white settlers while giving Indians protected territories in the West. It was an uneasy compromise between whites who wanted Indian land and those who wanted to protect Indian rights and perhaps encourage assimilation (Prucha, 1984, pp. 179–181). The most famous cases of removal were those of the southern tribes, but it also applied to tribes north of the Ohio River who had relatively small populations and were less well organized than tribes south of the Ohio River. The five largest southern tribes – Cherokee, Choctaw, Chickasaw, Creek, and Seminoles – were collectively known as the "Five Civilized Tribes" since they were agricultural and had adapted more European customs and technology. These tribes were forced from the Southeast in the years from 1820 to 1840 and received larger amounts of land in the Indian Territory (what is today Oklahoma), where they established self-governing republics. The Creek, Chickasaw and Choctaw moved within two years of the passage of the removal Act of 1830 (Barrington, 1998, p. 19). The largest tribe was the Cherokee, who were forced out of Georgia in 1838–1839 during the so-called "Trail of Tears." Prior to removal the Cherokee had achieved self-sufficiency on farms in Georgia and North Carolina (Wishart, 1995).

These eastern tribes are labeled as "immigrant tribes" on the map of major tribes taken from Utley (2003) (Fig. 7). After arriving west of the Mississippi, these tribes suffered raids from powerful plains tribes and some, notably the Cherokee and Creek, from internal disputes. The initial decades in Oklahoma were difficult. Presumably as these tribes became adjusted to their new homes and developed farms, conditions would have improved until 1865. This might account for the rise in average heights among recruits. During the U.S. Civil War, some factions of these Oklahoma tribes sided with the South and some with the North. But most of the organized tribal governments had southern sympathies; at the end of the war the tribes were stripped of territory in western Oklahoma which was turned into reservations for southern plains tribes.

Southern Plains and Texas

In the early nineteenth century, the southern plains were dominated by the Comanche. They developed an important trade network in which they acquired and sold horses. The growth in the number of horses led to differences in wealth – with wealthy men having large herds of horses and

Fig. 7. Major Indian Tribes in 1850. *Source*: Utley (2003, p. 5).

several wives. However, the large herds placed a strain on the grazing resources available to the tribe. The Comanche formed an alliance with the Kiowa and dominated the southern plains into what is today northern Mexico through the 1820s, raiding as well as trading with other tribes and

Mexican and American settlements. By the 1850s drought and the opening of overland trails led to a drastic decline in bison herds and led to periodic famines in the southern Great Plains. The population of the Comanche declined from roughly 20,000 in the 1820s to roughly 5,000 in the 1860s (Hämäläinen, 2003, pp. 844–845). This is reflected in the shorter stature of Comanche men (Prince & Steckel, 2003, p. 367; Steckel, 2010).

The Southwest

In the early nineteenth century the territory that is today Arizona and New Mexico (as well as several other western states) was part of Mexico. Some of the tribes in this region, particularly the Navajo, Apache, and Comanche, raided Mexican settlers, the agricultural tribes (such as the Pueblos and Yuma), and more nomadic tribes (the Ute) for goods, slaves, and horses. These tribes had horses and could trade with American traders for highly effective weapons. The Mexican government was never able to effectively contain these warlike tribes. Agricultural tribes allied themselves with the Mexicans and later the Americans in battles with the Navajo and other tribes (Lamar & Truett, 1996).

In 1848 the United States annexed a large territory, including Arizona and New Mexico, from Mexico at the end of the Mexican–American War. The U.S. army took over control of the sparsely settled region as well as taking over the frontier of Texas. Like the Mexican army had done, American troops built a series of forts and outposts to contain the raiders. In the thinly settled, harsh landscape, small bands of hostile Indians were able to evade the poorly paid and trained U.S. army (Utley, 1973, pp. 163–183). To deal with this, the United States increased its military presence in the region. This increased military presence could have led to better conditions for peaceful tribes after 1848, although there would have been more pressure on warlike tribes including the Navajo.

The Navajo remained a major military threat until about 1864, when they were defeated and confined to a reservation in southern New Mexico, Bosque Redondo, where conditions were harsh and the tribe survived on food provided by the U.S. army. Four years later the Navajo moved to a new reservation nearer their original home territory and remained at peace with the Americans thereafter (Prucha, 1984, pp. 451–453). Warfare continued in the Southwest until 1886. Tribes used the border with Mexico as a barrier. Tribes who moved into northern Mexico raided into the United

States and tribes based in the United States raided northern Mexico (Utley, 1973, pp. 344–398).

The Great Basin and Pacific Northwest

According to Table 2, only 277 Indians in the sample came from Idaho or Oregon and some of these would have been from nomadic tribes that had adapted to the arid Great Basin region. Since there were relatively few of these Indians in the sample, it is likely that they do not influence the pattern of heights in these data. Indians from Montana and Wyoming might be Crow, a mounted equestrian tribe who were often at war with neighboring tribes and would have been part of the struggle for control of the northern plains. Further west, tribes such as the Klamath had an economy based on hunter-gatherer existence that fit the more arid plateau. It is not surprising that they might have a poorer diet. The most famous fights in the Great Basin involved small desperate bands resisting being confined to reservations (Utley, 1973, p. 323).

CONCLUSION

Both the levels and trends estimated in this new sample are quite similar to the ones obtained from the Boas sample of Indians collected at the end of the 19th century. The trend describes a slightly inverted "U" shape with some increase in the late antebellum period and a slight subsequent decline after the Civil War. This implies that in spite of their considerable tribulations, the Native Americans were able to maintain and to some extent possibly even improve their nutritional status through the Civil War, though harder times followed for those born thereafter.

We find that the tallest Indian scouts were born during the American Civil War (1861–1865). Western settlement by whites greatly declined during the war, which reduced the pressure on tribal resources and exposure to diseases carried by migrants. This would have led to favorable conditions throughout much of Indian country. As discussed, the early 1860s saw the end of an intense campaign against the Navajo and their confinement on an arid reservation in southern New Mexico. It is possible that the pressure on the Navajo reduced the stress felt by other native groups in the 1850s and that the decline after the 1860s reflects the impact of the military defeat on the Navajo in particular.

The end of the Civil War saw an increased rate of white settlement in the West and would have placed added pressure on tribes for resources, as well as exposure to disease. The federal government began the first transcontinental railroad in 1863, during the war, and finished it in 1867. This split the bison herds and opened the way for their commercial slaughter as a source of leather. Settlers and miners also moved west to states like Colorado and Montana that previously had few white settlements. The bison herds on the northern plains were largely destroyed by white and Indian hunters by the 1870s, which greatly limited the food supplies of the Plains Indians.

The finding that the shortest Indian scouts were from Montana is consistent with the difficulties faced by Indians there. Many of them lived in villages and the men also used horses to hunt bison. Such villagers were exposed to raids by enemy tribes when the men went hunting. The Pawnee had a long tradition of fighting along with the U.S. military in wars against their enemies (Dunlay, 1982, p. 148). Other village tribes that combined hunting bison with village agriculture by women include the Ponca, Omaha, and Iowa. Similarly, scouts from the Midwest and Arkansas could also be from tribes that were exposed to raids by plains tribes. Indian scouts from Oregon may be from the more nomadic tribes in the Great Basin who faced a harsh environment.

In sum, the height of the Indian scouts serving in the U.S. army confirm that American natives were relatively tall in international comparison as they were taller than almost all European populations at the time with the exception of elite groups such as the British gentry (Komlos, 2007a). While at first glance this might appear to be surprising for a disadvantaged and poor minority population, the pattern appears less of a conundrum considering that they were living in close proximity to the land which tended to confer considerable nutritional advantages over urban populations throughout the world in the 19th century (Komlos, 2003).

That the proximity to the source of food conferred biological advantages has been found in many other data sets: "the tallest men in the Habsburg monarchy were born in the economically least developed lands .... Although technologically backward, the peasants were self-sufficient and lived on productive land that was not densely populated" (Komlos, 1985, p. 1156); "The fact that Swedes from the northern provinces born before 1850 were substantially taller than their more southern ... compatriots accords well with the status of the North as a frontier region, lightly populated and devoted to hunting and raising animals" (Sandberg & Steckel, 1987), and similarly for the United Kingdom: "The tall-but-poor anomaly also holds for other isolated pre-industrial populations" (Nicholas & Steckel, 1997, p. 115).[17] "Town dwellers, however, were generally at a disadvantage for procuring nutrients because they were farther from the source of food supply, and, unlike the rural population, were not paying farm-gate prices for agricultural products" (Komlos, 1998, p. 790).[18] In short, the nutritional status of Native Americans was commensurate with their preindustrial life style. To be sure, the food subsidies from the government must have contributed to the maintenance of their biological welfare.

However, the Indian men in both the scout and the Boas samples were among the shortest groups of the rural populations in the New World. Their height was closer to that of the urban populations who experienced a much heavier disease load than the Indians living in a low population density environment. One might characterize the implication of their height as rural poverty in the New World which still provided considerable advantages in terms of nutritional status in international comparison.

NOTES

1. For instance, for the Sioux sample the Kolmogorov–Smirnov test rejected normality at the 0.006 level and the Shapiro–Wilk test rejected it at the 0.02 level.

2. Furthermore, among the Cheyenne 41% of the recorded height of men were between 173 and 176 cm (68.1–69.3 in.), which is highly implausible in a normal distribution (Boas, 1895, p. 368).

3. This section draws extensively on Komlos and A'Hearn (2004).

4. IC-STATA version 10.

5. According to Utley there were less than 100,000 "hostile" Indians in 1866. Peaceful tribes had either chosen to accommodate themselves to the American presence, had already been defeated, or had been so terrorized by other tribes and disease that they did not have the strength to fight.

6. An example is the famous flight of the Nez Perce and Chief Joseph who were trying to escape into Canada. The last armed conflict of the Indian wars occurred in 1890 — the massacre by cavalry soldiers of Sioux Indians camped at Wounded Knee, South Dakota. The Indians who were camped there believed in the messianic ghost dance religion.

7. All extant observations were recorded.

8. The lower and upper limits are as follows: 1866(67:70), 1868(65:74), 1870 (66:72), 1871(66:74), 1872(63:74), 1873(60:74), 1874(60:69), 1875(66:71), 1876, (66:69), 1877(66:70), 1878(64:68), 1879(67:73), 1880(66:71), 1882(63:76), 1883(60:70), 1885(64:75), 1886(66:70), 1887(62:73), 1888(66:73), 1889(66:73), 1891(64:70), 1892 (66:72), 1894(64:72), 1896(66:72). Note that 0.01 inch was subtracted from the lower limit and 0.99 was added to the upper limit in order to retain observations on the height requirements.

9. The number of observations of this distribution does not equal the number noted in the regression on account of the fact that the regressions do not include data outside of the range required to be accepted into the military.

10. These 247 are not included in Table 2.

11. The number of observations thus excluded is 2,343 adults and 202 youth. These years are 1867, 1869, 1881, 1884, 1890, 1893, 1895, and >1996.

12. See footnote 8.

13. Only heights of men from Nebraska and Arkansas as well as those of herders were significant. They were consistently less than the average, but there were few observations in those categories in the sample (Table 2).

14. This specification includes adults only, with unconstrained estimation. With constrained estimation the increase is 0.81 in. ($p = 0.000$).

15. Rows 1 and 15 pertain to elites; 2–4, 9, 12, 14, 18 pertain to southerners and to convicts; both groups were taller than average; 6 pertains to an earlier period; 7–8, 13 were calculated incorrectly; 11, 16 are for an earlier period when men were taller; 17, 19 pertain to those living near bison herds.

16. While men in some tribes in the Boas sample were markedly taller than average, this was due to the fact that the samples were not random and taller men were more likely to be selected for the Boas sample.

17. "The situation of poor, isolated population being taller than a wealthy, more commercial population was not, then, unique to the Irish-English comparison" (Nicholas & Steckel, 1997, p. 115; see also Shay, 1994, Mokyr and O'Grada, 1994, Baten, 1996).

18. "Individuals who bought their food had to pay for transportation costs and for the efforts of middlemen, whereas subsistence farmers did not" (Komlos, 1989, p. 97).

ACKNOWLEDGMENT

We thank Richard Jantz for providing a copy of the "Boas sample." This paper was written while John Komlos was a fellow of the National Humanities Center.

REFERENCES

A'Hearn, B. (1998). The antebellum puzzle revisited: A new look at the physical stature of union army recruits during the civil war. In J. Komlos & J. Baten (Eds.), *Studies on the biological standard of living in comparative perspective* (pp. 250–267). Stuttgart: Franz Steiner Verlag.

A'Hearn, B. (2004). A restricted maximum likelihood estimator for truncated height samples. *Economics and Human Biology, 2*(1), 5–19.

Barrington, L. (Ed.). (1998). *The other side of the frontier: Economic explorations into native American history*. Boulder, CO: Westview Press.

Baten, J. (1996). Der Einfluss von regionalen Wirthschaftstrukturen auf den biologischen lebensstandard. *Vierteljahrschrift für Sozial- und Wirtschaftsgeschichte, 83*(4), 180—213.

Boas, F. (1895). Zur Anthropologie der nordamerikanischen Indianer. *Zeitschrift für Ethnologie, 27*, 366—411.

Bogin, B. (1999). *Patterns of human growth* (2nd ed.). Cambridge: Cambridge University Press.

Carlson, L. (1981). *Indians, Bureaucrats and land: The Dawes act and the decline of Indian farming*. Westport, CT: Greenwood Press.

Carlson, L. (1992). Learning to farm: Indian land tenure and farming before the Dawes act. In T. Anderson (Ed.), *Property rights, constitutions and Indian economies* (pp. 67—83). Lanham, MD: Rowman & Littlefield.

Carson, S. (2008). The effect of geography and Vitamin D on African American stature in the nineteenth century: Evidence from prison records. *The Journal of Economic History, 68*(3), 812—831.

Carson, S. (2009). African-American and white inequality in the 19th century American South: A biological comparison. *Journal of Population Economics, 22*(3), 757—772.

Cole, T. J. (2003). The secular trend in human physical growth: A biological view. *Economics and Human Biology, 1*(2), 161—168.

Cuff, T. (2005). *The hidden cost of economic development: The biological standard of living in Antebellum Pennsylvania*. Aldershot, UK: Ashgate Publishing.

Dunlay, T. W. (1982). *Wolves of the blue soldiers: Indian scouts and auxiliaries with the United States Army, 1860—1890*. Lincoln: University of Nebraska Press.

Greene, W. (1993). *Econometric analysis* (2nd ed.). Englewood Cliffs, NJ: Prentice Hall.

Hämäläinen, P. (2003). The rise and fall of plains Indian horse cultures. *The Journal of American History, 90*(3), 833—862.

Jantz, R. L. (1995). Franz Boas and native American biological variability. *Human Biology, 67*(3), 345—353.

Komlos, J. (1985). Stature and nutrition in the Habsburg Monarchy: The standard of living and economic development. *American Historical Review, 90*(4), 1149—1161.

Komlos, J. (1987). The height and weight of west point cadets: Dietary change in Antebellum America. *The Journal of Economic History, 47*(4), 897—927.

Komlos, J. (1989). *Nutrition and economic development in the eighteenth century Habsburg monarchy: An anthropometric history*. Princeton, NJ: Princeton University Press.

Komlos, J. (1992). Toward an anthropometric history of African Americans: The case of the free blacks in Antebellum Maryland. In C. Goldin & H. Rockoff (Eds.), *Strategic factors in nineteenth-century American economic history: A volume to honor Robert W. Fogel* (pp. 297—329). Chicago, IL: University of Chicago Press.

Komlos, J. (1998). Shrinking in a growing economy? The mystery of physical stature during the industrial revolution. *Journal of Economic History, 58*(3), 779—802.

Komlos, J. (2003). Access to food and the biological standard of living: Perspectives on the nutritional status of native Americans. *American Economic Review, 93*(1), 252—255.

Komlos, J. (2004). How to (and how not to) analyze deficient height samples: An introduction. *Historical Methods, 37*(4), 160—173.

Komlos, J. (2007a). On British Pygmies and giants: The physical stature of English youth in the 18th and 19th centuries. *Research in Economic History, 25*, 117—136.

Komlos, J. (2007b). Anthropometric evidence on economic growth, biological well being, and regional convergence in the Habsburg Monarchy, 1850–1910. *Cliometrica, 1*(3), 211–237.

Komlos, J., & Coclanis, P. (1997). On the puzzling cycle in the biological standard of living: The case of the Antebellum Georgia. *Explorations in Economic History 34*(4), 433–459.

Komlos, J. & A'Hearn, B. (2004, January). *On the bias-precision tradeoff: A practical guide to use of the restricted maximum likelihood estimator in historical height samples.* Discussion Paper 370, University of Munich, Department of Statistics, Sonderforschungsbereich 386.

Komlos, J., & Baur, M. (2004). From the tallest to (one of) the fattest: The enigmatic fate of the size of the American population in the twentieth century. *Economics and Human Biology, 2*(1), 57–74.

Lamar, H., & Truett, S. (1996). Greater Southwest and California to the 1880s. In B. G. Trigger & W. Wilcomb (Eds.), *The Cambridge history of the native peoples of the Americas, vol. I, North America, Part 2* (pp. 57–116). New York, NY: Cambridge University Press.

Mokyr, J., & O'Grada, C. (1994). The heights of the British and the Irish c. 1800–1815. In J. Komlos (Ed.), *Stature, living standards, and economic development* (pp. 39–59). Chicago, IL: The University of Chicago Press.

National Archives and Records Administration, Washington, D.C., Register of Enlistments in the U.S. Army, 1798–1914, Record Group RG094, Microfilm ID M233, Indian Scouts, 1866ff.

Nicholas, S., & Oxley, D. (1993). The living standards of women during the industrial revolution, 1795–1820. *The Economic History Review, 46*(4), 723–749.

Nicholas, S., & Steckel, R. H. (1997). Tall but poor: Living standards of men and women in pre-famine Ireland. *Journal of European Economic History, 26*(1), 105–136.

Prince, J. M. (1995). Intersection of economics, history, and human biology: Secular trends in stature in nineteenth-century Sioux Indians. *Human Biology, 67*(3), 387–406.

Prince, J. M., & Steckel, R. H. (2003). Nutritional success on the great plains: Nineteenth-century equestrian nomads. *Journal of Interdisciplinary History, 33*(3), 353–384.

Prucha, F. P. (1984). *The great father.* Lincoln: University of Nebraska Press.

Ruud, P. (2000). *An introduction to classical econometric theory.* Oxford: Oxford University Press.

Sandberg, L., & Steckel, R. H. (1987). Heights and economic history: The Swedish case. *Annals of Human Biology, 14*(2), 101–109.

Shay, T. (1994). The level of living in Japan, 1885–1938: New evidence. In J. Komlos (Ed.), *Stature, living standards, and economic development* (pp. 173–204). Chicago, IL: The University of Chicago Press.

Steckel, R. H. (1995). Stature and the standard of living. *Journal of Economic Literature, 33*(4), 1903–1940.

Steckel, R. H. (2010). Inequality amidst nutritional abundance: Native Americans on the great plains. *Journal of Economic History, 70*(2), 265–286.

Steckel, R. H., & Haurin, D. R. (1994). Health and nutrition in the American Midwest: Evidence from the height of Ohio National Guardsmen, 1850–1910. In J. Komlos (Ed.), *Stature, living standards, and economic development* (pp. 117–128). Chicago, IL: The University of Chicago Press.

Steckel, R. H., & Prince, J. M. (2001). Tallest in the world: Native Americans of the great plains in the nineteenth century. *American Economic Review, 91*(1), 287–294.

Sunder, M. (2004). The height of Tennessee convicts: Another piece of the antebellum puzzle. *Economics and Human Biology*, 2(1), 75—86.

Sunder, M. (2007). *Passports and economic development: an anthropometric history of the U.S. Elite in the 19th Century.* Unpublished Ph.D. dissertation, University of Munich, Munich.

Ubelaker, D. (1988). North American Indian populations size, A.D. 1500 to 1985. *American Journal of Physical Anthropology*, 77, 289—294.

Utley, R. M. (1973). *Frontier regulars: The United States army and the Indian 1866—1891.* New York, NY: Macmillan Publishing.

Utley, R. M. (2003). *The Indian Frontier, 1846—1890* (rev. ed.). Albuquerque, TX: University of New Mexico Press.

Whitwell, G., de Souza, C., & Nicholas, S. (1997). Height, health, and economic growth in Australia, 1860–1940. In R. H. Steckel & R. Floud (Eds.), *Health and welfare during industrialization* (pp. 379–422). Chicago, IL: The University of Chicago Press.

Wishart, D. (1995). Evidence of surplus production in the Cherokee nation prior to removal. *Journal of Economic History*, 55(1), 120—138.

Zehetmayer, M. (2011). The continuation of the antebellum puzzle: Stature in the US, 1847—1894. *European Review of Economic History*, 15(2), 313—327.

THE DISPERSION OF CUSTOMS TARIFFS IN FRANCE BETWEEN 1850 AND 1913: DISCRIMINATION IN TRADE POLICY

Stéphane Becuwe and Bertrand Blancheton

ABSTRACT

The principle of tariffs dispersion, or differential tariffs depending on country of origin, is well known. For instance, Canada adapted a double column of tariffs after 1846, Spain in 1877, and Switzerland in the 1880–1890s. But there has never before been a comprehensive measure for any national economy, to our knowledge. This contribution proposes an original and exhaustive measure of customs tariffs dispersion depending on the origin of imported products for France between 1850 and 1913. Part of this dispersion arises indirectly as the result of compiling the nomenclature – or the schedule of categories – for France's general trade chart. Our study nevertheless reveals the existence of direct discriminatory practices applied to certain countries for certain products. The creation of this measure yields important insights. First, tariff dispersion's evolution completes the analysis of the chronology of trade policy. Second, it is possible to link tariff discrimination, imports in particular sectors, and national production. In our opinion, the paper

Research in Economic History, Volume 30, 163–183
ISSN: 0363-3268/doi:10.1108/S0363-326820140000030004

should pave the way to work that reintroduces a country-specific dimension into the study of late 19th century commercial policy.

Keywords: Trade policy; tariffs; first globalization

JEL classification: N7

INTRODUCTION

Sources available at the French National Customs Museum (data relative to imports and duty received country by country) reveal substantial heterogeneity of "tariff practices." For one and the same heading, including those that are extremely disaggregated and, on the face of it, homogeneous, tariff rates could differ considerably according to country of origin. The principle of this dispersion, or discrimination by country, is well known. For instance, Canada adopts a double column of tariffs after 1846, and a triple column after 1906, Spain from 1877, Switzerland in the 1880—1890s, the United States adopts a double column with the Dingley tariff act in 1897, and Australia from 1902. But there has never before been a comprehensive measure of tariff dispersion for any national economy, to our knowledge. We have elected to take a deeper look along this research path to better understand French Trade policy. The historiography of French trade policy up until now has focused only on products in aggregate ignoring the country of origin. Quantitative studies around the theme of per-sector effective protection include Nye (1991), Irwin (1993), Broder (1993), Tena-Junguito (2006a, 2006b), Dormois (2006, 2007), and Lehmann and O'Rourke (2008). Qualitative studies of the role of pressure groups include Barral (1974), Smith (1980), Plessis (1993), Cadier-Rey (1997), Garrigues (2002), Todd (2008), among others.

For this study, we tapped into the *Tableau Général du Commerce et de la Navigation*, an annual publication, the title of which varies depending on the period. For nine countries, we collected data on the customs duty applied to all products included in the official nomenclature − or schedule of categories − every five years between 1850 and 1910. With these data we construct a measure of tariff dispersion. Our measure establishes the existence of substantial dispersion in French tariffs, and shows that this dispersion evolved significantly throughout the period. While in part this dispersion was the result of a systematic structural effect linked to the compiling of nomenclatures − or categories − for France's general trade chart, our study nevertheless reveals the existence of direct discriminatory practices applied to certain countries for certain products. We will show below that the proliferation of titles and the absence of harmonization of nomenclatures was a de facto way to penalize a specific partner and thus circumvent the clause of most favored nation.

This original result has major consequences for interpreting historical issues. First tariff dispersion's evolution between 1850 and 1913 casts light on the "trade policy regimes" at a point in time, and thus the measure introduces a new vision of French trade policy's chronology. Second an analysis of tariff dispersion deepens our understanding of the evolution of sectorally disaggregated international trade flows.[1] We use the case of international trade in wine to illustrate. The article thus shows the necessity of cross-referencing product and country factors when conducting an analysis of effective protection.

Our approach is rolled out in three stages. In an initial section, we present the data, propose a measurement of tariff dispersion and its dynamics, and show the appeal of analysing disaggregated data. In a second section, we use the constructed measure and its historical evolution to analyze the possible reasons for dispersion. In the third section, we show the importance of including an analysis of tariff dispersion for understanding historical issues in French trade relations.

THE DISPERSION OF TARIFF PRACTICES IN FRANCE (1850–1910)

Methodology and Data

To highlight the heterogeneity of tariff rates according to the origins of products, our approach has been as follows. We have considered nine countries: Great Britain, Germany, Italy, Spain, Belgium, Switzerland, Argentina, Russia, and the United States, which on average accounted for 60.77% of French imports (standard deviation of 5.29) and 43.64% of customs receipts (standard deviation of 7.51). The sample appears representative in terms of both intensity of flows and diversity (although mention should be made of the virtual absence of exotic foodstuffs[2]).

We have analyzed customs duties per product in the most disaggregated way possible, based on France's *Tableau Général du Commerce et de la Navigation*. The nomenclature for this primary source is indeed highly disaggregated: the number of products is in excess of 100 at the end of the period for Great Britain, Belgium, Germany, and Italy, and runs to several dozen for the other countries. We have worked on five-year data starting in 1850 and ending 1910, and also included the year 1893 to better appreciate the potential influence of the Méline tariff of January 1892. This means that 14 dates will systematically lie at the base of our calculations.

For each of these countries, data available on importations[3] and customs duties per product have made it possible to calculate mean customs duty rates per product and per country. From these figures we have been able to calculate the mean tariff rate and the dispersion figure, providing that the product was imported into France from at least three countries from the nine under consideration. Next, the selected products have been split into three categories: staples (or primary products, e.g., wool, plain timber, unrefined coal...); agricultural products (such as cereals and wine...); and processed products (machinery and engineering, hide and leather goods, silk fabrics...). This distinction aims to produce the bases for analysis in terms of real protection. For each of the three categories, the average rate of customs duty and the mean standard deviation coefficient for average rates of customs duty per product have been calculated. We calculate the dispersion index for one year as follows:

i: product, $i = 1 \ldots I$

j: country, $j = 1 \ldots J$

c: category (staples, agricultural product, processed product)

DD_{ij}: duties on imports of product i from country j

M_{ij}: imports of product i from country j

$DDM_{ij} = DD_{ij}/M_{ij}$: rate of duty customs by country

$DDM_i = \sum_{j=1}^{J} \frac{DDM_{ij}}{J}$; only if $J \geq 3$: average tariff

$DI_i = \sqrt{\sum_{j=1}^{J} \frac{(DDM_{ij} - DDM_i)^2}{J}}$: dispersion index of tariff duty by country

$DI_c = \sum_{i=1}^{I} \frac{DI_i}{I}$: dispersion index by category

This latter indicator is considered as an indicator of dispersion for custom duty rates per country and per product category.

A High Dispersion of Tariff Protections According to Country of Origin and Product Category

Fig. 1 presents the shifts in custom duty rates per class of product for the nine countries. The evolution of total average customs duty (ACD all products) is also given.

As evidenced by the calculation of the coefficients of correlation between these four curves, given in Table 1, shifts are somewhat similar. The exception, however, is that of the average customs duty for agricultural products and that for processed products. We will leave for later discussion in the paper the question of whether these differences in the evolution of nominal protection barriers between the agricultural and manufacturing sectors is evidence for the existence of a commercial policy.

Fig. 2 visualizes the evolution in dispersion across countries of customs duty rates for the three product categories. The average rate of dispersion over the period is 0.0156 for staples, 0.0466 for agricultural products, and 0.0416 for processed products. The average of tariff averages for each product category equal, respectively, 0.077, 0.1322, and 0.1131. Thus the coefficients of variation, equal to the ratio of the standard deviation to the average, is 0.4126 for staples, 0.3673 for agricultural products, and 0.3737 for processed products. These relatively large variations show that for one and the same product, the applied rate of customs duty is highly variable

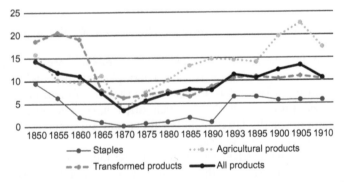

Fig. 1.   Shift in the Average Customs Duty Per Product Category. *Source*: Tableau Général du Commerce Extérieur de la France General, Musée National des Douanes, Bordeaux.

Table 1.   ACD Correlation Coefficients.

ACD Correlation	Staples	Agriculture	Transformed	Overall
Staples	1.000	0.618	0.593	0.851
Agriculture		1.000	0.105	0.382
Transformed			1.000	0.671
Overall				1.000

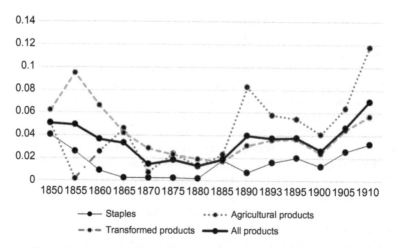

Fig. 2. Evolution in Dispersion Indicators. *Source*: Tableau Général du Commerce Extérieur de la France General, Musée National des Douanes, Bordeaux. Own calculations.

depending on the country of origin. This is one of the article's main findings.

Note that for staples, which typically have much more homogeneous nomenclatures (categories such as lead, wood, plain timber, and zinc, etc.), the coefficient of variation has a larger value than for agricultural products and processed products, both of which often have heterogeneous categories. Examples of the latter include rubber and gutta-percha structures, apparel, and sewn lingerie pieces.

Dispersion shows marked shifts over the period. From Fig. 2, we see that it falls from the start of the period with a low point of dispersion in 1880. From that point, dispersion increases until the end of the period.

An examination of Figs. 1 and 2 reveals a relatively similar evolution of the average customs duty and the dispersal indicator for each category of products. This fact is proven by calculating the correlation coefficients between these two variables, equal to 0.886 for the basic commodities, 0.888 for the processed products, and 0.569 for the agricultural products. The positive sign of the correlations suggests that dispersion increases when the level of protection rises and that, conversely, it decreases when protection decreases. The correlation between aggregate average customs and aggregate dispersion is not so high — only 0.48. For example, during the 1890s and the 1900s average customs rates decline but tariff dispersion increases.

This imperfect correlation suggests that tariff differentiation by country could be a second instrument of trade policy, one which complements the average tariff rate. We will discuss this further in the paper's last section.

Dispersion in Tariffs Per Country: Illustrations with Products

Here, we illustrate the concept of tariff dispersion with some examples. Figs. 3–5 show customs duty by country for the "machinery and engineering" category, the "wines" category, and for "plain timber" category. Significantly different rates prevail depending on the country exporting the product. Fig. 3 shows that American machinery seems to be taxed twice the amount of other countries between 1865 and 1875, and that the rate of customs duty imposed on American imports and machinery and engineering products remains higher than other countries at the end of the period between 1892 and 1910. Fig. 4 shows that in 1890, Italian wines were taxed at a rate five times higher than Swiss wines, and that the rate for Italian wines was also significantly higher than for Spanish wines. And finally Fig. 5 shows that Russian woods were taxed at rates three times higher than Swiss woods between 1893 and 1910.

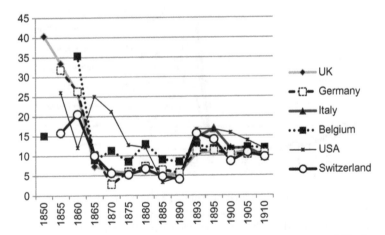

Fig. 3. Customs Tariffs (in Percent) Applied to the Machinery and Engineering Sector between 1850 and 1910, According to Country of Origin. *Source*: Tableau Général du Commerce Extérieur de la France General, Musée National des Douanes, Bordeaux. Own calculations.

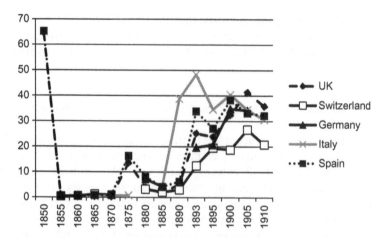

Fig. 4. Customs Tariffs (in Percent) Applied to the Wine Sector between 1850 and 1910, According to Country of Origin. *Source*: Tableau Général du Commerce Extérieur de la France General, Musée National des Douanes, Bordeaux. Own calculations.

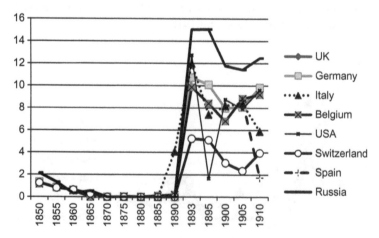

Fig. 5. Customs Tariffs (in Percent) Applied to Plain Timber between 1850 and 1910, According to Country. *Source*: Tableau Général du Commerce Extérieur de la France General, Musée National des Douanes, Bordeaux. Own calculations.

It is worth noting that we cannot systematically establish a link between variation in levels of protection per country and the shift in the flow of imports. In general, we will not see a decrease in imports from a country simply because customs rates from goods originating in that country have been increased. Each configuration must be analyzed individually. Broder (1993, p. 61) considers the case of agricultural machinery. His arguments help us to interpret the relative movements of tariff rates in machinery seen in Fig. 4. He writes, "the absence of any statistically detectable close link between the shift in customs duty and the evolution of imports is not comparable to neutrality of tariffs." If the purpose of such tariffs is to protect ageing and ineffective industry – in this case faced with peaks in demand – the result will be an increase in imports. There will be simultaneously a rise in tariffs and a rise in imports. To illustrate this point, note that between 1889 and 1903, a period when customs *barriers* for agricultural machinery was raised threefold, the value of imports of agricultural machinery *increased* eightfold. Three-quarter of imports of agricultural machinery came from the United States, the rest was imported from Germany and Great Britain. The rise in duties had the sole aim of aligning imported prices on excessively high home market prices.

EXPLANATIONS FOR DISPERSION OF TARIFFS: SYSTEMATIC ERROR VERSUS DISCRIMINATORY PRACTICES

How might we explain the dispersion of tariffs at any moment in time? How might that explanation allow us to better appreciate the full dynamics of trade policy? These are the questions we turn to in this section. First we explain how the creation of the trade nomenclature could indirectly introduce dispersion, and then we argue that in some cases the proliferation of categories masked intentional discrimination in violation of trade treaties' clause of most favored nation.

The Structure of Customs Nomenclatures

Tariff dispersion for particular categories arises almost necessarily from differences in the tariff schedule nomenclatures and trade flow nomenclatures. Consider the nomenclatures given in France's general chart of trade. This primary source has a relatively fine breakdown of the flows of imports. At the beginning of the 20th century, the nomenclature included 100 or more entries for France's main trading partners. Despite this significant disaggregation, certain headings still pooled a high number of products whose levels of taxation could be different. This was the case, for example, of entries for "machinery and engineering," "chemicals," "metal tools and structures," "pottery, glass, and crystal," "paper, carton, books, and engravings," and even "livestock." From 1892 to the end of the period, the general tariff for France comprised as many as 654 entries. Even seemingly specific and homogeneous heading included variants, giving rise to tariff differentiation according to quality, or even age for the "livestock" category.

Direct Discriminatory Practices

The differing evolution of the sectoral dispersion rates suggests a role for discriminatory practices. As noted in Fig. 2, the level of dispersion is almost identical for the three product categories, and the dispersion levels of the three product categories do not manifest greatly dissimilar evolutions. This being said, the evolutions are not exactly identical. Table 2 shows the correlation coefficients across the sectoral dispersal indices. Their relatively low values support differential sectoral paths of trade protection.

During a global tariff reduction, certain sectors will experience a larger decrease in rates than others, as was the case for industrial goods beginning in 1860; conversely, in the period of increased tariff pressure that began in 1881, agriculture received relatively more protection than other sectors. In these conditions, the evolution of the tariff dispersion in various sectors cannot be perfectly correlated. We will argue here that an important part of the decrease in dispersion following 1860 as well as the increase in dispersion which followed 1880, was the result of first the elimination of discriminatory tariffs, and then the gradual return of bilateral commercial treaties. The differing paths of dispersion across sectors will support this argument.

During the 19th century, commercial treaties were instruments of commercial policy, and they established preferential bilateral conditions at the

Table 2. Dispersion Indicator Correlation Coefficients.

	Staples	Agriculture	Processed
Staples	1.000	0.592	0.563
Agriculture		1.000	0.470
Processed			1.000

expense of unfavored countries, which were subject to a general tariff. Countries excluded from these bilateral treaties were, for this reason, beholden to the tenants of free trade. At the beginning of the period studied (1850), in France a flat rate prevailed dating back to 1791, which had been periodically modified by laws and decrees, and carried the traces of certain archaisms. These archaisms included trade restrictions which sometimes which penalized the competitiveness of French products, such as when raw materials were highly taxed, or there were prohibitions against the imports of intermediate inputs. Examples of the latter include prohibitions on the import of cotton wire or prepared skins. This system was associated with a high dispersal of tariffs.

The first important change in trade policy in our period is the Senatus Consulte of 1852, which gave the sovereign the right to sign and to execute commercial treaties without ratification by the Parliament. During the 1850s the imperial commercial policy consisted of decreasing trade rights. This changed with the Treaty of January 23, 1860 with Great Britain which defined a new flat rate, and eliminated prohibitions. Among the nine countries that we are studying, six signed treaties with France that included the most favored nation clause. These were Great Britain 1860, Belgium May 1, 1861, Zollverein March 29, 1862, Italy January 17, 1863, Switzerland June 30, 1864, and Spain June 18, 1865. Three countries were not partners in bilateral trade treaties. These were Argentina, the United States, and Russia.

The diffusion of the most favored nation's clause via Cobden–Chevalier's network of treaties, though for a time limited to a subset of countries, explains not only the reduction of the customs tariffs, but also the decrease of tariff dispersal following 1860 (Fig. 2). By nature, this clause implies, for the same product, a convergence of tariff levels for the countries that are in agreement. Thanks to these agreements, the customs duties were reduced in half, and because they remained in place for 10 years, they brought more certainty and stability to commercial relations. Insofar as these treaties were reciprocal and largely overlapping, they constituted a type of commercial, preferential, and "multilateral" trade agreement. Lampe (2009) establishes, like Accominotti and Flandreau (2005), that if the trade treaties signed within the Cobden-Chevalier network framework did not cause a total increase in international business between 1860 and 1875, they did nevertheless accelerate product differentiation and instigate a strong need for intra-European trade. The tendency of governments to be in favor of a more open commercial system disappeared rather quickly. The Great Depression, which began in 1873, accentuated the need for interior protection and slowed down the search for external outlets. The unification of Germany and Italy also modified the trade relations system in Europe, because each one of these two countries wanted to consolidate their new national unit by increasing their tariff revenue. On their side, the United States refused to belong to the European network of nondiscriminatory treaties, preferring to negotiate preferential bilateral agreements.

The European commercial treaties network started to disintegrate when it came time to renew the initial treaties signed in the 1860s. In 1871, the incipient Republic in France looked for a way to increase its financial resources through tariff policy by specifically raising the taxes on sugar and coffee. In March 1872, the treaties with England and Belgium ended and were restored via the conventions of July 1873, which thereafter expired in 1877. These events translated into a climate of rising commercial tension. In Spain and Italy, nominal protection increased from the mid-1870s. In Spain, the tariffs of July 1877 established a double column of rights, those for the products coming from a country with which Spain did not have trade agreements (taxed according to the provisions of the arencel Figuerola), and those for the products coming from a country benefiting from the clause of the most favored nation. For Italy, Federico (2006) highlights a turn point in 1877 when in July a new treaty was defined with France. In April 1878, Italy adopted a new flat rate.

The agricultural lobbyist groups, in front of the overseas cereal surge, solicited greater protection against the more competitive foreign products and encouraged other sectors, like the iron, steel, and textile industry, to do so as well. The reorientation toward a more protectionist commercial policy in Europe was confirmed by the increase of customs duties in Germany in 1879.

In France, protection increased with the 1881 administration, which instituted the law of May 7. This law combined a flat rate of a still relatively moderate level with and an even more advantageous schedule, which could vary according to the result of country-specific negotiations. The tariff of 1881 left for the majority of products room to maneuver equivalent to 24% of the negotiators fees (see Augier & Marvaud, 1911). Almost immediately, conventions were signed with Belgium October 31, 1881, Italy November 3, 1881, Spain February 6, 1882, and Switzerland February 23, 1882. At the same time France granted the clause of the most favored nation to Great Britain, Russia, and Germany, as they were required to do under article 11 of the 1871 Treaty of Frankfurt (see Arnauné, 1911).

Commercial policy in continental Europe became even more aggressive starting from the 1890s. The installation of the Méline tariff of 1892 in France reinforced protection, benefiting especially the agricultural sector. In addition to the increase in customs duties, more detailed and complex tariff lists appeared which accentuated uncertainty for traders. These tariff lists were made up of minimum and maximum rates. In France, minimal taxes were reserved for countries that had completed a bilateral treaty, which could only be modified by the decision of the Parliament, which was not the case for the tariffs applied within the framework of the former commercial treaties. The fact that the tariff lists were increasingly detailed was certainly due partly to the increase in product differentiation and the widening line of foreign goods, in particular of manufactured goods. Often this preoccupation with detail, however, was used with protectionist fines to reduce competition with foreign products. Until 1910, many tariff modifications intervened. France raised, for example, its customs protection in 1907 by adopting the "law of the lock." Under the terms of the latter, the government had the possibility of arbitrarily raising certain taxes, on agricultural products mostly. Parliament could only intervene afterwards. In 1910, the difference between the minimum tariff rates and the maximum tariff rates increased. Fig. 2 confirms the impact of these measures in terms of the increase in tariff dispersal, particularly in the agricultural product category.

The protectionist forces won control of many countries, which allowed governments to legitimately assert commercial restrictions onto other countries. As a result, the period from 1880 to 1890 was marked by episodes of strong commercial tensions related to treaty renegotiations, and isolated commercial wars, which further accentuated the tension within the commercial system. Between 1886 and 1892, France was in conflict with Italy, and the higher reprisal tariffs were applied rather than the flat rates. Federico (2006) emphasizes the disastrous character of this war with Italy. Between 1893 and 1895, an equally violent conflict put France in opposition with Switzerland; both countries were incapable of agreeing on a convention. France subjected the Swiss products to its flat rate between 1893 and 1895. Switzerland then subjected the French products to a tariff higher than the flat rate (the retention tariff), in particular in the wine sector and the clock industry (see Humair, 2004). Another conflict exploded between France and Spain following the imposition of the new flat rates of December 27, 1891 for Spain and the Méline tariff for France. Germany came into conflict with Russia (1893), Spain (1894–1896), and Canada (1894–1910); Austria experienced conflict with several Balkan states, such as Romania.

These various events led to the signature of bilateral commercial treaties which called into question the clause of the most favored nation. This meant not only an increase in tariff pressure, but also, more specifically, a more significant tariff dispersal than we noted at the beginning of 1880s (see Fig. 2). In short, for France, this discussion shows that tariff dispersal represents an increase in protection and/or international trade tensions due to commercial wars, which led to the signature of bilateral commercial treaties that mitigated the application of the most favored nation clause.

Tariff dispersion was not a French characteristic in particular. In addition to Spain the double grid system also prevailed in Switzerland from 1880 to 1890 (see Humair, 2004 for quantitative elements). The Germany of the Bismarck period developed a strategy that consisted in signing few commercial treaties and only granting reductions on products of which the partner is practically exclusive, so that the concessions would not benefit the countries Germany already granted the clause to. The rights were thus specialized gradually, which resulted in a limited role for the most favored nation clause.[4]

HISTORIOGRAPHIC CONSEQUENCES OF TARIFFS DISPERSION

Identifying the dispersion of customs tariffs has major consequences for historical issues. First tariff dispersion's evolution between 1850 and 1913 casts light on the "trade policy regime" in operation and, thus, introduces a new vision of French trade policy chronology. Second an analysis of tariffs dispersion may help understand the evolution of sectorally disaggregated international trade.

Tariffs Dispersion as an Indicator of International Trade Tensions

Tariff dispersion usefully complements an analysis of average tariffs rate when trying to set out a chronology of trade policy. More precisely, it can be used to identify trade policy regimes, that is to say phases characterized by the degree of activism and tension in international trade. Dispersion is a tool for identifying and analyzing the presence and extent of tariff discrimination, which is evidence of directed commercial policy.

Paul Bairoch (1972, 1993) widely relied on France's average tariff rate to provide a chronology of trade policies in Europe during the first globalization. Bairoch's chronology has been accepted by many historians. It is as follows:

1846–1860: maintenance of protectionism in continental Europe, until the Franco-British treaty (January 1860)

1860–1879: free-trade period, until the Bismarck tariffs (July 1879)

1879–1892: gradual return to protectionism

1892–1913: growing protectionism in Europe, starting with the Méline tariffs in France

We think an analysis of the French case using the dispersion index will identify only two different trade policy regimes. From the 1850s through the 1870s, the regime can be described as Ricardian as it is associated with a long secular decline in the tariff dispersion measure as rates became less discriminatory. Then, from the 1880s until the beginning of the World War I, the tariff dispersion measure starts to rise as trade policy changes focus toward bilateral relationships in the face of several trade conflicts.

Ricardian free trade is a unilateral policy: a country decides unconditionally to reduce tariffs barriers, like Britain did. In France, during the 1850s, the imperial power reduced the tariffs level. A lowered dispersion index between 1855 and 1860 confirms that a move toward generalized free trade was initiated before 1860, as Asselain (1994) and Accominotti and Flandreau (2005) have already pointed out. The spreading of most-favored nation clauses in the 1860s tends to reduce the level and dispersion of tariffs: dispersion drops to a low point in 1880 if we consider all products, while the average tariff rate is already increasing.

Beginning in the late 1870s, the unilateral Ricardian vision of free trade was called into question in Europe in favor of increasing protection from world competition and slowing down trading activity. Consequently, within the realm of foreign trade relations, a highly negotiated and strategic approach began to prevail (Becuwe & Blancheton, 2013).

After passing a law on a double tariff schedule in 1881, France experiences a new regime with a more strategic, bilateral, and negotiated approach. As a consequence, disputes arise between France and several of its partners: increasing dispersion is evidence of the strong tensions that occur during the period (see Fig. 2). It is interesting to note that dispersion gradually increases until 1910 for the all products categories (as well as the average across categories, see Fig. 1), whereas a study of only the average tariff rate would indicate a decline in protection after the mid-1890s.

At this point it is appropriate to review the analysis provided by some historical economists who minimized the protectionist nature of prewar policies. Messerlin (1985) argues that the measures France adopted after 1892 are not of a cumulative nature: they can be considered as decreasing protectionism. Messerlin even considered the years between 1896 and 1914 a new phase of liberalization. Asselain (1994), relying on the evolution of average tariff rates, also questions the protectionist nature of the 1892–1913 period. Dormois (2007) concurs; he also argues that the French trade policy after 1870 can hardly be described as protectionist.

Tariff Dispersion and International Trade Flows

To illustrate the usefulness of the concept of tariff dispersion in under-standing sectorally disaggregated trade flows, we will use the example of wine. One advantage is that it was a rather homogeneous category at the time. Wine was also a central element of French international trade (from 3% to 14% of the total value of exports), as well as a central focus in political debates during the Third Republic.

At the beginning of the 1860s, a devastating plague of phylloxera occurs in France and destroys the major part of the vineyards. French wine industries then face a period of underproduction. As a result, wine imports significantly increased during the years 1875–1885 (see Fig. 6). After the recovery, vineyards offer unexpected results around 1899–1900, thus leading to overproduction in 1905.

During the wine industry crisis, France imported wine from Spain and Italy. As a consequence, the industry started to play a more significant role in both countries exports. During the decade 1875–1885, the share of wine in total imports from Spain increased from 7.57% to 75.01%. A similar thing happens in regard to Italy. Wine's share rises from 1.08% in 1875 to 17.38% in 1880 and 16.41% in 1885. Fig. 7 shows that the share of Italian wine in French imports suddenly drops between 1885 and 1890. Spain experiences the same situation from 1890.

The explanation of this trend-reversal has to be found in tariff protec-tion applied by France toward both countries. Fig. 4 shows the evolution of tariffs applied on wine imports from Spain, Italy, and all other countries between 1850 and 1910. As Fig. 4 shows, higher tariff barriers are imple-mented between 1885 and 1890 for Italian products. This takes place in the

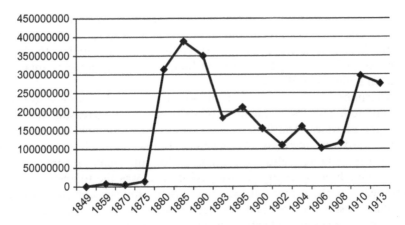

Fig. 6. Evolution of Imports of Wine (in France). *Source*: Tableau Général du Commerce Extérieur de la France General, Musée National des Douanes, Bordeaux. Own calculations.

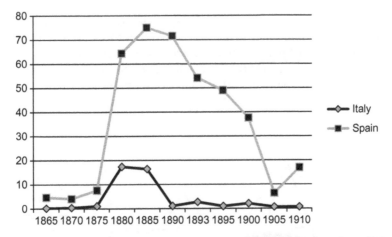

Fig. 7. Share of Wine Imports from Italy and Spain (in Percent). *Source*: Tableau Général du Commerce Extérieur de la France General, Musée National des Douanes, Bordeaux. Own calculations.

trade war that involves France and Italy from 1887 to 1910. Tariffs on Italian wine rise from 4.16% in 1885 to 38.78% in 1890, and to 48.38% in 1893. As a consequence, the share of Italy in total French imports of wine declines from 3% in 1880 to 0.36% in 1893. The Méline tariff in 1892 results in an increase of tariffs on Spanish products. Wine is particularly affected due to higher protection, from 6.22% in 1890 to 33.86% in 1893. Tariffs dispersion is important: in 1880, the same rate applies to the all countries. A few years later, tariffs on Italian and Spanish wines appear to be much higher than the average.

In response to the increase in imports, leaders had to choose between two different policies: reducing production costs or increasing the price of imported wines. The first strategy required considerable efforts and a shift toward new methods. At the time, France suffered from technical backwardness in agriculture (Lhomme, 1970), and significant investments would have been necessary to overpass it. This was the tougher solution. Obviously, tariff protection was an easier strategy, which permitted avoiding most constraints and sacrifices. Leaders opted for this "easy-lazy" solution. France sets up tariff discrimination toward close wine-producing countries, that is, Italy and Spain, as the increase of the dispersion index at the end of the period shows. This would have led to an increase in selling prices, thus probably favoring short-term benefits over long-term reforms.

Wine played an important role in Spanish exports. Consequently, a specific tariff discrimination that came in addition to the Méline tariff had a strong impact on Spanish foreign trade. Thus, examining the figure on the evolution of average tariffs per country (Fig. 8), it is not surprising to note a gap between Spain and other countries from 1890.

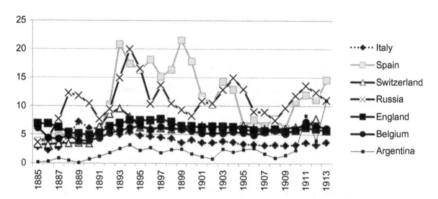

Fig. 8. Evolution of the Average Tariff by Country (in Percent). *Source*: Tableau Général du Commerce Extérieur de la France General, Musée National des Douanes, Bordeaux. Own calculations.

CONCLUSION

This article is the first to present a comprehensive measure of tariff dispersion for any national economy. This contribution has cast light on the extent of dispersion in France's customs tariffs, depending on the origin of products, between 1850 and 1913. A part of this dispersion is the result of a systematic error linked to the compiling of nomenclatures for France's general trade chart. But another part reveals the existence of discriminatory practices applied to certain countries for certain products. Separation of the two effects is even more delicate when the characterization of the products within nomenclatures is a tool of indirect discrimination.

In our opinion, the existence of this dispersion shows the need to cross-reference the product and country dimensions when implementing an approach in terms of effective protection. The country dimension has been completely obscured by empirical studies on this subject even though this was a time when the then geopolitical context made tariffs more of a political weapon than ever before.

We feel that this contribution should pave the way to work that reintroduces the country dimension into the study of late 19th century commercial policy. A per-country analysis is likely to shed light on arguments over commercial policy between 1870 and 1913, in a context of mounting international tensions.

NOTES

1. It should be noted that as the level of aggregation goes higher, the effects of tariff dispersion are more difficult to see.
2. Nye (1991) stresses that in theory, duties on exotic product have a distortional effect on the domestic market and should be considered as protective. For Irwin (1993), they are motivated solely by fiscal considerations and are not protective as long as there is no replacement product. Later work from O'Rourke (2006) and Tena-Junguito (2006a) showed that the key issue in the controversy between Nye and Irwin lay with the status of imports of alcohol by Great Britain (especially rum and wine). If these products were not considered to be exotic products, owing to the fact that British beer could be considered as a replacement product, then the view put forward by Nye would seem to be accurate.
3. As is customary in this type of enquiry, data on "special trade" have been retained, rather than those on "general trade" (which includes transit trade). Special trade relates more closely to the productive structure of the domestic economy.
4. Thus, the product labels appear in the French customs nomenclature like "Czechoslovakian crystals" or "Paris items."

ACKNOWLEDGMENTS

The authors thank participants at Economic History Society Congress (Oxford March–April 2012), participants at "European Trade Policies 1850–1913" meeting (Bordeaux March 2013) and J.-P. Dormois, C. Meissner, N. Nenovsky for valuable comments. Special thanks to Susan Wolcott for particularly helpful suggested revisions.

REFERENCES

Accominotti, O., & Flandreau, M. (2005). *Does bilateralism promote trade? Nineteenth century liberalization revisited.* CEPR Discussion Papers No. 5423.

Arnauné, A. (1911). *Le commerce extérieur et les tarifs de douane.* Paris: Alcan.

Asselain, J.-Ch. (1994). Faut-il défendre la croissance ouverte? *In post face Bairoch P. Mythes et paradoxes de l'histoire économique* (pp. 242–260). Paris: La Découverte.

Augier, C., & Marvaud, A. (1911). *Politique douanière de la France.* Paris: Alcan.

Bairoch, P. (1972). Free trade and European economic development in the 19th century. *European Economic Review, 3,* 211–245.

Bairoch, P. (1993). *Economics and world history: Myths and paradoxes.* Chicago, IL: University Press.

Barral, P. (1974). Les groupes de pression et le tarif douanier français de 1892. *Revue d'Histoire Economique et Sociale, 52,* 421–426.

Becuwe, S., & Blancheton, B. (2013). Les controverses autour du paradoxe Bairoch, quel bilan d'étape? *Revue d'Economie Politique, 123*(1), 1–27.

Broder, A. (1993). Le tarif de 1892 et les industries nouvelles: Une première approche. In *Le commerce extérieur français de Méline à nos jours* (pp. 53–65). Paris: CHEFF.

Cadier-Rey, G. (1997). Les chambres de commerce dans le débat douanier à la fin du XIXe siècle. *Histoire, Economie et Société, 16e Année, 2,* 279–298.

Dormois, J.-P. (2007). *The art of duplicity; or, did the third republic pretend to be protectionist while it actually wasn't really?* Hitotsubashi University Institute of Economic Research, Working Paper No. 153.

Federico, G. (2006). Protection and Italian development. Much ado about nothing. In J.-P. Dormois & P. Lains, (Eds.), *Classical trade protectionism 1815–1914: Fortress Europe (explorations in economic history)* (pp. 193–218). London: Routledge.

Garrigues, J. (2002). *Les groupes de pression dans la vie politique contemporaine en France et aux Etats-Unis de 1820 à nos jours.* Rennes: Presses Universitaires de Rennes.

Humair, C. (2004). Développement économique et état central (1815–1914). *Un siècle de politique douanière suisse au service des élites.* Berne: Peter Lang.

Irwin, D. A. (1993). Free trade and protection in the nineteenth-century Britain and France revisited. A comment on Nye. *Journal of Economic History, LIII,* 153–158.

Lampe, M. (2009). Effects of bilateralism and the MFN clause on international trade. Evidence for Cobden-Chevalier network 1860–1875. *Journal of Economic History, 69,* 1012–1040.

Lehmann, S. H., & O'Rourke, K. (2008). *The structure of protection and growth in the late 19th century*. NBER Working Papers No. 14493.

Lhomme, J. (1970). La crise agricole à la fin du XIXe siècle en France. Essai d'interprétation économique et sociale. *Revue Economique, 21*, 4, 521–553.

Messerlin, P. (1985). Les politiques commerciales et leurs effets de longue période. In B. Lassudrie-Duchene, & J.-L. Reiffers (Eds.), *Les protectionnismes* (pp. 71–89). Paris: Economica.

Nye, J. (1991). The myth of free trade Britain and fortress France: Tariffs and trade in the nineteenth century. *Journal of Economic History, LI*, 23–66.

O'Rourke, K. (2006). Measuring protection. A cautionary tale. In J.-P. Dormois & P. Lains (Eds.), *Classical trade protectionism 1815–1914: Fortress Europe (explorations in economic history)* (pp. 53–66). London: Routledge.

Plessis, A. (1993). Méline et la synthèse républicaine. In *Le commerce extérieur français de Meline à nos jours* (pp. 47–52). Paris: CHEFF.

Smith, M. S. (1980). *Tariff reform in france, 1860–1900: The politics of economic interest*. Ithaca, NY: Cornell University Press.

Tena-Junguito, A. (2006a). Assessing the protectionist intensity of tariffs in nineteenth-century European trade policy. In J.-P. Dormois & P. Lains (Eds.), *Classical trade protectionism 1815–1914: Fortress Europe (explorations in economic history)* (pp. 99–120). London: Routledge.

Tena-Junguito, A. (2006b). Spanich protectionism during the restauracion, 1875–1930. In J.-P. Dormois & P. Lains (Eds.), *Classical trade protectionism 1815–1914: Fortress Europe (explorations in economic history)* (pp. 265–297). London: Routledge.

Todd, D. (2008). *L'identité économique de la France. Libre-échange et protectionnisme 1814–1851*. Paris: Grasset.